ENVIRONMENTAL POLITICS AND POLICY IN THE WEST

ENVIRONMENTAL POLITICS AND POLICY IN THE WEST

REVISED EDITION

Edited by Zachary A. Smith and John C. Freemuth

UNIVERSITY PRESS OF COLORADO

Published by the University Press of Colorado
5589 Arapahoe Avenue, Suite 206C
Boulder, Colorado 80303

Printed in the United States of America

 The University Press of Colorado is a proud member of the Association of American University Presses.

The University Press of Colorado is a cooperative publishing enterprise supported, in part, by Adams State College, Colorado State University, Fort Lewis College, Mesa State College, Metropolitan State College of Denver, University of Colorado, University of Northern Colorado, and Western State College of Colorado.

∞ The paper used in this publication meets the minimum requirements of the American National Standard for Information Sciences—Permanence of Paper for Printed Library Materials. ANSI Z39.48-1992

Library of Congress Cataloging-in-Publication Data

Environmental politics and policy in the West / edited by Zachary A. Smith and John C. Freemuth. — Rev. ed.
p. cm.
Includes bibliographical references and index.
ISBN 978-0-87081-881-3 (pbk. : alk. paper) 1. Environmental policy—West (U.S.) I. Smith, Zachary A. (Zachary Alden), 1953– II. Freemuth, John C. (John Carter)
GE185.W47E58 2007
363.700978—dc22

2007018086

Design by Daniel Pratt

16 15 14 13 12 11 10 09 08 10 9 8 7 6 5 4 3 2

For Amy, Genevieve, and Alden

—*ZS*

And Sheri, Kenton, and Andrew

—JF

CONTENTS

PREFACE

The American West is a unique and highly interesting topic for a book on environmental politics and policy. We want to make it clear from the beginning, however, that something that might be obvious to most readers has actually been fought over and argued about for quite awhile. The argument is usually over how to resolve what Dan Kemmis calls the "perennial question" of whether California is really part of the West or something above and beyond. For the purpose of this book, and to keep many academic friendships intact, we have included California in our West.

This is the second edition of this anthology. We have made a number of important changes since the first edition was published in 1992. At that time the Clinton administration was just taking office and embarking on a series of policies that, in general, many thought were environmentally progressive and reflected a mature and powerful environmental movement. The Bush administration that followed reversed some of Clinton's policies and took a direction that was friendlier to industry and resource production. Environmentalists often found themselves on the defensive. Those changes, and reactions to them, are reflected in the chapters in this edition.

We use California as a starting point for a discussion about environmental politics and policy in the West and what has changed since the first edition of this book. California, like the rest of the western states that lie on and west of the 100th meridian, contains a good portion of U.S. public lands, reason enough to include the Golden State in this volume. Those lands have been argued about for many years, and, as Wallace Stegner once reminded us, the beginnings and early battlegrounds of the environmental movement lay deep within the context of public lands. Stegner said:

> Westerners live outdoors more than people elsewhere, because outdoors is mainly what they've got. . . . It is public land, partly theirs, and that space is a continuing influence on their minds and senses. It encourages a fatal carelessness and destructiveness because what is everybody's is nobody's responsibility. It also encourages, in some, an impassioned protectiveness: the battlegrounds of the environmental movement lie in the western public lands. Finally, it promotes certain needs, tastes, attitudes, skills. It is those tastes, attitudes and skills, as well as the prevailing destructiveness and its corrective, love of the land, that relates real Westerners to the myth. (Wallace Stegner, *The American West as Living Space* [Ann Arbor: University of Michigan Press, 1986], 81)

What it means to be considered a "conservationist," a "preservationist," and an "environmentalist" has clear reference to battles over parks, wilderness, forest policy, and range policy that have taken place largely in the West. For many of the states in the region, having at least 30 percent and sometimes well over 50 percent of their land base under federal management is a source of both economic benefit and long-lasting anger over distant decisions made with seeming disregard for more local concerns. Federalism has a distinct, deep, and controversial connotation in the West. At the same time, we would err if we thought of states as simply opposed to federal land management; their environmental policies can be quite progressive, as Robert Bartlett and Walter and Carolyn Baber tell us in Chapter 3. These authors also take issue with a common scholarly argument that effective state environmental policy must be "jumpstarted" by a thoughtful and benevolent federal government.

Public land battles since the early 1990s have been both familiar and new. Traditional resource development, seen by some as the "wise use" of much of the nation's natural bounty, remains a cherished value and sound public policy for many westerners. That is why it has been so difficult, as Charles and Sandra Davis suggest in Chapter 7, to revise one of the most important laws that reflects resource use—the General Mining Law of 1872. But in some policy arenas, notably forest policy, the language and terms of the debate over the purposes of national forests have changed. Now, arguments over whether to "log" or "thin" forests are made more in terms of "forest health" than of economic development. In a rhetorical sense, the language and perspective of environmentalism seem to have carried the day even when facing policies many would consider more sympathetic to traditional multiple use.

A century of fire suppression has placed these forests in conditions most foresters believe lie outside what scientists like to call their normal "range of variability." Hence forests need to be thinned and sometimes logged to restore them to the way they appeared before the era of complete suppression. While some environmentalists might argue that this is simply repackaging logging under more benign language and terms, nonetheless it appears that the terms of the debate have changed. Ironically, almost everyone on every side of this and many other environmental battles genuflects toward "best science" as a way to resolve the issue. Yet science itself is much more problematic, as Gregg Cawley and John Freemuth argue in Chapter 4.

The long-standing battle over wilderness remains as well, but it too has changed. Economic development has entered the equation as some federal land has been exchanged, auctioned, and transferred for various purposes as part of wilderness legislation. Several pieces of legislation affecting Nevada, such as the Southern Nevada Public Land Management Act of 1998 and the Clark County Conservation of Public Land and Natural Resources Act of 2002, are representative of this trend. In other states, however, such mechanisms are running into resistance, as the controversy over congressman Mike Simpson's proposed legislation for the spectacular Boulder–White Cloud region of Idaho would indicate. That legislation has proposed a number of small land conveyances to county and smaller towns while designating almost 300,000 acres of new wilderness. The conveyances have received both support and opposition from environmental groups, and they open a window into both wilderness politics and profound disagreements within the environmental community. To some environmentalists involved in crafting the legislation, the greater good of wilderness protection is worth a pragmatic concession or two. Others stand in opposition to any land transfer or conveyance, perhaps forgetting that some federal land boundaries were hardly the result of careful boundary drawing. Regardless, this sort of legislation seems to be a harbinger of future wilderness battles and suggests that wilderness politics may have changed.

Closely related to wilderness are the forest system's roadless lands. The Clinton administration attempted to protect almost all of those lands through the regulatory process. That attempt, coming late in his second presidential term, was quickly reversed by a Bush administration rule that placed much more decision-making authority in the hands of individual western governors. It was an interesting meld of quirky federalism and centralized rule making premised on the administrative presidency. In both cases those affected by the decisions sued, as groups have been doing over even the most remotely controversial public land decisions since the early 1990s. This has led to a growing movement to bring people together to try and work out differences—the collaborative resource movement. Of course, the stamp each president tries to put on the various federal agencies affects his budgets, priorities, and morale (see Chapter 2).

At times, familiar observations about the West and its public lands have been rendered simplistic. For some time now, those in the West have been hearing that the West is changing, that the "Old West" of resource extraction and development has been replaced by a "New West" of high-tech industries, footloose retirees, and the self-employed—all of whom hold a growing interest in amenity values of the public lands. To some observers, recreation has been heralded as more important than resource development. Closer examination reveals that it is not that simple. There are growing and divisive conflicts between recreationists. Cross-country skiers fight with snowmobilers; hikers complain about the noise from all-terrain vehicles (ATVs) and motorcycles. The mountain biking community is split over the concept of wilderness; some oppose new wilderness because it would prohibit bikes, others want bikes allowed in wilderness, and still others support the creation of new wilderness.

Many recreationists want to live in the West. Some of those who bike, hike, ski, and engage in other outdoor sports are newcomers to the West, drawn to its amenities. They become poster children for an influx of people throughout the entire region. Today, most western states are experiencing rapid growth. Data from the 2000 census place Nevada, Arizona, Utah, Colorado, and Idaho as the top five states for growth during the period 1990–2000, with no sign subsequently that the growth has slowed. With growth comes conflict between urban and rural citizens over such things as water allocation, funding for education, the economy, and so on.

Take water, for example. The template for modern water issues and policy is provided by Las Vegas. The city is already exploring the idea of obtaining groundwater from the northern part of the state, in an eerie reflection and evolution of the water politics of Los Angeles and Owens Valley during the 1920s (see Chapter 9 for a discussion of western water policy). But the city has also become a leader in water conservation. Still, its growth, and related water needs of cities such as Phoenix, San Diego, and so on, are forcing talk of revisiting the Colorado River Compact of the 1920s. While cities like Las Vegas seek water, others seek to remove dams that no longer serve their original purposes, a politics that would have been unheard of not long ago. Dan McCool provides two informative examples of dam removal and river restoration in Chapter 5. This is a political issue that will only grow over time.

Growth also brings increased air and water pollution problems, as well as the need for thoughtful land-use decisions. In cities throughout the West, growth is occurring at a rate many are ill-prepared to deal with. Some, such as Denver, are more sympathetic than they ever have been toward planned growth and public transportation. Hence, a book on western environmental issues must now include a discussion of sprawl and smart growth, so we have added a chapter on this topic by Matt Lindstrom and Hugh Bartling (Chapter 8).

As we were finishing our revisions, a perennial issue came to the fore once again that warrants some discussion. If space allowed, this issue would deserve expanded treatment in these pages. That issue is energy development and the renewed pressure to develop western public lands for oil and gas. The oil price shocks of 2005 have, not surprisingly, led to calls to develop more reliable sources of energy closer to home. The Republican-led Senate included in its budget bill for FY 2006 language that would allow the Alaska National Wildlife Refuge to be opened for oil and gas exploration, hoping to avoid a filibuster by placing the language in a bill that forbids filibustering. The Bush administration has also been supportive of oil and gas development. John Freemuth, during his tenure on the Bureau of Land Management's Science Advisory Board, heard presentations that focused on identifying legal and administrative obstacles to oil and gas development on federal public lands. Parts of western public lands hold tremendous oil resources locked within oil shale and tar sands, resources said to contain over 1 billion barrels of oil. The technology to recover the resource is yet to be fully developed, and recovery is highly dependent on the cost of oil. Yet the implications for the West could be enormous in terms of water use, population growth, economic benefits, environmental impacts, and such things as endangered species (see Chapter 6).

CHAPTER OVERVIEW

This book approaches environmental policy in the West from several directions. In Chapter 2, Leslie Alm provides a theoretical overview of various approaches to policy formulation and implementation, with special attention paid to the environment. Alm outlined this framework for the first edition of this book and has incorporated new material on environmental and natural resource policy that provides an updated perspective on public policy. He reminds us that the study of policy is embedded in the study of politics, and politics is very much about the struggle over ideas. In the case of environmental politics this is very much in evidence, as this arena is fundamentally concerned with how we ought to live among both ourselves and the other species that inhabit the planet. Alm also sets the context for environmental policy in the West by reminding us of the importance of the federal government's role in this region and the ongoing tensions and contradictions that remain within that role.

In Chapter 3, Matthew Cahn, Sheldon Kamieniecki, and Denise McCain-Tharnstrom discuss the myriad bureaucracies that affect the western United States. Here we begin to see in more depth the importance of the federal presence in this region of the country. The federal government manages about one-third of all land in the United States, and over 91 percent of the land under its jurisdiction lies in the thirteen western states. But, as these authors remind us, environmental protection also includes environmental regulation, and it is the Environmental Protection Agency that oversees much of that regulation, relying on environmental laws and state and local bureaucracies to implement what are usually complex, expensive, and controversial policies and regulations. While much of the general outline of these bureaucracies has not changed since the first edition of this book, their priorities, budgets, and capabilities certainly have.

Robert Bartlett, Walter Baber, and Carolyn Baber, in Chapter 3, examine the issue of policy innovation as it pertains to state environmental policy development in the western United States. This is a new chapter for this edition. The authors challenge the conventional wisdom of most policy scholarship that suggests, but never proves, that most innovative state-level environmental policy has been jumpstarted by federal government prodding. Instead, the authors suggest that both state and federal policy initiatives may well depend on more general phenomena. As a historical example, the first forest reserve was proclaimed by a state, followed by the large federal forest reserves, and both were likely dependent on the forces of progressivism and conservation ascendant at that time. The authors note instances where western states have fostered examples of policy innovation, especially as they strengthen what has been called their "civic base." Indeed, as the authors suggest, this may actually be a cutting edge of environmental policy as the federal government moves to adopt more collaborative approaches to making decisions.

Chapter 4, by Gregg Cawley and John Freemuth, delves into one of the oldest controversies in conversations involving federal land policy: the relationship of science and politics in managing federal lands. This controversy is as old as the federal land system but as new as the Bush administration's call for "best science." Science can be seen both as a method for studying phenomena that offers reliable and predictable explanations and as a sort of policy trump card that some would like to use to end discussion and debate. There are also different "sciences" that compete for primacy over the management of the federal estate. The authors tell us that "science as policy trump card" can often be problematic, especially when laced with hidden assumptions and value choices masked as mere science. The authors attempt to untangle these issues in the chapter.

Daniel McCool, in Chapter 5—also new to this edition—discusses the growing interest in and use of dam removal and river restoration in a region once described by Marc Reisner as a "Cadillac Desert" (*Cadillac Desert* [New York: Penguin Books, 1993]), McCool sees a new era dawning, where dam removal may, in some cases, be as important as new dam construction. He first provides a brief history of the reclamation era and takes that history into the present by showing how calls for river restoration have grown in scope and sometimes led to dam removals. He then provides two case studies of removals, the Matilija Dam in southern California and the Savage Dam on the Rogue River in Oregon, offering insights into lessons for politics and policy. He notes that there is likely to be growing demand for dam removal and restoration, a conclusion supported by arguments from groups who envision that great dams such as Glen Canyon and Hetch Hetchy might someday become candidates.

Chapter 6, revised for this edition by William Mangun, looks at wildlife management issues throughout the West, an appropriate topic for a region known for its spectacular wildlife and the endangered species issues that increasingly accompany it. Wildlife policy has evolved over time, and Mangun discusses that evolution. For westerners, the evolution toward endangered species protection is often highly controversial and a cause for anger. Mangun reminds readers, however, that the booming growth throughout most of the West will create habitat fragmentation issues for species in both urban and exurban areas.

Chapter 7, by Charles and Sandra Davis, discusses another perennial western issue—hard-rock mining—an issue framed by legislation passed the same year as the establishment of Yellowstone National Park: 1872. Hard-rock mining, as supported by the 1872 Mining Law, was originally seen as worthy of public support and subsidization because it would help boost the American economy. Although the 1872 law has not been greatly revised, it has become clear that mining can have deleterious environmental effects. The Davises note that reform has been difficult to achieve because of a subgovernment with a tight policy that has blocked serious reforms, at the same time noting that various presidential administrations have attempted to implement regulatory reforms. States, too, can play a role and, the authors say, can be the forum in which reform might be most likely to occur.

Matt Lindstrom and Hugh Bartling, in Chapter 8, point to the future of the West with their examination of growth and sprawl in the region. The American West is growing rapidly and becoming more urban. Smart growth movements have sprung up throughout the region. The growth is eating up farmland and edging up to the public lands that surround most western cities. Lindstrom and Bartling provide fascinating evidence of western growth. They also discuss the growing use of initiatives and referenda to protect open space and deal with transportation issues. What were once the problems of megacities like Los Angeles are increasingly problems throughout the region. In some ways, this may be the most important "new" western problem that will affect every other western issue to some extent.

Finally, and appropriately, in Chapter 9 Jaina Moan and Zachary Smith look at what many feel is the overarching, most resource-limiting, and most important western issue of all: water development, management, and allocation. Water constitutes a great paradox in the West. Developed mostly by federal dollars and expertise, water policy is administered primarily by individual states, in many of which bashing the federal government is a time-honored tradition. The authors take us through the history of water development in the West, bringing us to today's concerns over water quality and endangered species protection.

We intend this book to be a supplemental text for courses in environmental and natural resources policy and administration, as well as for other public policy and administration courses that focus on the West and its issues. We hope, as well, that we have presented our discussions in such a way that citizens interested in the West and its future can find something of interest to them. Each chapter can be read independent of the others if a reader is interested in one topic but not all. For this reason, the chapters exhibit some redundancy because each author felt there was background material that was important to understand in the context of his or her chapter. That redundancy will also make it clear to readers that these various chapters and their policy areas are indeed related to one another, that many U.S. policies have a common history, and that history matters a great deal to these authors.

Together, we have a combined professional experience of nearly fifty years working in, teaching in, and writing about the American West. We have come to know it well and, most days, would not want to live anywhere else. We hope this book enables the reader to better understand and appreciate this unique and special region.

ENVIRONMENTAL POLITICS AND POLICY IN THE WEST

CHAPTER ONE

THE POLICY PROCESS AND THE AMERICAN WEST: AN ENVIRONMENTAL PERSPECTIVE

Leslie R. Alm

Public policy making in the United States rests in a seemingly inexhaustible set of concepts and processes that have been described as predominantly "chaotic" (Birkland 2001, 3). The diligent student of American public policy must deal with the fact that public policy is said to be inclusive of all political activities and institutions, "from voting, political cultures, parties, legislatures, bureaucracies, international agencies, local governments, and back again, to the citizens who implement and evaluate public policies" (John 2003, 483). One must differentiate between federalism and separation of powers, between pluralism and elitism, and between fragmentation and incrementalism. Simply put, we are faced with the proposition that the sheer complexity of what is going on in public policy making precludes simple, straightforward, sequential explanations (John 2003).

There should be no doubt that the subfield within political science titled "public policy" is a dynamic and complex area of study. As James Anderson has noted: "Public policies in a modern, complex society are indeed ubiquitous. They confer advantages and disadvantages, cause pleasure, irritation, and pain, and collectively have important consequences for our well-being and happiness" (2003, 1).

When one adds environmental issues to this public policy mix, things become even more entangled. Environmental politics entails conflicts between value systems: conservation versus preservation, natural resources development versus environmental protection, individual property rights versus the government's right of eminent domain, and command-and-control regulatory systems versus market-oriented approaches. Such a combination makes for difficult reading and difficult analysis. More than two decades ago, Dean Mann—a highly respected environmental scholar—expressed the frustrations of dealing with environmental policy:

> Environmental policy is not an artifact of administrations, grandly enunciated by presidents, duly enacted by responsive legislatures, and efficiently administered by the executive establishment. It is . . . a jerry-built structure in which innumerable individuals, private groups, bureaucrats, politicians, agencies, courts, political parties, and circumstances have laid down the plans, hammered the nails, plastered over the cracks, made sometimes unsightly additions and deletions, and generally defied "holistic" or "ecological" principles of policy design. (1986, 4)

Within this environmental context I will add one final ingredient—the American West. The imagery and reality of the American West is undauntedly clear and contradictory. On the one hand, there is the majestic beauty of the mountains, deserts, and wilderness areas. On the other hand, there is the spirited and often fierce battle over the rights of a much-needed and scarce natural resource—water. Contrasting the vast open spaces is the booming growth in urban population centers. The frontier ethos of rugged individualism is offset by the dominance of and reliance on the federal government. These special characteristics make the West unique within the sphere of environmental policy making. To study environmental policy making in the United States is one thing. To study environmental policy making in the American West is distinctive in important and interesting ways. The following sections lay the groundwork for such a study.

OVERVIEW OF THE POLICY PROCESS

To comprehend western environmental policy making, it is necessary to have a basic understanding of the overall policy-making process.

Definition of Public Policy

Because the study of public policy is a fairly recent phenomenon within political science, we are still struggling to grasp the essence of exactly what it entails. In fact, it is a common technique to begin books about public policy by simply asking, "What is public policy?" James Anderson (2003), Clarke Cochran and colleagues (2003), and Thomas Dye (2002) have done just that. Anderson answers this question by stating: "A policy is defined as a relatively stable, purposive course of action followed by an actor or set of actors dealing with a problem or matter of concern" (2003, 2). Cochran and colleagues similarly observe that policy is "an intentional course of action followed by a government institution or official for resolving an issue of public concern" (2003, 1). Dye posits what may be the most straightforward and frequently cited definition: public policy is simply "whatever governments choose to do or not to do" (2002, 1).

While these definitions portray slightly different perceptions of exactly what the policy-making process entails, each contains a common theme—the idea that the making of public policy involves the government attempting to deal with society's problems. Viewed in this light, the study of public policy is firmly grounded in the study of politics (Birkland 2001) and in the question of how political communities struggle with ideas (Stone 1997). More to the point, public policy making is cast as "a contest over conflicting, though equally plausible, conceptions of the same abstract goal or value" (Stone 1997, 12). It is within this context that I will view the public policy process.

Analysis of Public Policy

One helpful way to visualize the policy-making process is to set up a specific framework of analysis. Fortunately, several good frameworks exist today. While there is a wide array of frameworks, from those grounded in historic-geographic and socioeconomic conditions (Hofferbert 1974) to those that emphasize individual actors and their preferences, interests, and resources (Kiser and Ostrom 1982), the most common framework has been to represent the policy-making process as a sequence of linearly connected stages (Bonser, McGregor, and Oster 2000; Cochran et al. 2003).

Policy making is seen as beginning in the agenda-setting stage, where issues are recognized as both worthy of government attention and within the legitimate scope of government action. From here the issue moves to the policy formulation stage, where a plan is developed to deal with the issue. In the next stage, policy adoption, a specific alternative or solution is chosen. Execution of the policy is completed in the implementation stage, where policy makers use a variety of policy instruments to ensure that their goals are achieved. After a period of time, a judgment is made regarding the success of implementation. This takes place in the evaluation stage. Finally, a determination is made as to whether the chosen plan of attack should be terminated, continued, or changed.

An offshoot of this policy-made-in-stages approach is based on the systems approach developed by David Easton (Robertson and Judd 1989). According to this approach, society makes demands of the government, the government reacts to these demands, and the end result is a specific policy, sometimes called a policy outcome. The societal demands involve specific types of political behavior, political culture, and ideology. Moreover, these demands are passed forward through such mechanisms as public opinion, interest groups, mass media, political parties, and community elites. The government policy-making structure is set up to view and deal with these demands within an institutional structure consisting of legislatures, elected executives, courts, and bureaucracy (including administrative agencies).

Essentially, the government processes the demands to produce public policy. The end results are called policy outcomes and consist of laws, executive orders, court rulings, regulations, enforcement actions, budgets, and taxes. This type of approach focuses specifically on institutions and political behavior both inside and outside those institutions.

While this focus on institutions and political behavior has remained a very popular approach, there has been some criticism that viewing public policy making through a simple sequence of stages is insufficient to grasp the true meaning and development of public policy. In other words, the policy-making process is now viewed as much too complex to be explained in such a straightforward manner (John 2003). The conceptual frameworks of John Kingdon (1995), Paul Sabatier and Hank Jenkins-Smith (1993), Frank Baumgartner and Bryan Jones (1993), and Elinor Ostrom (1990) are currently recognized as some of the most advanced approaches to the study of public policy, each, in its own way, addressing the complexities of public policy making (John 2003; Weschler 1991). The frameworks of Kingdon, Sabatier and Jenkins-Smith, and Baumgartner and Jones are grounded in the idea that policy is made through a series of complex interactions among participants, across time, and at multiple levels of government. Ostrom's framework challenges the more conventional approaches and posits that "communities rely on institutions that resemble neither the state nor the market, but are based on voluntary cooperation" (Weschler 1991, 489). Furthermore, as delineated in the next four paragraphs, these scholars portray their particular public policy constructs in a way that emphasizes a particular aspect of how policy changes over time.

Kingdon's (1995) approach conceptualizes policy making around enterprising policy entrepreneurs who make things happen within the context of three dynamic streams (problem stream, policy stream, and political stream) that merge at certain points in time (windows of opportunity) to possibly stimulate the production of a specific public policy. The problem stream consists of various mechanisms that bring problems to decision makers' attention. One such mechanism is the focusing event, which includes disasters, crises, personal experiences, and symbols. However, focusing events need to be understood within the context of preexisting perceptions, especially about past government actions. It is important to note that government officials do not address all problems. Hence, how and under what conditions problems are defined helps determine their status in the problem stream.

The Sabatier and Jenkins-Smith (1993) approach centers on advocacy coalitions as the primary determinants of public policy. Advocacy coalitions are defined as groups of actors from both private and public organizations at all levels of government who share a common set of values or beliefs. The policy process is viewed within a framework in which these advocacy coalitions attempt to manipulate the rules of government to bring about change that coincides with their beliefs. This activity takes place within the basic social structure and in accordance with the constitutional rules of the system.

The Baumgartner and Jones (1993) approach, founded within the agenda-setting process, is structured around the principle that political systems are never in a state of general equilibrium. Baumgartner and Jones depict the policy consequences of agenda setting as dramatic reversals rather than marginal revisions to the status quo. The generation of new ideas is viewed as creating an atmosphere such that policy monopolies (defined as structural arrangements supported by powerful ideas) are unstable over time. Policy is made in fits and starts, slow, then rapid, rather than in a linear, smooth way. Existing political institutions and issue definitions are viewed as key to the policy-making process, with issue definition, because of its potential for mobilizing the disinterested, seen as the driving force in the process, affecting both stability and instability.

The Ostrom (1990, 1999) approach is founded within political economy and rational choice theory, portraying policy within a framework in which decision makers repeatedly have to make decisions constrained by a set of collective-choice rules. Decisions are made based on incomplete knowledge, with policy makers gaining a greater understanding of their situations (and adopting their strategies) by learning from their mistakes. Ostrom's approach is designed to "shatter the convictions of many policy analysts that the only way to solve [common-pool resource] problems is for external authorities to impose full property rights or centralized regulation" (1990, 182). Through her critique of three conventional approaches (privatization, central regulation, and management by interested parties), Ostrom offers a picture of policy making in which communities voluntarily develop policy rules, a commitment to collective benefits, and successful mutual monitoring (Weschler 1991).

These approaches to the study of public policy making vary from looking at public policy as a linear process that takes place in definable stages, to the notion that it is the complex interaction of policy streams or policy subsystems that determines where we are going, to the notion that viable policy solutions exist outside mainstream approaches such as privatization and centralized government. While these conceptualizations are significant to the study of public policy, it still remains helpful to understand that the core of policy making lies in behavior that takes place within our policy institutions (legislatures, the presidency, courts, interest groups, administrative agencies, local governments, and political parties) and in behavior that takes place outside these political institutions (public opinion, voting, political culture, and political socialization).

American Public Policy

The previous section described several ways to view public policy making in general. However, the making of public policy in America is also strongly affected by several unique features of our democratic political system (Rushefsky 1990; Sussman, Daynes, and West 2002). American federalism—systems set up such that the national government shares power with the fifty states—has created a complex set of intergovernmental relations. Although each level's authority is set in constitutional law, the interpretation of that law has led to considerable competition among the different levels to establish and retain authority.

With three separate branches, each with primary responsibility for carrying out certain functions (e.g., legislature makes the law, executive executes the law, judicial interprets the law), it would seem that American policy is grounded in a finely defined model of government. But separation of powers means that the sharing of authority and the system of checks and balances ensures that each branch has some control over the others' powers. These shared powers include a high degree of both fragmentation and incrementalism.

Fragmentation underscores the redundancy and overlapping of authority between and among branches. For each issue there is generally no central point of control, leading to inconsistent and fractured policy making characterized by numerous points of access for interest groups to pursue their separate agendas. The incremental nature of American policy making prevents dynamic and innovative changes except on rare occasions. Most policy is based on the current or previous policy, with only small, incremental changes.

Finally, two divergent perspectives exist in the United States about who actually controls the power of governance. The pluralistic view argues that policy is made within a system based on multiple and competing interests and groups vying for control over any given issue. Participation comes from being a member of those interests or groups. In the elite theory of governance, participation is open only to the few who possess special characteristics such as wealth or institutional status.

Political stalemate appears to cause considerable disruption in American policy making. However, a careful analysis of how American public policy making works shows that the system was set up to be slow, deliberate, and often very confusing (Bosso 1987). It is a system based on an inherent faith in democratic institutions and founded on shared social, political, and cultural ideals. There is also a sharing of common problems. Urban decay, deteriorating infrastructure, increasing crime, and environmental degradation are just some of the problems common to all regions of America today. In the end, policy makers must deal with all aspects of American life, both good and bad.

OVERVIEW OF ENVIRONMENTAL POLICY MAKING

Environmental Policy Today

It has been almost two decades since the declaration that the world has entered a new era in environmental policy making—one that embraces a global conception of environmental degradation (Rosenbaum 1991) and a new generation of environmental problems (Vig and Kraft 1990). We are now functioning in an era marked by great complexity and diversity, one in which environmentalism is cast as "the most elaborate and segmented of our social issues" (Sussman, Daynes, and West 2002, 313). Emphasis has turned toward the internationalization of environmental problems and policy, as issues such as climate change, acid rain, geochemical flux, and control of toxic pollution are viewed more and more from a world, rather than a state, perspective (Bright 2003; Harrison and Bryner 2004; Rosenbaum 2002).

Yet despite these highly publicized changes in the environmental landscape, many of our nation's "old" environmental problems remain. Implementation of the Clean Air Act, cleanup of federal nuclear waste facilities, and the question of opening up more public lands to oil exploration continue to be vital areas of public policy concern. In the United States, as elsewhere in the world, we are still coming to terms with such environmental problems as air and water pollution, hazardous materials, and the preservation of public lands.

Moreover, because these environmental problems are inherently public problems, solutions must come from within the same policy-making process described earlier. The general pattern of decision making includes the government attempting to solve society's problems through a process of "high-stakes politics" (Scheberle 2004, 2). In this case, the problems happen to be environmental in nature.

Environmental policy making is inherently subject to the direct and indirect influence of those features that make American politics unique. In this regard, American federalism lies at the core of many environmental issues. Who should be responsible for hazardous waste siting and nuclear waste cleanup? Who should have the most say in how national forests are managed or preserved and whether Alaskan tundra should be opened for oil exploration? Who owns the rights to the precious water that flows through our western rivers? These questions can only be answered within a framework of intergovernmental cooperation and competition.

Environmental policy is fragmented in every sense of the word. Administrative agencies guard their turf with much resolve, leading more to competition than cooperation. Judges overrule executives. Executives defy regulatory directives. Redundancy and overlap abound in attempts to control our environmental heritage. Policy is anything but consistent, and innovative change occurs rarely. No environmental policy is left unscathed by the intricacies of these U.S. political characteristics. Whether the challenge comes from within the intergovernmental realm, through conflict between branches, from pressures of interest groups, or simply with the U.S. bureaucratic infrastructure, the policy outcomes reflect the values of the American system.

The words of Dean Mann remain an accurate description of the unique and complex aspects of environmental policy making in the United States:

> That the politics of environmental policymaking is a process of dramatic advances, incomplete movement in the "right" direction, frequent and partial retrogression, sometimes illogical and contradictory combinations of policies, and often excessive cost should come as no surprise to students of American politics. Environmental policies reflect the dominant structures and values of the American political system. (1986, 4)

Thus, we are left with the task of evaluating our nation's environmental policy within the confines of an institutional structure that embodies a unique and often fractionalized political system. We are attempting to resolve age-old environmental problems as well as dealing with a third generation of environmental problems. In addition, solutions to environmental problems, in the absence of fundamental institutional or constitutional change, can only be resolved through the public policy-making process as it now stands.

Tensions in the Environmental World

Having accepted the idea that environmental policy making in the United States reflects the dominant values of the American political system and also follows the same policy-making process that guides other governmental issues, it is time to recognize that environmental policy is singularly unique in many aspects. Several tensions exist in the world of environmental policy making that set it apart from other policy areas.

First, the prominence of the environmental ethos on the American agenda is a relatively new phenomenon, essentially beginning in the late

1960s and catapulting to the forefront during the 1970s (Hoberg 2001; Kline 2000). This relatively new interest in the environment has led to several competing value systems, each attempting to preserve its way of life. The most obvious is represented by the conflict between the development of our natural resources and environmental protection.

At a philosophical level, this conflict reflects differences between American interests that place their highest value on economic growth and those that place their highest value on environmental protection (Grant 2003; Rosenbaum 2002). The dominant American values of capitalism and the market system revolve around the belief that humans are the center of the universe and are responsible for managing the world around them. This value system represents growth, development, and the use of technology to foster these ideals. Environmentalists share a much different viewpoint. In the words of Walter Rosenbaum, "[E]nvironmentalism sharply criticizes marketplace economics generally and capitalism particularly, and denigrates the growth ethic, unrestrained technological optimism, and the political structures supporting these cultural traits" (2002, 28).

At a more practical level, this friction between values is apparent when we examine the concept of environmental protection. American preoccupation with economic growth and resource management, developed early on in the American experience, has given way to a new set of concerns that includes quality-of-life issues such as the environment (Vig and Kraft 2000). Although degrees of conflict exist, people are now being asked to choose between economic development and environmental protection. Pervading this decision choice are the questions of who should control our natural resources and which value should have a higher priority, economic growth or environmental protection. Policy debates over protecting old-growth forests in the Pacific Northwest, opening Alaska to oil exploration, siting a permanent nuclear waste facility in Nevada, and deciding whether dams should be removed to enhance the return of salmon to their spawning grounds are all representative of the larger argument between growth and environmental protection, between conservation/management and preservation.

A subset of the friction between economic growth and environmental protection is easily seen within the continuing and current debate between environmental groups and property rights advocates at the state and local levels (Bosso and Gruber 2006). This particular clash of values has been portrayed in the past by various wise use movements in the West and is currently reflected by the numerous court cases involving regulatory takings and land use that are prevalent in today's western states (O'Leary 2006). Furthermore, this particular value clash will likely be part of the environmental policy debate (especially in the West) well into the future.

Another area of tension revolves around the question of which method is most appropriate for carrying out environmental policy—government regulation or a market-oriented system (Meier, Garman, and Keiser 1998). Conflicts arise over which method is most efficient and which one leads to greater environmental protection. With the seemingly endless increase in environmental problems (endangered species, hazardous waste disposal, global warming, acid deposition), some believe it is only through governmental control and regulation that we can meet the demand for increased environmental protection. However, others reject this argument on the premise that environmental regulation is ineffective, inefficient, and out of control.

A current trend related to the tension between government regulation and market forces is the growing use of collaborative ecosystems management. As William Lowry has pointed out, "Perhaps the most promising third-stage proposals for resource policies are those that attempt collaborative, science-based resolutions to achieve innovative management of natural ecosystems" (2006, 320). Examples of such collaborative processes are especially prominent in western states, characterized by efforts with respect to old-growth forest ecosystems in the Pacific Northwest, efforts to reconcile natural preservation and development interests in the San Diego area, and adaptive management efforts to control the waters of the Colorado River (Lowry 2006).

A further tension present in American environmental policy making involves the science-policy linkage. Conventional wisdom posits that environmental questions are fundamentally questions of science (Carroll, Brockelman, and Westfall 1997; Underdal 2000). At the same time, some recognize that it is not easy to translate the findings of science into reasonable public policies (Skully 2003).

Along these lines, Walter Rosenbaum has characterized the science-policy nexus as a treacherous place to be because environmental issues compel public officials to make scientific judgments and scientists to resolve policy issues, and neither group is trained to make such judgments (2002). This tension between scientists and policy makers appears emblematic of all environmental policy making. As Rosenbaum observed, "The almost inevitable need to resolve scientific questions through the political process and the problems that arise in making scientific and political judgments compatible are two of the most troublesome characteristics of environmental politics" (2002, 125).

One last point must be made with respect to the recent emergence of environmental protection as a major American value: it is here to stay. Environmental protection has not only been acknowledged as one of the oldest social issues (Sussman, Daynes, and West 2002) as well as part of a new paradigm of social values (Milbrath 1984), but it has also been institutionalized into the American policy-making process. The establishment of the National Environmental Policy Act, environmental impact statements, the Council on Environmental Quality, and the Environmental Protection Agency bear witness to this fact. There should be no doubt in anyone's mind that environmental protection is now considered one of the core values of American society along with social justice, economic prosperity, national security, and democracy (Rosenbaum 2002; Vig and Kraft 2000).

OVERVIEW OF WESTERN ENVIRONMENTAL POLICY

Joel Garreau has characterized the American West as a region blessed with a "spirit-lifting physical endowment" and a repository for the "values, ideas, memories, and vistas that date back to the frontier" (1981, 302–303). The West continues to bask in a frontier image of mythic proportions (Hupp and Malachowsky 1993; Limerick 1987; Rudzitis 1996; Thompson 1998). It is characterized as having a wholly formed self-image defined by an idealistic and romantic western value system (Rothman 1999), a region where the "isolation, the struggle with nature, and the unpredictable opportunities fostered a resourcefulness, self-reliance, and spirit of working together" (Arrington 1994, 256).

This particular aspect of the western myth—the idea that it was the rugged, self-reliant individualist who built the West—remains strong today. More important, this myth fits in nicely with a particular aspect of the Mountain West's political culture—the long-established resentment of eastern interference in the western way of life. To this way of thinking, the role of the federal government in creating the conditions and expending the capital that allowed the West to grow and flourish is simply ignored (Barker, Freemuth, and Johnson 2002).

For years, writers have described a feeling of western alienation from national politics and discontent with the eastern establishment. References are often made to a "sense of disadvantage, exploitation, and betrayal" that permeates the West (Bartlett 1993, 111), as well as a "sense of helplessness bred of the perception that decisions in the West are made from the outside and that western communities have never been able to control their own destinies" (Wilkinson 1992, 301). The words of former Idaho governor Cecil Andrus, referring to national media coverage of issues such as the Endangered Species Act and forest fire prevention, reflect this sentiment: "There is a vastness west of the 100th meridian that you people don't understand. There is a culture out here that is different from Manhattan" (Andrus Center 2002, 1).

Those from outside the West seem to have trouble understanding this point of view. For example, in the keynote address at a conference concerning the national media's relationship to public policy and the West, former ABC World News anchor Peter Jennings summed up his view of the West's particular brand of federalism:

> I am somewhat puzzled at the tendency here in the West to be anti-government and even to only reluctantly acknowledge that the federal government and western development are incontrovertibly together. Without the government, western development would have been so different. . . . An objective person would argue that [the West] would have been a much poorer place without the federal government. (Andrus Center 2002, 51)

To understand why the West is truly unique in this regard, we need to look at only one statistic: the federal government owns nearly half of all the land area in the thirteen westernmost states, including half or more than half of the land in Nevada (83.1%), Alaska (67.9%), Idaho (62.5%), Utah (64.5%), Oregon (52.8), and Wyoming (49.9%); more than one-third the land in Arizona (45.6%), California (44.9%), Colorado (36.4%), and New Mexico (34.2%); and nearly one-third in Washington (28.5%) and Montana (28.5%) (Rosenbaum 2002, 308–309). This federal ownership has resulted in both an undue reliance and dependence on the federal government and a resentment of federal interference.

Critical decisions concerning the West's natural resources and lands have long been concentrated at the federal level. This control was greatly enhanced in the 1970s when Congress substantially increased its federal authority for developing and enforcing air and water quality standards, committed the federal government to retain ownership and management of public lands, and consolidated federal responsibility for energy development and planning (Francis and Ganzel 1984). This followed a long historical relationship during which the federal government had been almost singularly responsible for the development of western natural resources through the establishment of water supplies, grazing fees, timber roads, and access to minerals.

But this heavy dependence on the federal government by the West has been defined as one of necessity, not choice (Francis and Thomas 1991). The Sagebrush Rebellion of the 1970s (a movement centered on the demand that federal lands in the West be turned over to the states in which they lay) and the County Supremacy / Wise Use Movement of the 1990s (a movement centered on the demand that counties should have joint sovereignty over federal lands within their borders) have come to symbolize the strong antigovernment feelings in the West and the perceived federal interference in western values (Alm and Witt 1997; DeVine and Soden 1997; Layzer 2002). The tensions over property rights (described earlier) represent these same antigovernment sentiments that pervade many western states today.

As described earlier, the complex and contradictory set of intergovernmental relations, coupled with the frontier ethos of rugged individualism and antigovernment sentiment, have established the setting for environmental policy making in the West. At no time can the influence and impact of the federal government be overlooked. Many policy makers in the West truly believe the national-level government has declared a war on the West and have responded with anti-tax, anti-regulation, and anti-Washington rhetoric (Switzer 2004).

CONCLUSION

The heart of American public policy falls within the realm of government attempting to solve and ameliorate social problems. Western environmental policy making is no exception. It possesses the special policy characteristics that make the U.S. system unique. Policy is dependent on institutional structures, political behavior, intergovernmental relations, and the myriad elements that symbolize the American policy-making system. Furthermore, the West feels the effects of decentralization, a dynamic and shifting population base, the increased pressure of global influences, and the increased concern for quality-of-life issues such as environmental protection. Within this policy structure, the West has witnessed a significant increase in intergovernmental and value conflicts. The concepts that embody American federalism have been severely tested in the West.

The single factor that dominates western environmental policy making remains the high degree of influence, almost dominance, of the federal government. This is a direct result of the continued prominence of natural resources in western social, economic, and political life. Although there has been a substantial decline in dependence on a natural resource–based economy and an increased concern for quality-of-life issues, natural resources still define the texture of western environmental policy making.

The federal government owns over half of the West's land base and has historically played the major role in the development of the natural resources on those lands. While accepting the need for a federal presence in this development and enjoying the wealth that comes with royalties wrought from the extraction of resources, the West has still fostered a strong antigovernment rhetoric against federal interference. Moreover, with the federal government recently taking the lead in enforcement of environmental regulations, both the federal presence and antigovernment sentiment have expanded in scope.

A quick survey of some of the key issues at the top of the policy-making agenda in the western states verifies the increased tension among intergovernmental participants. Witness the extended controversies surrounding the designation of wilderness area, the use of snowmobiles in Yellowstone National Park, the battle over water rights in the midst of a prolonged drought, the question of opening additional Alaskan land to oil exploration, and the reintroduction of wolves to the Mountain West. A common thread running through all these issues is the West's desire to play a greater role in deciding its own fate and controlling its own destiny.

While the environmental ethos has gained a strong foothold in some western states, the vast majority of those states remain grounded in their heritage—natural resource extraction from a vast, beautiful, and bountiful landscape. This foundation makes it impossible to study environmental policy making in the West without considering both the imagery and reality of the West as a place dominated by rugged individualism and reliance on the federal government. Simply put, the West is a place where federalism meets environmental policy making head-on and where the battle for environmental supremacy remains tied to the opposing values of natural resource development and environmental protection. In the end, environmental policy making in the American West is an accurate reflection of the chaotic, dynamic value structures that mark public policy making in the United States.

REFERENCES

Alm, L., and S. Witt. 1997. "County Governments and Public Lands: A Review of the County Supremacy Movement in Four Western States." In B. Steel, ed., *Public Lands Management in the West*. Westport, CT: Praeger.

Anderson, J. 2003. *Public Policymaking* (5th ed.). Boston: Houghton Mifflin.

Andrus Center. 2002. *Dateline: The West*. Official Transcripts. Boise, ID: Andrus Center for Public Policy.

Arrington, L. 1994. *History of Idaho, Volume 2*. Moscow: University of Idaho Press.

Barker, R., J. Freemuth, and M. Johnson. 2002. "Proceedings from the 2002 Andrus Conference." In *Dateline: The West*. Boise, ID: Andrus Center for Public Policy.

Bartlett, R. 1993. "Political Culture and the Environmental Problematique in the American West." In Z. Smith, ed., *Environmental Politics and Policy in the West*. Dubuque, IA: Kendall/Hunt.

Baumgartner, F., and B. Jones. 1993. *Agendas and Instability in American Politics*. Chicago: University of Chicago Press.

Birkland, T. 2001. *An Introduction to the Policy Process*. Armonk, NY: M. E. Sharpe.

Bonser, C., E. McGregor, and C. Oster. 2000. *American Public Policy Problems*. Upper Saddle River, NJ: Prentice-Hall.

Bosso, C. 1987. *Pesticides and Politics: The Life Cycle of a Public Issue*. Pittsburgh: University of Pittsburgh Press.

Bosso, C., and D. Gruber. 2006. "Maintaining Presence: Environmental Advocacy and the Permanent Campaign." In N. Vig and M. Kraft, eds., *Environmental Policy: New Directions for the Twenty-First Century*. Washington, DC: CQ.

Bright, C. 2003. "A History of Our Future." In L. Starke, ed., *State of the World: 2003*. New York: W. W. Norton.

Carroll, J., P. Brockelman, and M. Westfall. 1997. *The Greening of Faith: God, the Environment, and the Good Life*. Hanover, NH: University Press of New England.

Cochran, C., et al. 2003. *American Public Policy* (7th ed.). Belmont, CA: Wadsworth.

DeVine, K., and D. Soden. 1997. "Changing Political Geometry: Public Lands and Natural Resources in Nevada." In B. Steel, ed., *Public Lands Management in the West*. Westport, CT: Praeger.

Dye, T. 2002. *Understanding Public Policy* (10th ed.). Upper Saddle River, NJ: Prentice-Hall.

Francis, J., and R. Ganzel. 1984. *Western Public Lands: The Management of Natural Resources in a Time of Declining Federalism*. Totowa, NJ: Rowman and Allanheld.

Francis, J., and C. Thomas. 1991. "Influences on Western Political Culture." In C. Thomas, ed., *Politics and Public Policy in the Contemporary American West*. Albuquerque: University of New Mexico Press.

Garreau, J. 1981. *The Nine Nations of North America*. Boston: Houghton Mifflin.

Grant, J. 2003. *Community, Democracy, and the Environment: Learning to Share the Future*. Boulder: Rowman and Littlefield.

Harrison, N., and G. Bryner, eds. 2004. *Science and Politics in the International Environment*. Boulder: Rowman and Littlefield.

Hoberg, G. 2001. "The Emerging Triumph of Ecosystem Management." In C. Davis, ed., *Western Public Lands*. Boulder: Westview.

Hofferbert, R. 1974. *The Study of Public Policy.* Indianapolis: Bobbs-Merrill.

Hupp, D., and J. Malachowsky. 1993. "The Politics of Polarization: Rural Divide." *Western States Center News* 10, 1–8.

John, P. 2003. "Is There Life after Policy Streams, Advocacy Coalitions, and Punctuations: Using Evolutionary Theory to Explain Policy Change." *Policy Studies Journal* 31, 481–498.

Kingdon, J. 1995. *Agendas, Alternatives, and Public Policies* (2nd ed.). New York: HarperCollins.

Kiser, L., and E. Ostrom. 1982. "The Three Worlds of Action." In E. Ostrom, ed., *Strategies of Political Inquiry*. Beverly Hills: Sage.

Kline, B. 2000. *First along the River* (2nd ed.). San Francisco: Acada Books.

Layzer, J. 2002. *The Environmental Case: Translating Values into Policy.* Washington, DC: CQ.

Limerick, P. 1987. *The Legacy of Conquest: The Unbroken Past of the American West*. New York: W. W. Norton.

Lowry, W. 2006. "A Return to Traditional Priorities in Natural Resource Policies." In N. Vig and M. Kraft, eds., *Environmental Policy: New Directions for the Twenty-First Century*. Washington, DC: CQ.

Mann, D. 1986. "Democratic Politics and Environmental Policy." In S. Kamieniecki, R. O'Brien, and M. Clarke, eds., *Controversies in Environmental Policy*. Albany: State University of New York Press.

Meier, K., E. Garman, and L. Keiser. 1998. *Regulation and Consumer Protection*. Houston: Dame.

Milbrath, L. 1984. *Environmentalists: Vanguard for a New Society*. Albany: State University of New York Press.

O'Leary, R. 2006. "Environmental Policy in the Courts." In N. Vig and M. Kraft, eds., *Environmental Policy: New Directions for the Twenty-First Century*. Washington, DC: CQ.

Ostrom, E. 1990. *Governing the Commons: The Evolution of Institutions for Collective Action*. New York: Cambridge University Press.

———. 1999. "Institutional Rational Choice: An Assessment of the Institutional Analysis and Development Framework." In P. A. Sabatier, ed., *Theories of the Policy Process*. Boulder: Westview.

Robertson, D., and D. Judd. 1989. *The Development of American Public Policy: The Structure of Policy Restraint*. Glenview, IL: Scott, Foresman.

Rosenbaum, W. 1991. *Environmental Politics and Policy* (2nd ed.). Washington, DC: CQ.

———. 2002. *Environmental Politics and Policy* (5th ed.). Washington, DC: CQ.

Rothman, H. 1999. "Tourism as Colonial Economy." In R. White and J. Findlay, eds., *Power and Place in the North American West*. Seattle: University of Washington Press.

Rudzitis, G. 1996. *Wilderness and the Changing American West*. New York: John Wiley & Sons.

Rushefsky, M. 1990. *Public Policy in the United States: Toward the Twenty-First Century*. Pacific Groves, CA: Brooks/Cole.

Sabatier, P., and H. Jenkins-Smith. 1993. *Policy Change and Learning*. Boulder: Westview.

Scheberle, D. 2004. *Federalism and Environmental Policy* (2nd ed.). Washington, DC: Georgetown University Press.

Skully, M. 2003. "Of Patronage and Exploitation." *Chronicle of Higher Education* 49, B13.

Stone, D. 1997. *Policy Paradox*. New York: W. W. Norton.

Sussman, G., B. Daynes, and J. West. 2002. *American Politics and the Environment*. New York: Longman.

Switzer, J. 2004. *Environmental Politics: Domestic and Global Dimensions* (4th ed.). Belmont, CA: Thomson/Wadsworth.

Thompson, J. 1998. *Forging the Prairie West: The Illustrated History of Canada*. Toronto: Oxford University Press.

Underdal, A. 2000. "Science and Politics: The Anatomy of an Uneasy Partnership." In S. Andesen et al., eds., *Science and Politics in International Regimes*. Manchester: Manchester University Press.

Vig, N., and M. Kraft. 1990. *Environmental Policy in the 1990s*. Washington, DC: CQ.

———. 2000. *Environmental Policy: New Directions for the Twenty-First Century*. Washington, DC: CQ.

Weschler, L. 1991. "Taming the Common Pool." *Journal of Public Administration Research and Theory*: J-PART 1, no. 4, 488–492.

Wilkinson, C. 1992. *The Eagle Bird: Mapping a New West*. New York: Vintage Books.

CHAPTER TWO

BUREAUCRACY, POLITICS, AND ENVIRONMENTAL POLICY IN THE AMERICAN WEST

Matthew A. Cahn, Sheldon Kamieniecki, and Denise McCain-Tharnstrom

The West is blessed with the majority of America's remaining natural resources, which are widely dispersed across the entire region. These resources are extremely valuable, and they require government monitoring and, in many cases, regulation. The federal government manages millions of acres of forests, national and state parks, and areas of scenic beauty, which include coastal regions, mountain ranges, and vast deserts. Many government agencies are also responsible for overseeing the extraction of oil, coal, natural gas, uranium, and a long list of metals and minerals. The federal government, therefore, plays a major role in natural resource management in this area of the country.

Most federally owned public land is in the West; of the 674,267,000 acres of public land owned by the federal government, over 613 million acres are in the West (U.S. Census Bureau 2002). In fact, over 91 percent of all federally owned lands are in thirteen western states (Alaska, Arizona, California, Colorado, Hawaii, Idaho, Montana, Nevada, New Mexico, Oregon, Utah,

Washington, and Wyoming). The federal government owns over 30 percent of total land in California, Colorado, Montana, New Mexico, Oregon, and Washington; over 50 percent of total land in Alaska, Arizona, Idaho, Utah, and Wyoming; and over 90 percent of total land in Nevada (U.S. Census Bureau 2002). These vast state lands are managed by competing federal agencies for multiple uses, including natural resource extraction, grazing, logging, and recreation. Federal control over so much of the West has presented unique issues not faced by eastern states. This and other factors have resulted in a complex intergovernmental environmental policy arena that is considerably more intricate than those in other regions of the country.

In addition, the West has a number of environmental problems that are the result of the use of natural resources, population growth, and economic expansion. Numerous abandoned mines, for example, have become toxic waste sites and require costly abatement measures. Air and water pollution are acute problems in some parts of the West. Efforts to protect the environment often involve a host of federal, state, and local government offices.

Government control over western environmental policy springs, in part, from the strong environmental protection values many Americans share and, in particular, from their appreciation of the West's natural beauty (Kamieniecki 2006). In part because of federal ownership of much western land, the West contains most of the nation's undeveloped landscapes. The spectacular beauty of the Pacific coastline, the old-growth forests, desert vistas, and scenic mountain ranges are among the many ecosystems preserved in the numerous western national parks, including Yosemite, Sequoia, and Yellowstone. Over a century ago, citizen concern for protecting the natural surroundings of the West spawned the conservation and preservation movements, whose followers viewed the western lands as a national resource requiring federal protection and management to ensure their preservation for future generations. Many new westerners share these views and express strong environmental protectionist values (Klyza 1996, 2001). These values, coupled with growing populations and increased scarcity of water and usable state land, have resulted in the creation of numerous state agencies to oversee environmental protection. California and Oregon, in particular, have become known for their environmental activism and regulatory leadership.

Other westerners, however, are fiercely supportive of states rights and eschew federal control for independence (Davis 2001; Layzer 2002). The West has historically attracted "rugged individuals" who took risks to settle the arid western plains and mountains. Growth and opportunity were rewards for aggressive actors who seized water rights, rerouted rivers, and logged forests. The region's natural beauty and less dense populations attracted and retained many westerners; nonetheless, a love for the natural beauty that surrounds them cannot support the local economies or pay for much-needed public services (e.g., education and health care). Political tension has grown as the new bloc of voters prioritizes recreation, aesthetics, and tourism over traditional western views of local control and use of natural resources. Accordingly, western environmental politics reflects value conflicts involving environmental and economic protectionism, federal authority versus states' rights, public versus private ownership, and scarcity issues. These deep conflicts, with their roots in the history of the development of western environmental policy, set the backdrop for intergovernmental tension and bureaucratic turf wars over the direction of western environmental policy and natural resource management. Sorting out the environmental policy bureaucracy in the West is not easy, but it is essential to do so to understand fully the various political dimensions of natural resource management in this part of the country.

This chapter analyzes the environmental and natural resource policy bureaucracy in the West. The chapter begins with a brief review of the development of federal environmental policies over time, focusing especially on those policies that have impacted the West. The study then discusses the intricate web of agencies that comprise the policy bureaucracy, with particular attention paid to the influence of the U.S. Environmental Protection Agency (EPA) and federal natural resource agencies in the western states as well as the development of state environmental bureaucracies. The impact of ideology, politics, and bureaucratic agendas on environmental policy making is also discussed. Finally, the future direction bureaucratic politics and policies might take in this area of the country is examined.

EARLY EVOLUTION OF A NATIONAL ENVIRONMENTAL POLICY

The early environmental movement began in the West. Among other things, it resulted in the establishment of Yosemite Valley State Park in 1860 and the creation of Yellowstone National Park in 1872. Early environmentalists were split between conservationists, who favored controlled development of environmental resources, and preservationists (such as the San Francisco–based Sierra Club, founded in 1892 by John Muir), who focused on preserving public lands and wilderness areas. The prevailing federal view, that lands were a national resource available for public and private use, dominated until 1916, when the preservationists scored a victory with the creation of the National Park Service. This permitted the transfer of public lands from the Forest Service to the Park Service, where the lands were protected by the agency's mandate to preserve and protect public lands and wilderness areas. National parks were created, in part, because federal officials thought the land on which they were located had little economic value. For the next few decades, tension between the two mandates focused environmental concern on multiple-use management of public lands. Under the administration of the Departments of the Interior (DOI) and Agriculture, public lands were set aside for recreation, ranching, forestry, mining, wilderness, and wildlife refuges.

Concern later expanded from conservation and preservation to pollution protection. By the 1940s and 1950s, public alarm over water pollution had grown, and Congress passed federal water protection acts over the vetoes of Presidents Harry Truman and Dwight Eisenhower. Although both presidents thought water protection legislation might harm agriculture and urban development and would cost too much, Congress and the public were becoming increasingly concerned about the continued availability of clean water. In 1961, the U.S. Senate Select Committee on National Water Resources sought national regulation of water irrigation as an alternative to flood-control dams as part of a revitalized water resources development program (Caulfield 1989).

Contemporary environmental concern in the West and elsewhere coincided with the new policies of President John F. Kennedy. Kennedy voiced concern over depleting natural resources in his "Special Message to the Congress on Natural Resources," delivered February 23, 1916. He outlined the need for federal legislation to protect air, water, forests, topsoil, wildlife, seashores, and public lands for recreational use.

President Lyndon Johnson continued Kennedy's environmental initiatives. In September 1964, Johnson signed the Land and Water Conservation Fund Act and the Wilderness Act into law. The Water Quality Act, establishing the Federal Water Pollution Control Administration, was enacted in 1965. The first Clean Air Act was adopted in 1965, and the Air Quality Act was passed in 1967. By October 1968, Johnson had approved the Wild and Scenic Rivers Act, the National Trails System Act, the establishment of North Cascades National Park, and the establishment of Redwood National Park (Caulfield 1989). In one way or another, these laws have dramatically influenced environmental politics and policy in the West and have placed large tracts of western land under tighter federal regulation.

In contrast to the Kennedy and Johnson administrations, the Nixon administration was more supportive of economic expansion than of environmental protection and natural resource conservation. His appointment for secretary of DOI was Walter Hickle who, as governor of Alaska, was more concerned with development than with environmental protection. To satisfy the Senate Interior Committee, Nixon ultimately appointed Russell Train, president of the Conservation Foundation, as undersecretary of the DOI. Although Nixon generally tended to favor economic growth over environmental protection, he was not prepared to fight a Congress or a public alarmed about the nation's air and water quality and natural resources. Public concern over the dangers of pollution was perhaps most clearly expressed on Earth Day in April 1970. Thousands of people demonstrated and protested the lack of effective government action to improve environmental quality. As a result of this concern, President Nixon supported the creation of the EPA in 1970, with a mission to protect human health and safeguard the air, land, and water upon which life depends.

PASSAGE OF THE NATIONAL ENVIRONMENTAL POLICY ACT

Nixon also suggested that a Council on Environmental Quality (CEQ) be created instead of adopting a legislative proposal for a National Environmental Policy Act (NEPA). However, NEPA passed Congress in 1969 and was signed into law by President Nixon. NEPA formally established the CEQ and was the first comprehensive federal legislation designed to protect environmental quality. According to the legislation, the federal government must now use all practicable means and measures, including financial and technical assistance, to protect the natural environment. NEPA makes environmental protection a national goal and requires preparation of detailed environmental impact statements (EISs) for evaluating all federal programs. Actions by federal agencies that oversee natural resources in the West (and elsewhere) have been guided by NEPA mandates.

In the 1970s nearly all federal agencies were required to develop some capabilities of environmental analysis under NEPA, which required that EISs be prepared for all major federal decisions that significantly affect environmental quality. The CEQ outlined detailed requirements for developing the EIS, which were enforced by the federal courts. Provisions for public hearings and citizen input permitted environmental and community groups to challenge agency actions, often by filing suits questioning the contents and adequacy of the EIS. As a result, agencies had to change significantly their project designs and, more generally, the way they do business (Bartlett 1989). The EIS has been used extensively in the western states because of the sharp increase in population growth and land development.

AGENCIES WITH ENVIRONMENTAL OVERSIGHT

Over thirty-five years after the creation of the EPA, environmental policy efforts are still uncoordinated and divided among numerous and diverse executive departments and agencies. While the EPA is responsible for much of the regulatory enforcement effort at the federal level, a number of other agencies oversee the use of natural resources in the West and elsewhere. Many natural resource agencies, bureaus, and services share overlapping responsibilities and conflicting goals. As a consequence, disputes between these entities are common.

Each cabinet-level department is responsible for maintaining the environmental integrity of programs within its jurisdiction. The DOI manages distinctly different types of resources: public lands, energy, and minerals (Bureau of Land Management—BLM)); national parks, preserves, and recreation areas (National Park Service); and wildlife (U.S. Fish and Wildlife Service). The Department of Agriculture oversees forestry (U.S. Forest Service) and soil conservation. These and other resources are abundant in the West, which contains nearly 70 percent of U.S. national forests, over 90 percent of public lands, and more than fifty national parks (U.S. Census Bureau 2002; U.S. Forest Service 2004; U.S. National Park Service 2005).

The Department of Commerce oversees oceanic and atmospheric monitoring and research. The State Department deals with international environmental agreements. The Justice Department is responsible for pursuing litigation for violations of environmental regulations. The Department of Defense is responsible for control of pollution created by or within defense facilities and, with the help of the U.S. Army Corps of Engineers, oversees civil works construction and dredge-and-fill operations. Many military bases are located in the West, are seriously contaminated, and require expensive abatement. The Department of Energy (DOE) coordinates energy policy and oil and gas research and development. The Office of Conservation and Renewable Energy, located within the Department of Energy, oversees

Table 2.1. Major Congressional Committees with Oversight Responsibility for Environmental Policy and Natural Resource Management Relevant to the Western States

United States House of Representatives

Committee	*Oversight Responsibility*
Agriculture	Soil conservation, forestry, pesticide policy
Commerce	Air quality, nuclear waste, drinking water, pesticide control, hazardous and toxic waste
Resources	Public lands, natural resources, national parks, wilderness areas, energy and nuclear waste disposal, water, oceanography, fisheries, endangered species, coastal zone management, mining
Transportation and Infrastructure	Water pollution, rivers and harbors, Superfund and hazardous waste cleanup, hydroelectric power
Science	Global climate change, environmental research and development, energy research

United States Senate

Committee	*Oversight Responsibility*
Agriculture, Nutrition, and Forestry	Soil conservation, forestry, pesticide policy, nutrition
Commerce, Science, and Transportation	Oceanography and marine affairs, coastal zone management, fisheries, some wildlife
Energy and Natural Resources	Energy, nuclear waste, national parks and recreation areas, wilderness, scenic rivers
Environment and Public Works	Air, water, and noise pollution; toxic and hazardous waste; nuclear waste; fisheries; wildlife; endangered species; ocean dumping; solid waste

energy conservation programs and studies the effects of acid rain and carbon dioxide associated with the burning of coal. Finally, the Department of Transportation manages mass transit, roads, and aerial noise pollution. The various federal agencies that deal with environmental and natural resource problems rarely communicate with one another or coordinate their efforts.

Many different federal agencies can be simultaneously responsible for a given environmental issue. For example, the Nuclear Regulatory Commission (NRC), the EPA, the Department of Energy, the DOI, the BLM, the U.S. Geological Survey, and the Department of Transportation have various policy roles involving the management of low-level waste, a major issue in the western United States. Congress has made almost no effort to coordinate agency environmental administration. Such a lack of coordination, while allowing the development of various levels of expertise in different departments, has also permitted a huge federal environmental and natural resource policy bureaucracy to develop. In addition to being inefficient, this situation sometimes leads to serious conflicts between agencies (e.g., the EPA and the BLM over water quality issues). This has particularly impacted the natural resource–rich West.

THE WHITE HOUSE

A number of environmental entities exist within the executive office of the president whose activities have the potential to affect western states, including the CEQ, the Office of Environmental Policy, and the Office of Federal Environmental Executive. The White House has largely ignored these offices since the beginning of the Reagan administration. Only the EPA has remained a strong executive agency force in environmental policy making. Overseeing policies and programs concerning air and water pollution, pesticide control, radiation, solid waste, and toxic and hazardous waste, the EPA is clearly the most visible environmental agency within the federal government, and its rules and standards significantly affect western states.

STRUCTURE AND ROLE OF THE ENVIRONMENTAL PROTECTION AGENCY

The structure of the EPA is unique from other agencies. It is the only regulatory agency that is not under the jurisdiction of a cabinet-level department. The agency enjoys legislative autonomy and authority to a much greater extent than other agencies and commissions. Legislation such as the Clean Air and Clean Water acts specifically outlines the agency's power and scope within these two policy domains (Meier 1985). The EPA has its own laboratories and research offices to help monitor environmental conditions and compliance.

Environmental programs are typically federalized, with states taking central enforcement responsibilities and the EPA taking an oversight role. The agency is organized into ten regions, with each regional headquarters having jurisdiction over the included states. The western states are covered by three regions. Region eight is centered in Denver and includes Colorado, Utah, Wyoming, Montana, North Dakota, and South Dakota. Region nine is based in San Francisco and includes California, Nevada, Arizona, and Hawaii. Region ten is headquartered in Seattle and oversees Washington, Oregon, Idaho, and Alaska. Currently, the EPA employs approximately 18,000 people nationwide to develop and enforce regulations authorized by federal environmental laws, perform environmentally related research, and sponsor voluntary pollution prevention and conservation partnerships and programs.

WESTERN STATES ENVIRONMENTAL BUREAUCRACIES

The environmental bureaucracy is not confined to the federal level. As with other states throughout the country, western states have established a firm foundation of agencies that work to maintain and improve environmental quality and conserve natural resources. As Table 2.2 illustrates, the specific environmental policy bureaucracy differs from state to state. Most western states have created a lead environmental agency. In addition to environmental protection agencies, state departments of food and agriculture regulate pesticides, while departments of health are typically responsible for assessing the health risks of exposure to chemicals.

Responsibility for controlling different types of pollution and natural resources is still divided among various bureaucratic entities within individual states. Nonetheless, it is possible to identify relevant agencies in seven areas: general environmental affairs, air quality, water development and water quality, solid waste management, hazardous materials management, natural resource management, and wildlife management. States have established agencies to oversee these areas in order to comply with federal guidelines and standards. State agencies also help address local environmental problems unique to each state. In some states, such as California, state standards actually exceed federal standards (e.g., air quality requirements).

State agencies typically work closely with other municipal, county, statewide, and federal agencies to develop environmental quality plans and accomplish abatement goals. On occasion, however, some state agencies have taken a leadership role in national environmental problem solving. The Oregon Department of Energy is currently working with other federal and Oregon agencies to build an experimental ocean-wave energy power project (Environmental News Network 2005). California's Air Resources Board, a division of the California Environmental Protection Agency (Cal-EPA), has continually led the nation in air pollution control measures.

As illustrated by Table 2.2, the creation of lead environmental agencies has not generally consolidated state bureaucratic oversight of environmental issues. Western states have assigned responsibility for the four environmental areas to as few as four and as many as nineteen different entities. California

Table 2.2. Environmental Agencies in the Western States

Agency	*State*	*State*	*State*
	Alaska	**Arizona**	**California**
Environmental Affairs	Department of Environmental Conservation (DEC)	Department of Environmental Quality (DEQ)	California Environmental Protection Agency (Cal-EPA)
Air	Air Quality Division (DEC)	Air Quality Division (DEQ)	Air Resources Board (Cal-EPA)
Water	Division of Water (DEC) Division of Mining, Land and Water (Department of Natural Resources) Division of Environmental Health Drinking Water Program (DEC)	Department of Water Resources Water Quality Division (DEQ)	Department of Water Resources California Coastal Commission Water Resources Control Board (Cal-EPA) California Watershed Council
Solid Waste	Division of Environmental Health Solid Waste Program (DEC)	Waste Programs Division (DEQ)	Integrated Waste Management Board (Cal-EPA)
Hazardous Materials	Division of Environmental Health Solid Waste Program (DEC) Division of Spill Prevention and Response (DEC)	Waste Programs Division (DEQ)	Integrated Waste Management Board (Cal-EPA) Department of Toxic Substances Control (Cal-EPA) Office of Environmental Health Hazard Assessment (Cal-EPA)
Natural Resources	Department of Natural Resources	Department of Mines and Mineral Resources Natural Resources Division (State Land Department)	Resources Agency
Wildlife	Department of Fish and Game	Game and Fish Department	Department of Fish and Game

	Colorado	Hawaii	Idaho
Environmental Affairs	Department of Natural Resources (DNR) Department of Public Health and Environment (DPHE)	Department of Health (DOH)	Department of Environmental Quality (DEQ)
Air	Air Pollution Control Commission (DPHE)	Clean Air Branch (DOH)	Air Quality Division (DEQ)
Water	Division of Water Resources (DNR) Ground Water Commission Water Conservation Board Water Quality Control Division (DPHE)	Commission on Water Resource Management (DLNR) Water Quality Management Program, Environment Planning Office (DOH) Clean Water Branch (DOH) Safe Drinking Water Branch (DOH) Wastewater Branch (DOH)	Department of Water Resources Water Quality Division (DEQ)
Solid Waste	Hazardous Materials and Waste Management Division (DPHE)	Solid and Hazardous Waste Branch (DOH)	Waste Management and Remediation Division (DEQ)
Hazardous Materials	Hazardous Materials and Waste Management Division (DPHE)	Office Of Hazardous Evaluation and Emergency Response (DOH) Noise, Radiation, and Indoor Air Quality Branch (DOH) Solid and Hazardous Waste Branch (DOH)	Hazardous Waste Program, Waste Management and Remediation Division (DEQ)
Natural Resources	Department of Natural Resources (DNR)	Department of Land and Natural Resources (DLNR)	Department of Lands
Wildlife	Division of Wildlife (DNR)	Division of Forestry and Wildlife (DLNR) Animal Species Advisory Commission (DLNR)	Department of Fish and Game

continued on next page

Table 2.2—*continued*

Agency	*State*	*State*	*State*
	Montana	**Nevada**	**New Mexico**
Environmental Affairs	Department of Enviromental Quality (DEQ) Board of Enviromental Review	Department of Conservation and Natural Resources (DCNR) Enviromental Commission	New Mexico Environmental Department (NMED)
Air	Air Quality Permitting, Compliance Division (DEQ) Air Quality Planning, Prevention, and Assistance Division (DEQ) Air Pollution Control Advisory Council Clean Air Advisory Committee	Division of Enviromental Protection (DCNR)	NMED
Water	Public Water Supply Program (DEQ) Permitting and Compliance Division (DEQ) Planning, Prevention, and Assistance Division (DEQ) Water Pollution Control Council Statewide TMDL (Total Maximum Daily Load) Advisory Group Water Resources Division (DNRC)	Division of Enviromental Protection (DCNR)	NMED
Solid Waste	Integrated Waste Management (DEQ) Solid Waste Task Force (DEQ) Pollution Prevention Bureau (DEQ)	Division of Enviromental Protection (DCNR)	NMED
Hazardous Materials	Hazardous Waste Program, Permitting and Compliance Division (DEQ) Hazardous Waste Site Cleanup Bureau (DEQ)	Division of Enviromental Protection (DCNR)	NMED

	Montana *(continued)*	**Nevada** *(continued)*	**New Mexico** *(continued)*
Natural Resources	Department of Natural Resources and Conservation (DNRC)	Division of State Lands (DCNR) Advisory Board on Natural Resources	Energy, Minerals, and Natural Resources Department State Land Office
Wildlife	Fish, Wildlife, and Parks	Division of Wildlife Natural Heritage Program (DCNR) Wildlife Commission Wild Horses Commission	Department of Game and Fish

	Oregon	**Utah**	**Washington**
Environmental Affairs	Department of Enviromental Quality (DEQ)	Department of Enviromental Quality (DEQ)	Department of Ecology (DOE)
Air	Air Quality Division (DEQ) Air Quality Board	Division of Air Quality (DEQ)	Air Quality Program (DOE)
Water	Water Resources Department Watershed Enhancement Board Water Quality Control Division (DEQ) Water Resources Commission	Division of Drinking Water (DEQ) Division of Water Quality (DEQ) Division of Water Resources (DNR)	Water Quality Program (DOE) Water Resources Program (DOE)
Solid Waste	Land Quality Division (DEQ)	Division of Solid and Hazardous Waste (DEQ)	Solid Waste Program (DOE)
Hazardous Materials	Land Quality Division (DEQ)	Division of Solid and Hazardous Waste (DEQ) Division of Radiation Control (DEQ)	Hazardous Waste and Toxic Reduction Program (DOE) Nuclear Waste Program (DOE)
Natural Resources	Department of State Lands	Department of Natural Resources (DNR) Conservation Commission	Department of Natural Resources
Wildlife	Department of Fish and Wildlife	Division of Wildlife Resources (DNR)	Department of Fish and Wildlife

Source: Review of each state's online description of its departments and agencies. Web sites visited April–August 2004.

was one of the first states to establish a lead agency to oversee nearly all policies concerning toxic waste cleanup, pesticide regulation, and air and water pollution control (Paddock 1991). Even so, California continues to have one of the most complicated networks of government bodies dealing with environmental issues in the nation. For example, water pollution and resources issues are managed by the California Department of Water Resources, two different Cal-EPA departments (the State Water Resources Control Board and the Office of Environmental Health Hazard Assessment), and, to a lesser degree, the Department of Fish and Game, the Coastal Commission, the California Integrated Waste Management Board, the California Watershed Council, and the Department of Health and Toxic Substances Control. This network has become so cumbersome that Governor Arnold Schwarzenegger's government reform panel considered consolidating these agencies, along with hundreds of other state boards and agencies, to reduce bureaucratic inefficiencies and oversight costs.

BUREAUCRATIC THEORY AND BUREAUCRATIC GOVERNMENT

The implementation of many environmental policy objectives requires a coordinated group effort involving different agencies across various levels of government. This need for interagency cooperation challenges each agency's unique bureaucratic structure within which it sets goals, accomplishes tasks, and measures effectiveness. Max Weber has defined bureaucratic organization as a specific hierarchy of offices each with a specialized task, with each task specifically defined (Weber 1946). This hierarchy is structured somewhat like a pyramid, with authority diffused as one moves down the bureaucratic ladder. This rational organizational model, with its top-down centralized management strategies, views organizations as a series of tightly coupled means-ends chains between small and fairly stable levels of hierarchy (March and Simon 1958).

U.S. society has changed considerably since the beginning of the twentieth century when Weber and other early organizational theorists were promoting a formal hierarchical view of the world and its organizations. Today, society is composed of more people, increased communication and information access, and sophisticated workforce needs. Underpinning modern organizational theory is the belief that hierarchical central bureaucracies do not function well in today's information-rich, knowledge-intensive society and economy (Gore 1993; Osborne and Gaebler 1992). Decision making is more decentralized and vulnerable to directional changes at various organizational levels. Further, when considering the environmental policy process, Weber's notion of a rational bureaucracy is accurate only in part. While bureaucratic organizations allow for the effective implementation of nationwide programs, such organizations are vulnerable to manipulation. Weber's assumption that everyone within the bureaucracy will share the ideology of the bureaucratic culture is suspect. In fact, serious disagreement often exists as to the agency's goals. Thus, internal agency power rests, among other things, on the ability to achieve agreement on the goals necessary for policy formulation, implementation, and evaluation.

As with any policy process, resources are available to help maximize one's power within the bureaucracy. The basic resources necessary for administrative power are knowledge, access, and charismatic leadership (Neustadt 1980; Rourke 1984). Knowledge is necessary for two reasons. First, knowledge of the bureaucratic process allows one to navigate the various offices and agencies responsible for environmental policy. Second, technical expertise is necessary to make decisions in complicated areas. Access to agency administrators is not assured; consequently, one's ability to gain access is crucial in acquiring bureaucratic influence. Charismatic leadership may allow an administrator to mobilize support and loyalty among agency staff. Equally important, one's ability to mobilize support among peers within the bureaucracy may similarly influence the procedural agenda (Cobb and Elder 1983; Kerwin 2003).

These resources of power undermine notions of a completely rational bureaucracy, as does the recognition that public-sector bureaucratic decision making frequently reflects the power and energy of the agency's politically dominant coalition. Political appointments allow the White House to control the agency's agenda. Further, since environmental policy is not controlled by a single bureaucracy and is shaped instead by multiple agency actors, the particular policy goals of any given bureaucracy are often undermined or negated by the conflicting goals of other agencies and actors involved in the given policy issue. Opposing agencies are frequently competing for financial resources and do not have shared ideologies. The decentralization of environmental and natural resource management among various entities has created a policy web characterized by uncertainty and undermined by political bargaining. This is true at both the federal and state levels of government and colors environmental and natural resource policy outcomes in the West.

BUREAUCRATIC POWER AND ENVIRONMENTAL POLICY

Two bureaucratic tools have evolved along with environmental policy. First, and perhaps most significant, is the notion of "scientific regulation" (Schmandt 1984; Layzer 2002). Such regulation is based on the application of the best available technologies in resolving environmental problems, without regard to cost. Regulation based primarily on scientific information was supplemented by Ronald Reagan's Executive Order #12291, requiring all agencies to include a cost-benefit calculation in decision making. Although cost-benefit analysis can produce results that differ from findings based on science, scientific investigation still provides a fundamental basis for policy analysis.

The second tool is the "administrative hammer" (Rosenbaum 1995). Hammer clauses, such as those included in the 1984 Hazardous and Solid Waste amendments, ensure that policy is carried out the way Congress intended by stipulating specific standards and explicit deadlines for implementation (Cohen and Kamieniecki 1991; Cohen, Kamieniecki, and Cahn 2005). Such tools make it difficult for agency administrators (and target groups) to delay implementation and compliance, and they often contain rules and standards more stringent than those the agency is required by law to adopt. Congress has also required citizen participation and extended legal standing to citizens, allowing the public to bring suit against agencies if policies are not carried through (McSpadden 1995; O'Leary 1993, 2003).

In exploring bureaucratic implementation of environmental policy, it is possible to illustrate the functions and interrelationships among environmental agencies. Typically, policy is first initiated in Congress. Air pollution policy, for example, might originate in the House Commerce Committee or the Senate Committee on the Environment and Public Works. After congressional adoption and presidential approval, air policy falls under the jurisdiction of the EPA. In the case of the Clean Air Act, the EPA is responsible for identifying and monitoring air pollutants, as well as enforcing air pollution regulations. Denver and southern California historically have the worst air quality of any areas of the West, and the EPA increasingly pressures state and local leaders in Colorado and California to comply with federal air quality standards (Kamieniecki, Cahn, and Goss 1991). The state environmental agencies charged with implementing EPA air regulations may pass their own standards and create state regional entities to monitor and enforce air quality, such as California's air quality management districts.

Other environmental policy–area bureaucratic networks are similar, although agency jurisdiction may differ. In the context of forest preservation policy, for example, the bureaucratic trail is simpler. After becoming law, forest policy becomes the domain of the Forest Service within the Department of Agriculture. The Forest Service has been deeply involved in managing much of the forestland in several western states (Kamieniecki, Cahn, and Goss 1991).

Policy implementation problems occur when state or regional standards, or both, conflict with or subvert federal requirements. The federal courts may be drawn in, or Congress may reenter the arena, to represent constituent or regional interests. California, several other states, and a number of western cities, for example, have adopted policies to reduce greenhouse gas emissions and control climate change because of a lack of action at the federal level (Rabe 2004). The automobile industry has sued California, arguing that this issue falls under federal, not state, jurisdiction. Another problem has been the EPA's refusal to support state implementation of standards designed to meet federal air quality goals. President George W. Bush, for example, supported industry efforts to relax California's automobile emission standards to reduce smog in southern California (*Engine Manufacturers Association and Western State Petroleum Association v. South Coast Air Quality Management District et al.* 2004).

At the regional level, various agencies and governments may attempt to reduce jurisdictional conflicts by creating an interagency committee or workforce charged with addressing a particular environmental issue. States may even enter into an interstate compact, a formal contractual arrangement setting forth regional policy goals and delineating various agency contributions. This commonly occurs around shared water issues, although the largest compact system concerns regional low-level radioactive waste disposal. Three western states—California, Oregon, and Washington—are currently attempting to forge a regional agreement to cut greenhouse gas emissions from the region's power plants by 2020 to combat global warming (Eilperin 2005).

POLITICS OF THE FEDERAL ENVIRONMENTAL POLICY BUREAUCRACY

With the maze of agencies and departments that oversee various aspects of the environmental bureaucracy, policy is vulnerable to manipulation. To protect against this, a number of mechanisms have been set in place. The

EPA's strong commitment to environmental regulation, nurtured and supported by congressional and court action over the years, makes it difficult for polluting industries to "capture" the agency (Rosenbaum 2005). Other barriers include specific statutory language that bans members of the regulated industry from serving in certain agencies. The Surface Mining Control and Reclamation Act (SMCRA) of 1977, for example, includes a clause that prohibits the Office of Surface Mining Reclamation and Enforcement from hiring anyone who previously worked with any federal agency involved in the development of coal or any other mineral resources (Rosenbaum 2005). Montana, Wyoming, and other western mining state governments have generally benefited from this provision of the law.

Yet such protection is not always enough. The environmental commitment that evolved throughout the 1960s and 1970s culminated under President Jimmy Carter. During his tenure, SMCRA, the Comprehensive Environmental Response, Compensation, and Liability Act of 1980 (also known as Superfund), and the Low Level Radioactive Waste Policy Act of 1980 were passed. The executive branch's environmental agenda shifted fundamentally, however, with the election of Ronald Reagan.

The EPA and environmental policy in general stagnated under the Reagan administration's opposition to additional environmental regulations and his ideological support for western private-property rights over long-standing national environmental policy aims. For the first time in history, agency administrators strongly opposed attempts to improve environmental quality. Reagan's appointment of James Watt as secretary of DOI and Anne (Gorsuch) Burford as administrator of the EPA slowed environmental policy making. Watt was president of the Mountain States Legal Foundation, a corporate law firm in Denver that specialized in bringing suit against government regulations on behalf of pro-development interests. Eleven of Watt's top sixteen Interior officials had previously been associated with the industries regulated by Interior: oil, mining, timber, livestock, and utilities (Kenski and Ingram 1986). This slowed progress toward natural resource conservation in the West.

The DOI's primary goal under Watt was to ease regulations concerning the development of public lands, in most cases inside western states. Watt also sought to accelerate energy and mining extraction on federal lands, including opening national parks to mining (McCurdy 1986). Watt's public support of the Sagebrush Rebellion (i.e., western state demands to be awarded control over federal lands inside their borders) in the early 1980s focused national attention on western dissatisfaction with federal environmental policies. Congress and the federal courts blocked many administration reforms, signifying the political and legal schism that existed over the control and use of public lands in the West.

Like Watt, Anne Burford brought the Reagan administration's philosophy of deregulation and increased development to the EPA. A former Colorado legislator, Burford was a corporate attorney whose clients generally opposed environmental laws. As EPA administrator she sought to reduce regulatory requirements and standards in most areas.

To sidestep the pro-environment culture that had been bred in the agency since the era of William Ruckelshaus, Burford instituted a number of procedural changes. For example, she frequently held unannounced meetings when discussing policy with regulated industries. The lack of public notice successfully precluded public comment (Rosenbaum 2005). In addition, Burford centralized all decision making within her office, effectively paralyzing staff activities (Cohen 1986). Burford initiated a "policy criterion" in decision making concerning the release of program money. This was most evident in Rita Lavelle's refusal to release a large Superfund award to clean up the Stringfellow site in southern California, one of the most dangerous hazardous waste sites in the country. As director of the Office of Toxic Substances within the EPA, she withheld cleanup funds to help defeat then California Democratic governor Jerry Brown in his U.S. Senate race (Rosenbaum 2005).

The Reagan administration pressured the EPA to cut back regulation and enforcement. The Office of Management and Budget (OMB), which oversees all policy implementation, pushed the EPA to revise existing rules, arguing that their economic costs outweighed their financial benefits. This allowed the OMB to become a partner in environmental policy making. Such influence had the effect of reinterpreting congressional intent without actually altering legislation (Rosenbaum 2005).

Under Burford the EPA suffered substantial budget cuts, reorganization of staff, and policy changes that effectively reversed many previous advances. Between 1980 and 1983, the staff was cut from over 11,000 to just over 9,000, and EPA's non-Superfund budget was cut by 12 percent (Cohen 1986). After she received highly negative publicity for her actions and suffered severe credibility problems, Reagan pressed Burford to resign and reappointed William Ruckelshaus, the agency's first administrator under Nixon, to head the EPA. In summary, during his eight years in office, President Reagan cut the EPA's budget, ignored the CEQ, provided legal advantages to businesses and private-property owners, and introduced cost-measure evaluation that pitted long-term environmental damages against short-term profit losses.

President George H.W. Bush, elected in 1988 with a campaign promise to be an "environmental president," disappointed many with his general lack of support for additional environmental policies and his procedural posturing to manipulate the environmental bureaucratic system. Although the Bush administration was generally more supportive of environmental initiatives than the Reagan administration had been (e.g., he helped push through the Clean Air Act of 1990), he remained closely aligned with industry throughout his term. Vice President Dan Quayle chaired the "Council on Competitiveness," a little-known committee that reviewed, and often killed, regulations that had been developed and approved by independent regulatory agencies and cabinet-level departments. Under the premise of protecting America's "competitiveness" from overly burdensome regulations, the council served as a nonjudicial means for industry to challenge regulations. While Bush's appointment of William Reilly as EPA administrator was widely seen as a gesture to the environmental community, most of his other appointees were largely unsympathetic to environmental concerns.

The election of Bill Clinton and Al Gore in 1992 introduced a substantial change in the bureaucratic culture of executive environmental agencies. Almost immediately after taking office, President Clinton disbanded the Council on Competitiveness. His EPA administrator, Carol Browner, had a positive record as head of Florida's Department of Environmental Regulation, and the EPA strengthened under her leadership. Like President Bush before him, Clinton called for elevating the EPA to a cabinet-level department, and, while no formal change was made, Browner sat in on cabinet meetings. Bruce Babbitt, Clinton's secretary of DOI, was president of the League of Conservation Voters and had a solid environmental record as governor of Arizona. As head of the DOI, Babbitt supported restoration of the Florida Everglades and adopted new, creative approaches to ecosystem management. He suffered a major political setback early in his tenure, however, when Clinton, in the face of fervent western political opposition, publicly withdrew his support for Babbitt's campaign to raise grazing fees on public lands to private market levels.

President Clinton and Vice President Gore led an effort to reform environmental bureaucracy as part of their broader attempt to "reinvent government." In attempting to streamline the EPA's cumbersome bureaucracy and make it more responsive to public needs, the administration urged decreased reliance on command-and-control regulation in favor of market-based incentives for pollution control; it also created policy collaborative strategies involving industry, trade associations, and the public. Administrator Browner created new regulatory negotiation techniques and methods of stakeholder inclusion in rule-making procedures. Under her tenure the EPA gained policy momentum with a focus on initiatives designed to increase flexibility, reduce unnecessary regulations, and facilitate both cross-media and public-private policy making. Finally, Clinton's Executive Order #12866 (1993) replaced Reagan's executive orders on regulatory cost-benefit analysis, which favored short-term economic interest over long-term environmental benefits, with a new policy approach that emphasized cost-effectiveness while including environmental, equitable, and public health considerations.

Clinton administration initiatives generally furthered environmental protection and natural resource management in the western states. Unable to reform the General Mining Law of 1872 earlier in his administration, Clinton later tried to alter the law through administrative rules he could enact without obtaining congressional approval (Clinton 2004). At the end of his administration, for example, the DOI adopted a regulation that gave the BLM the authority to veto proposed mining projects that would do "significant irreparable harm" to public lands. Mining tends to produce dangerous pollutants (e.g., arsenic) that often find their way into soil and nearby lakes, rivers, and streams. This action was intended to protect water and soil quality. In addition, to the dismay of congressional legislators from western states, he banned road building in 43 million acres of national forests and approved a rule severely limiting commercial logging on 54 million acres of national forestlands (Kamieniecki 2006). In the last two years of his administration, relying largely on his executive order power under a controversial use of the 1906 Antiquities Act, Clinton acted alone to create numerous national monuments and expand three others, bringing under federal protection an additional 5.9 million acres of land. According to Rosenbaum, "Altogether, Clinton's land legacy would be more than fifty million acres of new or newly protected public domain and the designation of sixty-five million acres of existing public forest land in Washington, Oregon, Idaho, and Montana as roadless areas, thereafter off-limits to commercial timbering" (Rosenbaum 2005, 312).

The election of George W. Bush in 2000 led to an effort to weaken existing environmental rules and natural resource protection. President Bush used economic conditions and California's energy problems in early 2001 as evidence of a policy crisis and successfully called for the relaxation of environmental regulations that allegedly inhibited the nation's economy, particularly in the industrial and energy sectors. Immediately after taking office in 2001, his newly appointed secretary of the interior, Gale Norton, suspended the Clinton rules on mining, and in October 2001 she officially rescinded the BLM's authority to veto environmentally dangerous projects. In 2003 the EPA relaxed rules and thereby made it easier for thousands of old power plants, refineries, and factories to expand or upgrade their facilities without installing more effective (and costly) pollution-control equipment.

Bush also took the unprecedented step of creating an "in-house" interagency task force, led by the DOE, which acted as a liaison between the industry and DOI field officers for the sole purpose of expediting BLM issuance of drilling permits on federal lands. This task force was charged with increasing energy production and transmission by expediting governmental reviews related to energy projects, particularly those associated with pipelines (Executive Order #13302, 2003). As a result of the task force's intervention, as well as senior administration officials' directives to federal employees to accelerate energy development, critics believed the BLM had begun to ignore environmental safeguards in an effort to develop and increase sources of energy (Miller, Hamburger, and Cart 2004). As the vast majority of public lands are located in the West, the environmental impacts of the energy and pipeline projects have been borne almost exclusively by western states.

The Bush administration has been exceptionally active in its pursuit of policies favoring logging and mining interests. Declaring that the devastating 2002 wildfire season in the West was the result of a national forest health crisis, Bush unveiled his Healthy Forest Restoration Act, which has subsequently opened national forests (largely located within the western United States) to "thinning" by the timber industry. Environmentalists and scientists agreed that changes in forest policy were required to reduce large wildfires; however, they did not agree that increased thinning and logging was the solution. Further, the initiative weakened the environmental review process used to evaluate the need for thinning, prompting some critics to charge that it was a thinly veiled attempt to increase logging. Many scientists and policy analysts remain skeptical as to whether the bill will live up to its goal of significantly reducing forest fires and the damage they cause.

In April 2002 President Bush announced that his administration intended to overhaul the Northwest Forest Plan adopted by the Clinton administration. Dale Bosworth, chief of the Forest Service, argued that the plan's cumbersome and costly procedures have held logging far short of projected levels and rendered the Forest Service ineffective. Environmental groups disagreed with Bosworth and contended that the plan barely does enough to protect wildlife, given the results of recent scientific research.

In July 2004 the Bush administration proposed new forest rules that could lead to logging, mining, and oil and gas development in remote areas that had been protected under a policy adopted in the last days of the Clinton presidency. The new rules allow state governors a significant say in the management of natural resources in remote areas of the country, primarily in twelve western states. Under the new rules, governors can petition the federal government either to maintain road-building bans on all or part of the affected forestland or to open the land to road construction, whether for logging, mining, gas or oil development, or off-road vehicle use. Giving individual state governors this much influence in the management of public lands owned by the entire nation represents a major departure from past practice. Environmentalists worry that future decisions on the use of public lands will reflect the will of narrow state and local economic interests rather than the advice of forest conservation scientists and the views of the American public.

ENVIRONMENTAL POLICY AND POLITICS IN THE WESTERN STATES

Previous research has shown that the commitment to environmental protection varies across the states. A state's financial resources and institutional capacity, among other things, often determine its ability to enforce regulations. States that are densely populated or highly industrial, such as California, tend to have greater challenges and may therefore exceed federal guidelines and standards (e.g., on clean air policy) (Davis and Lester 1989).

Christopher Duerksen has ranked states' environmental commitment based on twenty-three factors, ranging from congressional voting records for federal policies to specific regulatory programs within each state (Duerksen 1983). The thirteen western states were ranked from best to worst (out of a possible top score of 63): California (46); Oregon (42); Washington (39); Montana (37); Idaho (28); Colorado (26); Arizona (24); Alaska, Utah, and Wyoming (23 each); Nevada (22); New Mexico (18); and Hawaii (11). When ranked by per capita expenditures in 1986, a different picture emerges: Alaska ($326); Wyoming ($135); Montana ($69.55); Idaho ($51.97); California

($50.70); Oregon ($49.01); Washington ($38.80); Utah ($24.60); New Mexico ($24.59); Colorado ($22.26); Nevada ($21.77); Hawaii ($19.21); and Arizona ($15.19) (Davis and Lester 1989; Lester 1989).

When controlling for environmental degradation (i.e., severity of pollution problems and the need for environmental regulation), state rankings in environmental commitment shift: Oregon, Washington, Montana, California, Hawaii, Colorado, Arizona, Utah and Wyoming, Nevada, Idaho and New Mexico (Davis and Lester 1989). The implementation of environmental protection in western states appears to be based on the degree of environmental degradation, type of industry within each state, economic strength, and political culture.

Fredriksson and Milliment's (2002) recent study of strategic interaction in environmental policy making found that the environmental policies of all states, particularly western states, have been shown to be influenced by the policies of their contiguous and regional neighbors. States are responsive to the policy changes of contiguous neighboring states within a two- to five-year window while responding to changes in abatement costs in regional neighbors over a five-year period. Western states are particularly responsive to neighboring states' environmental policies, especially when actions involve the adoption of programs that require higher abatement costs, such as in the areas of air and water pollution control.

In comparing the West to the rest of the country, western states spend more per capita on environmental improvements: six of the top eight states in money spent per capita are in the West, and eleven of the thirteen western states are in the top 50 percent. The mean per capita expenditure on environmental improvement nationwide (including the West) was $33.50 in 1988. In the western states, the mean per capita expenditure was $65.31 (Lester 1989).

As state involvement in environmental issues has grown, so has state dissatisfaction with the constraints imposed by federal statutes and regulations. The inadequacy of federal funding (e.g., unfunded mandates), perceived federal micromanagement of state environmental programs, and federal constraints on state flexibility to set policy have contributed to increased tension between Washington, D.C., and the states. The western section of the Council of State Governments has been particularly active in pressing the federal government to reduce its regulatory control over federal lands in the western region and has issued numerous resolutions in support of curtailing federal regulation of public lands (Council of State Governments

West 2003). These include calls for Congress to decrease federal landholdings in the West and claims for greater federal compensation for the private use of public lands within state borders. States believe they should receive additional funds from such activities as mining, grazing, and logging on public lands located inside their borders.

A major conflict between the West and the federal government has been over the creation of a national high-level radioactive waste disposal facility at Yucca Mountain, Nevada. The nation, to date, lacks a permanent repository for the burgeoning amount of dangerously deteriorating nuclear wastes currently stored at nuclear power plants. Nevada has strongly opposed hosting the facility, arguing that the safety of a permanent repository for high-level radioactive waste at Yucca Mountain is questionable. The DOE—the agency charged with oversight of the facility—and Congress, however, have continued to press for completion of the site. Despite being allocated up to $20 million a year to manage the site, Nevada officials have reacted with outrage, and the state has filed numerous lawsuits seeking to bar completion of the facility.

Western states sometimes find themselves in conflict with states from other regions of the country over environmental policy. For example, West Virginia and other high-sulfur coal states have continually opposed the adoption of strict air pollution standards and attempts to control acid rain. Federal efforts to control air pollution, however, have forced old coal-burning electric generating plants to use low-sulfur coal, which is primarily mined in Montana, Wyoming, and Colorado. Western states supported the Clean Air Act Amendments of 1990, which require the burning of low-sulfur coal by old electric generating plants located primarily in the Midwest. These regulations have contributed to the near death of the coal industry in West Virginia and other parts of Appalachia that produce high-sulfur coal. High-sulfur coal states continue to lobby Congress to relax the rules regulating coal use.

CONCLUSION

The adoption of many environmental and natural resource policies by federal and state governments has led to the formation of a complex policy subsystem. Today, state and local governments play a critical role in the implementation and enforcement of federal law, and many have taken the lead in formulating their own environmental programs (Kamieniecki, Cahn, and Goss 1991). Clearly, future environmental and natural resource policies will require greater coordination by agencies at all levels of government if they are to be effective.

Bureaucratic politics in the West is likely to become even more contentious in the future. Not all western states have the financial resources to absorb the costs of new environmental protection and natural resource conservation programs and still continue to provide essential services to growing populations. This may make it increasingly difficult for western states to afford to implement expensive policies. Demand for the transfer of federal lands to the states, which intensified during the early Reagan years in the form of the Sagebrush Rebellion, is likely to continue in the coming years. Increased representation in Congress by the western states will undoubtedly give regional business interests and state government bodies greater leverage in disputes with federal agencies over the use of natural resources. How such disputes are resolved will depend upon, among other things, the level of continued public support in the West and elsewhere for pollution control and natural resource conservation.

REFERENCES

Bartlett, Robert V. 1989. *Policy through Impact Assessment: Institutionalized Analysis as a Policy Strategy.* New York: Greenwood.

Caulfield, Henry. 1989. "The Conservation and Environmental Movements: An Historical Analysis." In James P. Lester, ed., *Environmental Politics and Policy: Theories and Evidence.* Durham, NC: Duke University Press.

Clinton, Bill. 2004. *My Life.* New York: Alfred A. Knopf.

Cobb, Roger, and Charles Elder. 1983. *Participation in American Politics: The Politics of Agenda Building* (2nd ed.). Baltimore: Johns Hopkins University Press.

Cohen, Steven. 1986. "EPA: A Qualified Success." In Sheldon Kamieniecki, Robert O'Brien, and Michael Clark, eds., *Controversies in Environmental Policy.* Albany: State University of New York Press, 1986.

Cohen, Steven, and Sheldon Kamieniecki. 1991. *Environmental Regulation through Strategic Planning.* Boulder: Westview.

Cohen, Steven, Sheldon Kamieniecki, and Matthew A. Cahn. 2005. *Strategic Planning in Environmental Regulation: A Policy Approach That Works.* Cambridge, MA: MIT Press.

Council of State Governments West. 2003. Resolution #2003-3 "Withdrawal of Federal Land Managers Guidance Which Impedes Needed Energy Projects"; Resolution #2002-01 "Resolution Urging the United States Congress to Compensate Western States for the Impact of Federal Land Ownership on State Education

Funding"; Resolution #99-3 "Calling for the Development of a Western Platform on Natural Resource Issues"; Resolution #99-4 "Urging Congress Not to Increase Its Land Holdings"; Resolution #98-6 "Urging EPA and U.S. Congress to Refrain from Defining Carbon Dioxide as a Pollutant"; Resolution #97-2 "National Monument Fairness Act."

Davis, Charles (ed.). 2001. *Western Public Lands and Environmental Politics* (2nd ed.). Boulder: Westview.

Davis, Charles, and James P. Lester. 1989. "Federalism and Environmental Policy." In James P. Lester, ed., *Environmental Politics and Policy: Theories and Evidence*. Durham, NC: Duke University Press.

Duerksen, Christopher. 1983. *Environmental Regulation of Industrial Plant Siting.* Washington, DC: Conservation Foundation.

Eilperin, Juliet. 2005. "Three States Seek Emissions Pact." *The Washington Post*, August 24, A2. At www.washingtonpost.com, site accessed August 26, 2005.

Engine Manufacturers Association and Western State Petroleum Association v. South Coast Air Quality Management District et al. 2004. 541 US 2004, #02-1343, U.S. Supreme Court, April.

Environmental News Network. 2005. "Scientists Try to Harness Wave Energy." August 26. At www.enn.com/today_PF.html?id=8632, site accessed September 5, 2005.

Executive Order #13302. 2003. *Federal Register* 68, no. 97. Presidential Documents. May 15.

Fredriksson, Per G., and Daniel L. Milliment. 2002. "Strategic Interaction of Environmental Policy across the U.S. States." *Journal of Urban Economics* 51, 101–22.

Gore, Al. 1993. *Creating a Government That Works Better and Costs Less: Report of the National Performance Review.* Washington, DC: U.S. Government Printing Office.

Kamieniecki, Sheldon. 2006. *Corporate America and Environmental Policy: How Often Does Business Get Its Way?* Palo Alto, CA: Stanford University Press.

Kamieniecki, Sheldon, Matthew Cahn, and Eugene Goss. 1991. "Western Governments and Environmental Policy." In Clive S. Thomas, ed., *Politics and Public Policy in the Contemporary American West.* Albuquerque: University of New Mexico Press.

Kenski, Henry, and Helen Ingram. 1986. "The Reagan Administration and Environmental Regulation: The Constraint of the Political Market." In Sheldon Kamieniecki, Robert O'Brien, and Michael Clark, eds., Controversies in Environmental Policy. *Albany: State University of New York Press.*

Kerwin, Cornelius M. 2003. *Rulemaking: How Government Agencies Write Law and Make Policy* (3rd ed.). Washington, DC: CQ.

Klyza, Christopher McGrory. 1996. *Who Controls Public Lands: Mining, Forestry, and Grazing Policies, 1879–1990.* Chapel Hill: University of North Carolina Press.

———. 2001. "Reform at a Geological Pace: Mining Policy on Federal Lands." In Charles Davis, ed., *Western Public Lands and Environmental Politics* (2nd ed.). Boulder: Westview.

Layzer, Judith A. 2002. *The Environmental Case: Translating Values into Policy.* Washington, DC: CQ.

Lester, James P. 1989. "A New Federalism? Environmental Policy in the States." In James P. Lester, ed., *Environmental Politics and Policy: Theories and Evidence.* Durham, NC: Duke University Press.

March, James G., and Herbert A. Simon. 1958. *Organizations.* New York: John Wiley.

McCurdy, Howard. 1986. "Environmental Protection and the New Federalism: The Sagebrush Rebellion and Beyond." In Sheldon Kamieniecki, Robert O'Brien, and Michael Clark, eds., *Controversies in Environmental Policy.* Albany: State University of New York Press.

McSpadden, Lettie. 1995. "The Courts and Environmental Policy." In James P. Lester, ed., *Environmental Politics and Policy: Theories and Evidence* (2nd ed.). Durham, NC: Duke University Press.

Meier, Kenneth. 1985. *Regulation: Politics, Bureaucracy and Economics.* New York: St. Martin's.

Miller, Alan C., Tom Hamburger, and Julie Cart. 2004. "A Changing Landscape: White House Puts the West on a Fast Track for Oil, Gas Drilling." *Los Angeles Times*, August 25, 1A.

Neustadt, Richard. 1980. *Presidential Powers.* New York: John Wiley and Sons.

O'Leary, Rosemary. 1993. *Environmental Change: Federal Courts and the EPA.* Philadelphia: Temple University Press.

———. 2003. "Environmental Policy in the Courts." In Norman J. Vig and Michael E. Kraft, eds., *Environmental Policy: New Directions for the Twenty-First Century* (5th ed.). Washington, DC: CQ.

Osborne, David, and Ted Gaebler. 1992. *Reinventing Government: How the Entrepreneurial Spirit Is Transforming the Public Sector.* New York: Penguin Group, Penguin Books USA.

Paddock, Richard C. 1991. "Wilson Picks Cal-EPA Chief." *Los Angeles Times,* January 30, A3.

Rabe, Barry G. 2004. *Statehouse and Greenhouse: The Emerging Politics of American Climate Change Policy.* Washington, DC: Brookings Institution Press.

Rosenbaum, Walter A. 1995. "The Bureaucracy and Environmental Policy." In James P. Lester, ed., *Environmental Politics and Policy: Theories and Evidence* (2nd ed.). Durham, NC: Duke University Press.

———. 2005. *Environmental Politics and Policy* (6th ed.). Washington, DC: CQ.

Rourke, Francis. 1984. *Bureaucracy, Politics and Public Policy* (3rd ed.). Boston: Little, Brown.

Schmandt, Jurgen. 1984. "Regulation and Science." *Science, Technology, and Human Values,* no. 1, 23–38.

U.S. Census Bureau. 2002. Statistical Abstract of the United States: 2003, No. 360. "Total and Federally Owned Land by State: 2002." At http://www.census.gov/prod/2004pubs/03statab/geo.pdf, site accessed July 13, 2004.

U.S. Forest Service. 2004. U.S. Department of Interior Forest Service Land Areas Report as of September 30, 2004. "National and Regional Areas Summary." At http:\\www.fs.fed.us/land/staff/lar/LAR04/table1.htm, site accessed September 5, 2005.

U.S. National Park Service. 2005. U.S. Department of Interior Parks and Recreation. At http://www.nps.gov/parks.html, site accessed September 5, 2005.

Weber, Max. 1946. "Bureaucracy." In H. H. Gerth and C. Wright Mills, eds., *From Max Weber: Essays in Sociology.* New York: Oxford University Press.

CHAPTER THREE

INNOVATION IN STATE ENVIRONMENTAL POLICY: A VIEW FROM THE WEST

Robert V. Bartlett, Walter F. Baber, and Carolyn D. Baber

> The problem is not just what we don't know, but what we do know that ain't so.
>
> —James Clarity and Warren Weaver, "What Folks Don't Know"; William Safire, "Beware of Certitude"

The conventional wisdom about state environmental policy holds that prior to the 1970s the states had been lethargic, even irresponsible, with little policy capacity and no political will or incentive to undertake new policies, much less exacting ones. Indeed, a general characterization of states before the 1970s holds them to have been "backwaters for the worst excesses of American politicians and bastions for the most shameful of American policies" (Lowry 1992, 10). The states were "mired in corruption, hostile to innovation, and unable to take a serious role in environmental policy out of fear of alienating key economic constituencies" (Rabe 2003, 295). Because "states failed to act" (Dwyer 1995, 1185) and federal "efforts to prod states to act had failed" (Percival 1995, 1144), in the 1970s the federal government undertook numerous massive initiatives on behalf of environmental protection, many of which subsequently depended on state implementation and provided for optional, subsidized state participation. These new federally established opportunities and subsidies forced and inspired extensive environmental policy capacity building by the states. This occurred as the states were already engaging in numerous institutional and constitutional reforms (Van Horn 1989). Thus by the early 1980s, when the federal government began to seek actively to devolve environmental responsibilities to the states, the states were able and willing to respond.

By the late 1980s scholars were beginning to point to the "resurgence of the states" (Bowman and Kearney 1986) and were situating states at the "cutting edge of environmental policy" and innovation (Rabe 2003; Van Horn 1989). Even so, into the early years of the twenty-first century, state initiative and innovation continue to be facilitated by federal policies, grants, technical assistance, data collection, research, and coordination (Rabe 2003). If anything, this "jumpstart" explanation is assumed to apply even more in the conservative western states than in the more populated, economically diverse, and greener East.

Yet this conventional wisdom contains troubling anomalies, not the least of which is that it offers no explanation for the many instances of state environmental policy innovation that have not been the result of prodding by the federal government. The jumpstart explanation seems to derive in part from two widespread analytical biases of environmental policy scholars. One of these biases is "Washington centeredness," which assumes that because so much environmental policy seems to be linked to Washington, D.C., it must be the primary stimulus, either proximately or ultimately, for any state policy activity that occurs. A second analytical bias involves giving short shrift to history. Even pioneer efforts to assess state pollution control policies offer unsupported claims that prior to 1970, "states made little systematic progress in the fight against pollution (Lowry 1992, 15) and that "most states paid little attention to environmental protection" (Ringquist 1993, 20). But in fact the states, including western states, were environmental policy innovators for decades prior to the 1970s, with many significant accomplishments to their credit, and they would continue to innovate in innumerable ways beyond the demands and incentives of federal policies and in policy areas barely touched by federal efforts.

Environmental policy innovation is best understood as a phenomenon in which both the federal government and the states respond to historical forces, the same forces that drive modern environmentalism and the emerging outlines of the environmental problematique. Much of the innovation in environmental policy has always occurred at the state level, and this is true in the West as much as anywhere.

CONVENTIONAL WISDOM: THE "JUMPSTART" HYPOTHESIS

From the early 1600s to the mid-nineteenth century, the virtually unchallenged discourse that guided the relationship between Americans and their natural environment was grounded in the idea of manifest destiny. We were ordained, so this theory held, to spread across the entire North American continent, subdue it, and turn it to the purposes of humans. This ideology is represented graphically in the official seals of several states, providing a concrete image of the aspirations of the population at the time each seal was adopted (Brulle 2000). The same ideology, especially strong in the West, was represented functionally in the attitudes and actions of the political elites that dominated state politics during the rapid expansion of the United States in the nineteenth century.

It has long been understood that elite interest groups are most powerful when they exist in a jurisdiction characterized by weak party competition, a legislature that lacks sophistication and cohesion, and a population that is predominately poor, rural, and agricultural. Under these circumstances, present to a far greater degree in state capitals than in Washington, the interests of the powerful and well organized generally prevail over those of the general population (Zeigler and Baer 1969). The earliest research on interest groups in politics recognized that organization represents concentrated power and concentrated power can exercise a dominating influence when it encounters power that is diffused and therefore weaker (Latham 1952). As an example, the lengthy and detailed character of state constitutions has been interpreted as evidence of this domination by organized groups (Froman 1966). Local elites who are attentive to state politics tend to manifest more conservative values and are more suspicious of government generally (Jennings and Zeigler 1970). In short, business groups have long been the most powerful interests in state legislatures (Wahlke 1962).

As a consequence of the dominance of state legislatures by business interests, the states have a history of adopting economic development policies that undermine their ability to provide social services and protect the public health (Donahue 1997). In the absence of strong federal mandates, states would seem to have little incentive to impose regulatory burdens on business that would put them at a competitive disadvantage with respect to neighboring states in attracting industry (Rowland and Marz 1982). In fact, states would have an incentive to engage in a "race to the bottom" by competing with one another to offer business the least demanding regulatory system that could be devised (Swire 1996).

National regulatory policy has been seen as a reaction to this perceived deficiency in state politics. Most states, it has been argued, show neither the will nor the administrative capacity to address the pervasive and growing problems of the environment. They risk competition from one another if they impose stricter standards on their business communities. They lack the inherent authority to address trans-boundary problems such as air and water pollution (Andrews 1999). Federal environmental policies, according to this view, represent an "implicit social contract" under which the federal government assumes authority to set minimum standards but also provides technical assistance and funds to defray the costs of implementing the new standards (Andrews 1999).

In addition to eliminating interstate competition and providing technical and financial support, federal standard setting provides the states with political cover in dealing with their business communities. State regulators can argue that their actions are necessary to forestall more onerous direct federal intervention. This tactic led then Environmental Protection Agency (EPA) Administrator William Ruckelshaus to characterize the EPA as the "gorilla" in the states' enforcement closet (Stanfield 1984). For all these reasons, according to Barry Rabe (1999), a good deal of the most innovative state-level activity has been stimulated (and financially underwritten) through federal initiatives. And so was born the view that for states to pursue innovative environmental policies, a federal mandate, incentive, or some other form of "jumpstart" is required. The bad news was that states could not be expected to show initiative. The good news was that they were willing to respond affirmatively to federal proposals, especially those accompanied by a dowry.

No marriage is perfect, however. Federal environmental initiatives often create their own opposition at the state level (Brulle 2000). This has seemed especially true in the West. As an example, federal efforts to establish and expand the system of national forests have given rise to strong local opposition. As early as 1897, protests against President Grover Cleveland's creation of thirteen new national forests drew an estimated 30,000 people to the bustling crossroads of Deadwood, South Dakota (Robbins 1962). Later actions by Theodore Roosevelt to further expand the forest system prompted Public Lands Conventions in 1911 and 1914, as well as other protest efforts that died away only with the advent of World War I (Richardson 1962). And President Bill Clinton announced the creation of a new national monument in Utah from a politically safe distance on the Arizona rim of the Grand Canyon.

There is a similar history of state opposition to federal innovation in the area of grazing on western federal lands. Early opposition to federal grazing fees, led by Senator Robert Stanfield of Oregon, was not immediately successful (Cawley 1993). Later efforts by Senators Pat McCarran of Nevada and Alan Robertson of Wyoming ultimately led to the replacement of the U.S. Grazing Service by the comparatively weaker Bureau of Land Management (Graf 1990). Thus, through most of its history the so-called Sagebrush Rebellion could achieve no better than a stalemate in the face of federal determination to actively manage federal land resources in the public interest. The resulting frustrations have led state-based opponents of federal land management to form the inaptly named Wise Use Movement. Wise use is a loosely knit affiliation composed largely of academic property rights advocates, national anti-environmental organizations, and radical county supremacists who (ironically) represent a greater threat to state and local civil servants than to the federal government (Cawley 1993; Switzer 1997).

Against this historical backdrop of state and local efforts to frustrate federal environmental initiatives, proponents of the jumpstart theory of state environmental innovation might be forgiven for believing that strong federal leadership will always be necessary if progress is to be made. Thus the wave of environmental activism that swept America in the 1970s focused its energy on the nationalization of a system of political relationships long held by citizens, communities, and state and local governments. In some states, well-established bodies of state administrative law (combined with common-law enforcement of individual rights) were replaced by a new arsenal of complex federal statutes. Elsewhere, emerging federal law required the construction of administrative mechanisms that did not fit with existing patterns of environmental and land-use governance (Cepola and Yandle 1997). So, prompted by federal mandates and subsidies, the states began to develop their own environmental regulatory agencies, programs, and technical expertise. They did so to carry out the new federal mandates and, in a few cases, to go further with their own initiatives in response to federal leadership and the public support for environmental protection it had promoted (Andrews 1999). This provided the states with their first federal jumpstart as innovation in Washington promoted reaction in state capitals.

The jumpstart hypothesis (which is never presented as a hypothesis but rather as an irrefutable conclusion) has it that the status of states with respect to environmental protection began to change dramatically only after 1970. Prior to that time, according to proponents of the hypothesis, only a few states (like California with respect to air pollution) had Progressive environmental policies. That laxity, in fact, is held to have contributed to the federal government's determination to act. The federal initiative, so the theory goes, awakened new environmental sensibilities within the states and led to the development of regulatory capacities at that level (Rosenbaum 2002). Along with these new environmental capacities, however, came a "new degree of ambivalence" in the federal-state relationship (Andrews 1999). For jumpstart proponents, this explains (at least in part) the states' poor record as followers of the federal lead on the environment. For example, states' performance in enforcing the Clean Air Act has been questioned (Ringquist 1993). Significant differences have also been observed among the states in both their approach to measuring water pollution and their willingness to take enforcement action (General Accounting Office 1996). And wide variations persist in state spending on the environment (Council of State Governments 1999). All of this is used to support the view that the federal government is essential to environmental protection, both to initiate policy and to monitor its implementation at the state and local levels.

As the legal power of federal regulatory agencies such as the EPA increased, so did federal dependence on delegation of program implementation responsibilities to the states (National Academy of Public Administration 1995). But as states assumed more responsibility for implementing federal programs, relations between the states and the EPA worsened, and the EPA responded by increasing the intensity of its oversight activities (Davies and Mazureck 1998). The resulting frustration in state capitals contributed to the election of Ronald Reagan and the eventual control of Congress by the Republican Party. But, like so many other rear-guard actions against the future, the anti-environmentalism of the "Reagan Revolution" was able to achieve no better than a stalemate (Hays 1987). Extension of federal authority to protect the environment was prevented, and federal subsidies to the states were significantly reduced (contributing to the problem of unfunded mandates).

An "advantage" of the jumpstart hypothesis thus becomes evident—all evidence confirms it. As the federal role in environmental protection is reduced, either the states step forward to assume a greater leadership role or they lapse back into the bad habits of the past. Either way, jumpstart advocates have a ready argument. Should the states show continued and growing leadership, they would be declared the new heroes of federalism (Rabe 2003), and Washington's wisdom in administering a second jumpstart (both administrative and political) by withdrawing from the environmental arena would be confirmed.

If the states stumble, however, the jumpstart hypothesis is once again vindicated. The failure of states to carry on in the absence of federal leadership reaffirms the notion that ongoing federal involvement is essential (Stewart 1977). It lends additional credence to the arguments that environmental interests are underrepresented at the state level (Swire 1996) and that states are primarily motivated to export, rather than solve, their environmental problems (Dwyer 1995). This, in turn, explains why many Clinton-era initiatives to give states more freedom to innovate were used to "streamline" operations rather than to foster actual environmental improvements (Davies and Mazureck 1998). And it explains why states balked at having the federal government use serious environmental performance measures to evaluate their effectiveness under the National Environmental Performance Partnership system (General Accounting Office 1999). The jumpstart hypothesis is irrefutable.

UNCONVENTIONAL WISDOM: THE "HISTORIC FORCES" HYPOTHESIS

The jumpstart hypothesis has it that state environmental innovation is the dependent variable and that the predominant independent variable is federal action (or deliberate inaction). To simply reverse the theory, arguing that state actions drive federal responses, might work in the limited circumstance, for example, in which complete indifference to the environment in state capitals would require federal action sooner or later or where aggressive but diverse state initiatives inspire federal preemption and regulatory rationalization. But this theory has too limited a range of application (virtually nonexistent) to be useful, even if it made sense generally (which it is not clear that it does).

A better competing hypothesis is that both state and federal innovations in environmental policy are dependent variables that result from some more general phenomena. To describe that general phenomenon, it is necessary to correct some historical and conceptual misimpressions proponents of the jumpstart hypothesis tend to perpetuate.

First is the notion that the federal government goes where the states fear to tread. Across a wide range of environmental issues, however, states have beaten the federal government to the punch. Beginning in the early 1800s, the establishment of urban and state parks offered the first glimpse of the environmental preservation movement (Huth 1957). The first governmental action to establish a forest preserve was taken by the state of New York in 1885, six years before passage of the federal Forest Reserve Act (Dana and Fairfax 1980). Although today the issue of wildlife protection is associated with the federal Endangered Species Act, the wildlife protection movement in America was born in state and local organizations that promoted the adoption of numerous state laws prior to the first federal statute on the subject (Brulle 2000). Pioneering efforts to address urban sprawl and growth management have been undertaken in western states such as Oregon in the absence of any leadership or support from the federal government (Layzer 2006). States began developing comprehensive resource management agencies in the 1950s, even though the federal government was engaged in little activity on environmental issues at that time (Hays 1987).

Today, the future of resource conservation efforts such as endangered species protection can best be illustrated not by federal efforts but by innovations like the San Diego Multiple Species Conservation Program (MSCP). The MSCP is a comprehensive habitat conservation program created pursuant to the federal Endangered Species Act (1973), the California Endangered Species Act (1970), and the California Natural Community Conservation Plan Act (2002). It is a consortium of county, city, and special-district actors designed to conserve native vegetation communities and their associated animal populations across a 900-square-mile planning area. The MSCP represents a significant departure from the traditional federal approach of protecting individual species, offering the possibility of protecting entire habitats while reducing the impact of regulation on the economic health of human communities (California Department of Fish and Game 2003).

Moreover, state and local regulation of pollution predates federal regulation by many decades (Davies and Mazureck 1998) and can trace its origins to the activities of state urban health and sanitation commissions immediately prior to and during the Civil War (Brulle 2000; Melosi 1981). A burst of legislative activity in the late 1960s and early 1970s did give the federal government the dominant role in setting pollution control standards and greatly strengthened the federal role in environmental enforcement (Davies and Mazureck 1998). But air, water, and solid waste problems in major urban areas had prompted action at the state level long before the federal government addressed those issues (Melosi 1981). A 1905 U.S. Geological Survey report found that every state but three had water pollution laws, with a majority—including most western states— imposing "general" or "severe" restrictions (Goodell 1905). Many states provided strong policy tools, as thirty-three of them revised their water pollution control laws between 1945 and 1951 (Andreen 2003a, 2003b; Weiss 1951). With regard to state air pollution policy, pollutants generally recognized as such before 1970, including particulate matter and sulfur dioxide, were declining markedly by the time the Clean Air Act was passed, which first gave the federal government a major direct role in regulation (Goklany 1999).

At the beginning of the twenty-first century, virtually all states have gone beyond federal requirements in at least some environmental areas, and in many areas states have assumed the role of policy leadership (John 1994). As an example, western states have led the way in the development of tiered regulatory systems that reward firms for adopting Environmental Management Systems with a reduced regulatory burden (Speir 2001). California has created two regional stakeholder involvement groups to aid in implementing its Environmental Management System Innovation Initiative (California Environmental Protection Agency 2000). Arizona has adopted strong requirements for documenting compliance with environmental statutes, as well as other performance goals, as part of its Voluntary Environmental Performance Program (Arizona 2000). New Mexico has established an Inter-Agency Environmental Justice Task Force by executive order, with the goal of developing an environmental justice program that is a model for other states (Rankin 2006). Oregon has the nation's most fully developed tiered regulatory system, offering as many as four levels of participation, each with progressively richer incentives for progressively superior performance (Speir 2001). Oregon is also one of several states that "have recognized climate change as a serious environmental threat and have responded with multiple programs that explicitly establish greenhouse gas reduction as a state policy goal" (Rabe 2004, 5).

Since 2000, Nebraska, North Dakota, Oklahoma, and Wyoming have passed legislation creating programs for sequestering carbon through agricultural practices (Rabe 2004). Western states have undertaken a patchwork of other initiatives, and the Western Governors' Association has called for increased energy efficiency and new sources of renewable energy (Reese 2005). Major experiments in adaptive governance are under way, perhaps more than in other regions, as the West grapples with diverse challenges such as endangered species, forest use, and grazing practices (Brunner et al. 2005).

All of this points to a considerable level of environmental policy entrepreneurship at the state level (Carpenter 2001) and a determination to respond to the severity of environmental problems with innovative programs (Sapat 2004). But how do we explain this apparently independent innovation in the face of the jumpstart hypothesis and its less than flattering characterization of state politics?

When it comes to developing Progressive environmental policy, state politics has been criticized for a lack of both *motivation* and *capacity*. The race-to-the-bottom argument is nothing if not a critique of the incentives faced by state policy makers in the environmental arena. But that argument may be flawed in several ways. First, the problem of lax environmental standards resulting from competition among states for business may have been exaggerated simply because the costs of environmental compliance are actually fairly modest. Such costs as exist may be swamped by other, far more significant elements in the overall business climate (Donahue 1997). Moreover, it is far from clear that federal standards are always an improvement over state requirements (Revesz 1997). In fact, by the early 1970s business was turning to the federal government for regulatory relief in the form of federal preemption of state authority (Hays 1987). Western states in particular have exceeded federal mandates in several areas. The higher automotive emissions standards in California are a venerable example. More recently, California's Proposition 65 (1986; requiring consumer warnings about the presence of toxic and carcinogenic chemicals) has led to a significantly greater reduction of environmental toxins in California than has been achieved nationwide, without the imposition of additional emission controls (Environmental Defense Fund 2000). In Oregon, the governor has set the goal of achieving environmental sustainability by the year 2025 (Oregon 2000, 2001, 2003).

The picture may be similar when it comes to states' capacity for environmental innovation. The sensitivity of state politics to elite interest manipulation may have been overblown. The interest group profile is probably larger and more diverse in most states than the jumpstart theory assumes, and when various interest groups provide input into the regulatory process, it is far less likely that any one will dominate (Teske 2003). This may explain Alka Sapat's finding (2004) that interest group activity is unimportant in explaining state-level environmental innovation regarding hazardous waste. In addition to the diversity of modern interest groups at the state level, the expertise-driven character of environmental policy making affords state professionals considerable independence from stakeholders (Borins 1998). Interest group influence appears to be attenuated by the information asymmetry that exists between legislators and bureaucrats charged with policy development and implementation (Sapat 2004).

States also appear to follow environmental innovations of other nearby states, perhaps because of overlapping ideology or the geographic spillover of specific environmental problems (Teske 2003). As a consequence, many state environmental officials have become highly skilled actors without ties to or reliance on resource-based industry groups. The result has been a new level of initiative and efficacy, as when Arizona wildlife officials sought protection for the Mexican spotted owl in the southwest region of the Forest System or the return of the California condor to the north rim of the Grand Canyon (Nelson 2001).

Other general trends in state government may also be helping the cause of environmental innovation. William Lowry has documented a revitalization of state government that he attributes to more equitable legislative representation, urbanization, increased public participation, improved finances, greater governmental openness, and policy competition among the states (Lowry 1992). When combined with greater administrative professionalism and institutional resources, these developments provide many key requisites of policy innovation (Sapat 2004). Western demographic trends in particular have reduced state economic reliance on resource-based industries, contributed to a rise in environmental activism, and prompted greater support among state officials for environmental protection (Klyza 2001). And it is increasingly clear that state legislative action is responsive to a growing ideological mandate for environmental protection (Teske 2003).

Broad public support for environmentalism may not guarantee the success of any particular innovation (much less every one). But it does provide the foundation for creative, bottom-up environmental policy development that is genuinely independent of federal mandates (John 1994). Against this Progressive backdrop, much of the alleged local resistance to federal environmental mandates appears in a different light. For example, organizations associated with the so-called Wise Use Movement are predominantly funded by large resource extraction and manufacturing firms. They are oligarchic internally rather than democratic. In short, they are classic examples of "astroturf" anti-environmental lobbyists pretending to be "grassroots" citizens groups (Brulle 2000). In fact, this may go some way toward explaining the desperation and shrillness of many in the movement, as well as its efforts to nationalize its issues.

The genuine public support for environmental protection, even if it exists as a generalized sentiment rather than as preferences for specific policies, creates the essential preconditions for environmental innovation. Public opinion is the dominant influence on policy making in the American states (Erikson, Wright, and McIver 1993). Thus, it should not be surprising that states exceeding EPA air quality or air monitoring standards include Arizona, Montana, Nevada, Utah, and Wyoming, in addition to California and Washington (Potoski 2001). Even in Montana, a supposedly conservative western state, Stillwater Mining Company found it necessary to go well beyond state and federal environmental standards to overcome resistance to a new facility from state officials, ranchers, and grassroots environmental groups (Moomaw 2001). All of these outcomes are evidence that state politics does precisely what it is supposed to do: it translates public opinion into a general ideological direction that largely determines the outcome of environmental policy making, regardless of whether the issue is how to comply with a federal mandate or deal with a strictly intrastate issue (Erikson, Wright, and McIver 1993).

This perspective makes better sense of a variety of observations about the states' responses to both environmental challenges generally and to federal leadership. The states did not, in the 1960s and 1970s, suddenly step on the gas after idling for decades. Rather, they "extended the long-standing trend toward professionalism and centralization" in regulatory policy (Teaford 2002, 201). By the 1980s the states began to resent close federal government oversight, as they became increasingly competent and professional and as federal funding became less important to state pollution control efforts (Davies and Mazureck 1998). At about the same time, the EPA began to decentralize significantly, taking on more of a regional emphasis. This approach has proven more effective than a centralized approach in that it allows for more integrated enforcement, permitting, and planning and for greater responsiveness to regional differences (Andrews 1999). It has also led to more cordial relations between regional EPA officials and state environmental administrators and to a resulting increase in the ability of the state-federal partnership to implement federal policy (Scheberle 1997). This, of course, makes good sense from the state perspective. But it is also in the long-term interest of the EPA. As the largest and most egregious pollution problems are brought under control, attention is turning to the small and dispersed sources that can only be controlled through effective action at the state and local levels (Davies and Mazureck 1998). Thus, federal dependence on state resources and expertise is only likely to increase with time.

There are other reasons to believe the future of environmental protection lies with the states as much as with the federal government. Environmental innovation in the future is likely to emphasize voluntary compliance systems, economic incentives, and devolution (Borins 1998). While always subject to the criticism that they represent appeasement of the business lobby, these are features of a new approach to environmentalism. Dewitt John (1994) has advanced the notion that some of the most promising and innovative developments in environmental policy are occurring at the state and local levels. He argues that a bottom-up approach to environmental protection has the potential to reduce disputes over the factual bases of policy making and replace interminable legal action with consensus building.

John's "civic environmentalism" offers the opportunity to bridge a gap that has limited the effectiveness of state and local environmentalism for decades. Lacking a sufficiently broad environmental perspective, local environmental groups have rarely coalesced into the wider environmental movement. Only in recent years has this strain of environmentalism begun to connect with the preservationist and conservationist movements at the national level, movements local activism also spawned in an earlier era (Melosi 1981). A parallel development can be seen at the level of government institutions, as state environmental agencies are beginning to undertake collective action through the Environmental Council of the States. This trend suggests that the states have the capacity to take the lead in addressing complex environmental problems without waiting for the federal government to take the lead (Sussman, Daynes, and West 2002).

One example of the regulatory innovation this bottom-up form of environmentalism makes possible is the use of Environmental Management Systems (EMSs) in a tiered structure of regulation. EMSs are comprehensive programs that encourage Progressive reductions in pollutants across a range of emissions, discharges, and waste disposal practices that (if effectively implemented) would clearly produce results that complement traditional command-and-control regulation of individual pollutants and media and produce superior results to command and control alone (Speir 2001). Successful implementation of EMSs is far from assured. But it clearly relies on voluntary compliance and a nuanced approach to planning and enforcement that only the states and localities are likely to achieve.

A WESTERN PERSPECTIVE ON ENVIRONMENTAL FEDERALISM

Our argument to this point suggests that the appropriate balance of federal and state initiative in environmental policy may not ultimately be found through constitutional or institutional analysis. After all, since the earliest days of the Republic, the federal government has been deeply involved in public activities not specifically delegated to it by the Constitution (Elazar 1962). And there has never been a time when it was possible to put neat labels on discrete federal, state, and local functions (Grodzins 1967).

This is not to say, however, that there are no environmental challenges that are most appropriately federal and others more likely to be addressed successfully by the states. For example, there are times when uniform national standards are important, as when the economies of scale involved in producing a specific product require that it meet only one set of environmental standards (as in the case of automobiles). But attempting to arrive at specific requirements for the *process* by which that product meets a uniform standard (for example, by specifying a specific emission control technology) may be less desirable. Attempting to impose a uniform process standard across jurisdictions may have the undesirable effect of creating an artificial competitive advantage in jurisdictions that perform well on other, unregulated aspects of the production process (such as infrastructure and education investment) unrelated to environmental issues (Revesz 1997). In this example, we must puzzle out whether we want infrastructure and education spending to affect (or be affected by) outcomes that previously seemed only to balance the economy and the environment.

This sort of quandary has confronted environmentalists and government officials for decades. But it poses a peculiar problem. The problem is not that we fail to understand what regional or central governments do best; nor are we confused about the economic and ecological issues at stake. We are, rather, at odds over what collective and individual choices related to environmental protection we want to reward and to punish. This is precisely the complex of problems that gave birth to California's Quincy Library Group (QLG). This grassroots effort was prompted by a desire to preserve both forest and community health while reducing the level of rancor in local political discourse. Founded by a forester for Sierra Pacific Industries, a county supervisor, and a local environmental attorney, QLG brought together a broadly representative group of stakeholders to develop a "community stability proposal" intended to protect environmental values while limiting impacts on the local economy. Collaborative groups like QLG were rare in the mid-1990s, but there are hundreds of them today in the West (Davis 2001; Sagoff 1999; Weber 2003). Their long-term efficacy has yet to be determined. But in their understanding of the complexity of natural resource issues and the necessity for broadly based responses to those issues, groups such as the QLG provide an example of western environmentalism that is not only more genuine than the Wise Use Movement but also more helpful and more hopeful.

To the extent that environmental questions come to be understood in this way by a broad cross-section of the population, we will discover new environmental issues at every turn. We will be required to use new information in new ways and to think about environmental, economic, social, and political values on an equal footing. The federal regulatory structure will not disappear, but there will be increased opportunity for independent state and local initiative. Exploiting these new environmental opportunities will require a "much stronger civic base, as individuals, communities, and many businesses come to understand and believe that they can prosper while protecting environmental values" (John 1994, 302). That new civic base, and the new forms of state politics it produces, are already clearly evident if one looks west. Westerners have always been political innovators, and in the broad realm of environmental policy that is certain to continue both in response to, and in spite of, the actions of the federal government.

REFERENCES

Andreen, W. L. 2003a. "The Evolution of Water Pollution Control in the United States: State, Local, and Federal Efforts, 1789–1972, Part 1." *Stanford Environmental Law Journal* 22 (January), 146–200.

———. 2003b. "The Evolution of Water Pollution Control in the United States: State, Local, and Federal Efforts, 1789–1972, Part 2." *Stanford Environmental Law Journal* 22 (June), 216–294.

Andrews, R.N.L. 1999. *Managing the Environment, Managing Ourselves: A History of American Environmental Policy*. New Haven, CT: Yale University Press.

Arizona. 2000. *Voluntary Environmental Performance Program*.

Borins, S. 1998. *Innovating with Integrity*. Washington, DC: Georgetown University Press.

Bowman, A.O.M., and R. C. Kearney. 1986. *The Resurgence of the States*. Englewood Cliffs, NJ: Prentice-Hall.

Brulle, R. J. 2000. *Agency, Democracy and Nature*. Cambridge, MA: MIT Press.

Brunner, Ronald D., et al. 2005. *Adaptive Governance: Integrating Science, Policy, and Decision Making*. New York: Columbia University Press.

California Department of Fish and Game. 2003. *San Diego Multiple Species Conservation Program*. At http://www.dfg.ca.gov/nccp/mscp/mscp_home.htm, accessed July 2, 2003.

California Environmental Protection Agency. 2000. Environmental Management System Innovation Initiative.

Carpenter, D. 2001. *The Forging of Bureaucratic Autonomy*. Princeton, NJ: Princeton University Press.

Cawley, R. M. (1993). *Federal Land, Western Anger: The Sagebrush Rebellion and Environmental Politics.* Lawrence: University Press of Kansas.

Cepola, K., and B. Yandle. 1997. "Western States and Environmental Federalism: An Examination of Institutional Viability." In T. Anderson and P. Hill, eds., *Environmental Federalism*. Lanham, MD: Rowman and Littlefield.

Clarity, James F., and Warren Weaver Jr. 1984. "What Folks Don't Know." *New York Times,* October 18, 14.

Council of State Governments. 1999. *Resource Guide to State Environmental Management* (5th ed.). Lexington, KY: Council of State Governments.

Dana, S. T., and S. K. Fairfax. 1980. *Forest and Range Policy: Its Development in the United States* (2nd ed.). New York: McGraw-Hill.

Davies, J. C., and J. Mazureck. 1998. *Pollution Control in the United States: Evaluating the System*. Washington, DC: Resources for the Future.

Davis, S. 2001. "Fighting over Public Lands: Interest Groups, States, and the Federal Government." In C. Davis, ed., *Western Public Lands and Environmental Politics*. Boulder: Westview.

Donahue, J. 1997. *Disunited States: What's at Stake as Washington Fades and the States Take the Lead*. New York: Basic Books.

Dwyer, J. P. 1995. "The Practice of Federalism under the Clean Air Act." *Maryland Law Review* 54, 1183–1225.

Elazar, D. 1962. *The American Partnership: Intergovernmental Cooperation in Nineteenth-Century United States*. Chicago: University of Chicago Press.

Environmental Defense Fund. 2000. *Air Emissions of Specific Toxic Chemicals 1988–1997, Trend for U.S. and California: Carcinogens and Reproductive Toxins*. New York: Environmental Defense Fund.

Erikson, R. S., G. C. Wright, and J. P. McIver. 1993. *Statehouse Democracy: Public Opinion and Policy in the American States*. New York: Cambridge University Press.

Froman, L.A.J. 1966. "Some Effects of Interest Group Strength in State Politics." *American Political Science Review* 60, 952–962.

General Accounting Office. 1996. *Water Pollution: Differences among the States in Issuing Permits Limiting the Discharge of Pollutants*. Washington, DC: General Accounting Office.

———. 1999. *Collaborative EPA-State Effort Needed to Improve New Performance Partnership System*. Washington, DC: General Accounting Office.

Goklany, I. 1999. *Clearing the Air: The Real Story of the War on Air Pollution*. Washington, DC: Cato Institute.

Goodell, E. B. 1905. *A Review of the Laws Forbidding Pollution of Inland Waters in the United States*. Water-Supply and Irrigation Paper No. 152. Washington, DC: U.S. Geological Survey, U.S. Government Printing Office.

Graf, W. L. 1990. *Wilderness Preservation and the Sagebrush Rebellions*. Savage, MD: Rowman and Littlefield.

Grodzins, M. 1967. "The Federal System." In A. Wildavsky, ed., *American Federalism in Perspective*. Boston: Little, Brown.

Hays, S. P. 1987. *Beauty, Health, and Permanence: Environmental Politics in the United States 1955–1985*. Cambridge, UK: Cambridge University Press.

Huth, H. 1957. *Nature and the American: Three Centuries of Changing Attitudes*. Berkeley: University of California Press.

Jennings, M. K., and H. Zeigler. 1970. "The Salience of American State Politics." *American Political Science Review* 64, 523–535.

John, D. 1994. *Civic Environmentalism: Alternatives to Regulation in States and Communities*. Washington, DC: CQ.

Klyza, C. M. 2001. "Reform at a Geological Pace: Mining Policy on Federal Lands." In C. Davis, ed., *Western Public Lands and Environmental Politics* (2nd ed.). Boulder: Westview.

Latham, E. 1952. "The Group Basis of Politics: Notes for a Theory." *American Political Science Review* 46, 376–397.

Layzer, Judith A. 2006. *The Environmental Case: Translating Values into Policy* (2nd ed.). Washington, DC: CQ.

Lowry, W. R. 1992. *The Dimensions of Federalism: State Governments and Pollution Control Policies*. Durham, NC: Duke University Press.

Melosi, M. V. 1981. *Garbage in the Cities: Refuse, Reform, and the Environment, 1880–1980*. College Station: Texas A&M University Press.

Moomaw, W. R. 2001. "Expanding the Concept of Environmental Management Systems to Meet Multiple Social Goals." In G. Conglianese and J. Nash, eds., *Regulating from the Inside: Can Environmental Management Systems Achieve Policy Goals?* Washington, DC: Resources for the Future Press.

National Academy of Public Administration. 1995. *Setting Priorities, Getting Results: A New Direction for EPA*. Washington, DC: National Academy of Public Administration.

Nelson, L. 2001. "Wildlife Policy." In C. Davis, ed., *Western Public Lands and Environmental Politics*. Boulder: Westview.

Oregon. 2000. *Development of a State Strategy Promoting Sustainability in Internal State Government Operations*. Salem: Governor of Oregon.

———. 2001. *Oregon Sustainability Act*. Salem: State of Oregon.

———. 2003. *A Sustainable Oregon for the 21st Century*. Salem: Governor of Oregon.

Percival, R. V. 1995. "Environmental Federalism: Historical Roots and Contemporary Models." *Maryland Law Review* 54, 1141–1182.

Potoski, M. 2001. "Clean Air Federalism: Do States Race to the Bottom?" *Public Administration Review* 61, no. 3, 335–342.

Rabe, B. G. 1999. "Federalism and Entrepreneurship: Explaining American and Canadian Innovation in Pollution Prevention and Regulatory Innovation." *Policy Studies Journal* 27, 288–306.

———. 2003. "Power to the States: The Promise and Pitfalls of Decentralization." In Norman J. Vieg and Michael E. Kraft, eds., *Environmental Policy: New Directions for the Twenty-First Century*. Washington, DC: CQ.

———. 2004. *Statehouse and Greenhouse: The Emerging Politics of American Climate Change Policy*. Washington, DC: Brookings Institution.

Rankin, Adam. 2006. "State Agencies Convene Environmental Justice Task Force." U.S. Federal News Service, March 31.

Reese, April. 2005. "States Lead Charge against Global Warming." *High Country News*, October 17, 14.

Revesz, R. 1997. "Federalism and Environmental Regulation: A Normative Critique." In J. A. Ferejohn and B. R. Weingast, eds., *The New Federalism: Can the States Be Trusted?* Stanford, CA: Hoover Institution Press.

Richardson, E. 1962. *The Politics of Conservation: Crusades and Controversies 1897–1913*. Berkeley: University of California Press.

Ringquist, E. J. 1993. *Environmental Protection at the State Level: Politics and Progress in Controlling Pollution*. Armonk, NY: M. E. Sharpe.

Robbins, R. 1962. *Our Landed Heritage: The Public Domain 1776–1936*. Lincoln: University of Nebraska Press.

Rosenbaum, W. A. 2002. *Environmental Politics and Policy* (5th ed.). Washington, DC: CQ.

Rowland, C. K., and R. Marz. 1982. "Gresham's Law: The Regulatory Analogy." *Policy Studies Review* 1, 572–580.

Safire, William. 2004. "Beware of Certitude." *New York Times*, June 30, 23.

Sagoff, M. 1999. "The View from Quincy Library: Civic Engagement in Environmental Problem Solving." In R. K. Fullinwider, ed., *Civil Society, Democracy, and Civic Renewal*. Lanham, MD: Rowman and Littlefield.

Sapat, A. 2004. "Devolution and Innovation: The Adoption of State Environmental Policy Innovations by Administrative Agencies." *Public Administration Review* 64, 141–151.

Scheberle, D. 1997. *Federalism and Environmental Policy: Trust and the Politics of Implementation*. Washington, DC: Georgetown University Press.

Speir, J. 2001. "EMSs and Tiered Regulation: Getting the Deal Right." In G. Coglianese and J. Nash, eds., *Regulating from the Inside: Can Environmental Management Systems Achieve Policy Goals?* Washington, DC: Resources for the Future Press.

Stanfield, R. L. 1984. "Ruckelshaus Casts EPA as 'Gorilla' in States' Enforcement Closet." *National Journal,* May 26, 1034–1038.

Stewart, R. 1977. "Pyramids of Sacrifice? Problems of Federalism in Mandating State Implementation of National Environmental Policy." *Yale Law Journal* 86, 1196–1272.

Sussman, G., B. W. Daynes, and J. P. West. 2002. *American Politics and the Environment.* New York: Longman.

Swire, P. 1996. "The Race to Laxity and the Race to Undesirability: Explaining Competitive Failure among Jurisdictions in Environmental Law." *Yale Law and Policy Review* 16, 112–156.

Switzer, J. V. 1997. *Green Backlash: The History and Politics of Environmental Opposition in the U.S.* Boulder: Lynne Rienner.

Teaford, J. 2002. *The Rise of the States: Evolution of American State Governments.* Baltimore: Johns Hopkins University Press.

Teske, P. 2003. "State Regulation: Capture Victorian-Era Anachronism or 'Re-enforcing' Autonomous Structure?" *Perspectives on Politics* 1, 291–306.

Van Horn, C. E. 1989. "The Quiet Revolution." In C. E. Van Horn, ed., *The State of the States.* Washington, DC: CQ.

Wahlke, J. 1962. *The Legislative System.* New York: John Wiley and Sons.

Weber, E. P. 2003. *Bringing Society Back In: Grassroots Ecosystem Management, Accountability, and Sustainable Communities.* Cambridge, MA: MIT Press.

Weiss, M. D. 1951. *Industrial Water Pollution: Survey of Legislation and Regulations.* New York: Chemonomics.

Zeigler, H., and M. Baer. 1969. *Lobbying: Interaction and Influence in American State Legislatures.* Belmont, CA: Wadsworth.

CHAPTER FOUR

SCIENCE, POLITICS, AND FEDERAL LANDS

R. McGreggor Cawley and John C. Freemuth

A variety of factors make the western United States unique, but perhaps the most important is the amount of land owned by the national government. As a quick measure of this factor, roughly 46 percent of the total land base of the twelve western states (we are not including Hawaii) is federal land (over 60% in some cases), whereas only about 4 percent of the land base of the rest of the nation is federal land. As should be obvious, then, decisions about how the federal estate will be used create an array of issues that are a main feature of western political discourse. In this chapter we address one of the central knots in conversations about federal land policy—the argument over the relationship between science and politics in determining how the federal estate should be managed.

The standard understanding of this matter portrays science as an activity that produces objective *facts* and politics as an activity driven by subjective *values*. This view poses the question: Should land-use decisions be based on objective facts or subjective values? On the face of it, the answer seems relatively straightforward—objective facts are the better basis for federal land-use decisions. Almost all participants in federal land policy debates invoke this answer when they call for "best science" rather than "best values" to guide land management decisions. We will argue, however, that this question is more complicated than it might appear.

For example, if we accept the definition of science as an activity that produces objective facts, it helps us decide what *could* be done, but it is not necessarily helpful for deciding what *should* be done. Stated differently, science can tell us the likely consequences associated with a clear-cut in a national forest. But the decision as to whether the clear-cut should be allowed is a judgment about what is more valuable to us—timber or undisturbed forest.

And herein is the complication with the politics side of the equation. In a democratic society, there are multiple definitions of "us." Wilderness interests view undisturbed forests as more valuable than timber; the inverse would be true of timber interests. Both positions represent expressions of subjective value. In pressing their claims, moreover, both wilderness and timber interests argue that they represent the view of the general public (another definition of "us"). The problem here is that while "the public" is one definition of us, it seldom expresses a single value position.

Indeed, as Robert Nelson suggests: "It has become apparent in recent years that the prospects for the progressive governing scheme actually depended on something the progressives mostly took for granted: the existence in American life of a set of common values and a strong sense of national community. . . . The idea of one set of values and one administrative design for all the United States is not only flawed but increasingly seems an outright impossibility" (Nelson 1995, xix). While we do not disagree with Nelson, we think there might be another way to understand the underlying logic of the Progressive conservation movement.

The conservation movement emerged in the early twentieth century and was animated by a belief that the demands of industrialization combined with fears of resource depletion required turning management of the federal estate over to a cadre of trained experts "applying scientific and technical principles" (Hays 1999, 265). The current Bush administration offers confirmation of this script: "We need to employ the best science and data to inform our decision-making" (White House July 2004). The change that has occurred between the time of the conservation movement and the present has taken place in the area of politics.

For example, Gifford Pinchot was a leading spokesperson for the early conservation movement and an advocate for scientific management, yet he also understood that "[w]hat went in America wasn't somebody's say-so. It was the widespread, slow-moving pressure of public opinion." Thus, before the management of the federal estate could be turned over to professionals, the "ingrained habit of mind of the best part of a hundred million people . . . had to be changed" (Pinchot 1974, 20 and 29). These statements seem to suggest that Pinchot viewed a common set of values not as a given but as something that had to be created. And Pinchot was not alone in this belief. In an 1891 lecture, Woodrow Wilson argued that an important part of the Progressive governing scheme was to "help make up the general mind, *to form it to the right ideals and purposes*" (Wilson 1891, 366 [original emphasis]; see also Cawley 1998).

These comments suggest that Progressives at the beginning of the twentieth century did not believe objective facts produced by science would by themselves necessarily lead to a common set of values. Facts were important, but something else was needed to change the public's mind. To gain an understanding of what that "something else" might have been requires thinking about two related, but different, roles science occupies in our public discourse.

On the one hand, science is a process—"the scientific method"—for studying phenomena that produces reliable and predictable explanations based on objective facts. This aspect of science is a very useful land management tool. But on the other hand, science occupies a broader role. Dwight Waldo captured the essence of this broader role when he noted: "The imperative of higher law is always conceived as derived from what is most valid, most powerful, most highly honored. Historically, this has most frequently been God. But in the late nineteenth- and early twentieth-century America it has often been SCIENCE" (1984, 157 [original emphasis]). Science as higher law (which we will call science to distinguish it from scientific method) emerges from scientific method, but it assumes a different role. Science presents objective facts in ways that make it seem as though it can inform the question of not only what *could* be done but also what *should* be done.

The possibility we want to raise, then, is that while the Progressives were clearly interested in using scientific method as a foundation for governing, they also believed science could create a common set of values and, through that, political support. But this view raises another issue. Understood as higher law, would science, of necessity, need to be unchanging? If the

Progressive era invoked science to create a common set of values and science has remained a central component of the discourse, why is this approach not working today?

To answer this question requires several steps. First, we will offer examples that help demonstrate how the scientific method leads to a changing science. Second, we will explore how a changing science creates different ways of thinking about what government should do. And finally, we will suggest how all of this gives us a better understanding of the current state of federal land policy.

SCIENTIFIC METHOD AND SCIENCE

One way to think about what we are calling science is in terms of theory. For instance, evolution theory is built on facts produced by scientific method, but it arranges those facts into a story about the history of life on the planet. The evolution story, in turn, provides an explanation for what has happened, what could happen, and perhaps what should happen. We will return to evolution theory later in the chapter, but for now let us consider the curious story of malaria as an example of the interaction between science and scientific method.

Although the disease had been described by ancient Egyptians, an Italian physician, Giovanni Lancisi, coined the name "malaria" in 1717. The prevailing theory (science) at that time was that air caused disease. Combining this theory with data (scientific method) suggesting that people living close to swamps were more likely to contract the disease, Lancisi speculated that the cause was swamp gas or "bad air" (in Italian, *mal aria*). To our modern eye Lancisi's theory may appear quaint, if not a touch silly, but at the time it was viewed as plausible scientific explanation. Roughly 100 years later, the research of Louis Pasteur gave support to an alternate theory—that disease was actually caused by microorganisms. Building on Pasteur's work, Alphonse Laveran conducted further research in the 1880s, demonstrating that malaria was actually caused by a parasite; roughly 10 years later Sir Ronald Ross established that the parasite was carried by mosquitoes. Read one way, this story offers concrete evidence of how the scientific method can help provide useful answers for serious problems. At the same time, it reveals important lessons about the dynamic character of science.

Because science is based on scientific method, the explanation it provides is always constructed on the basis of available data (facts). In consequence, as scientific method produces more data, there is always the possibility that existing explanations will need to be revised. Sometimes the revisions simply add more detail to existing explanations; other times, they may lead to a very different explanation. Thus, Lancisi's work may appear quaint to us today, but it was based on the science of his day. Pasteur added more data, and science changed.

At first glance, this brief discussion of malaria may seem unrelated to federal land policy. But let us suggest two examples that provide a bridge. Writing in the early twentieth century, against a backdrop of catastrophic forest fires in the western United States, Pinchot observed: "[I]n the early days of forest fires . . . [i]t was assumed that they came in the natural order of things, as inevitably as the seasons or the rising and setting of the sun." In consequence, "[A]ny opposition was hopeless and any attempt to control them not merely hopeless but childish." Pinchot then assured his readers: "Today we understand that forest fires are wholly within the control of men [sic]" (1967, 44–45). In short, Pinchot invoked science to buttress his claim that fire suppression was part of good forest management practices. And as we discuss later, a change in science now suggests that forest fires may, in fact, be part of the natural order of things.

A second example is the Preble's Meadow jumping mouse (PMJM). Scientific studies in the 1950s concluded that the PMJM was a distinct subspecies. In the 1990s other scientific studies determined that the PMJM was threatened with extinction. Since part of the PMJM's habitat included western rangeland, the possibility of protecting it under the auspices of the Endangered Species Act (ESA) was perceived as a threat to livestock grazing in the West. In 1998, after following the process defined by ESA, the U.S. Fish and Wildlife Service listed the PMJM as endangered. In 2003 a team of scientists at the Denver Museum of Nature and Science published the results of a study that suggested the PMJM is not a distinct subspecies. The primary difference between the earlier and more recent studies is a rather dramatic improvement in genetic research. Stated differently, the conclusions of the recent study simply reflected the availability of more, perhaps better, data. Advocates of the PMJM believed their claim was supported by science. However, rather than accept the new studies as representing more data that need to be considered in the decision process, they have recently challenged the validity of the studies. It could be that the studies were flawed, but it could also be that, like the forest fire example, science has simply changed, and continues to change, our understanding of the situation.

What these examples demonstrate is the dynamic interaction between science and scientific method. At the same time, they also point to potential problems associated with linking management with science. On the one hand, the dynamic character of science means that management policies based on it must also be dynamic. At the beginning of the twentieth century, science supported fire suppression policies; now science supports "let it burn" policies. On the other hand, the dynamic character of sciences also impacts its utility as an authoritative foundation for political claims.

If, as these examples suggest, changes in science affect the way we understand things, then we might suspect that the same would be true about our thinking regarding the role of government. It is widely recognized that the role of government in this country changed rather dramatically at the beginning of the twentieth century as a result of the Progressive movement. In the next section, we will explore how the idea of *progress* represented a change in science and, through it, a different way of thinking about the role of government.

NEWTON, DARWIN, AND THE CONSTITUTION

During the 1912 presidential campaign, Woodrow Wilson (the Democratic Party candidate) delivered a speech entitled "What Is Progress." At one point Wilson exclaimed: "Progress! Did you ever reflect that that word is almost a new one?" (1961, 39). Campaign speeches tend to be heavy on rhetoric and light on careful analysis. The word "progress" was certainly not "new" in the early 1900s. Nevertheless, the kind of progress Wilson was thinking about did represent a new definition that emerged from a change in science. Equally important, Wilson's views demonstrate how science has informed us about the role of government.

Wilson noted that that the drafters of the U.S. Constitution "were scientists in their way—the best way of their age" (1961, 41). But the drafters lived in the age of Newtonian theory, and, in consequence, they viewed government and politics as "a variety of mechanics" (Wilson 1961, 41). The example he used was the system of checks and balances that is a key component of the Constitution. Newtonian theory described the solar system in terms of "how by the attraction of gravitation the various parts are held in their orbits." He then asserted that the drafters viewed "Congress, the Judiciary, and the President as a sort of imitation of the solar system" (Wilson 1961, 41). In contrast, the dominant thought at the beginning of the twentieth century was organized around Darwinian theory, which meant government was no longer viewed as a "machine, but a living thing. . . . No living thing can have its functions offset against each other, as *checks*, and live. On the contrary, its life is dependent upon their quick co-operation, their ready response to the commends of instinct or intelligence, their amicable community of purpose" (Wilson 1961, 42 [emphasis added]).

We think Wilson's comments help provide a different way of interpreting the underlying logic of the Progressive movement. Returning to Nelson's comment, discussed earlier, the Progressives were animated by "a common set of values and a strong sense of national community." But rather than matters taken for granted, Progressives believed the public had to be convinced that its vision represented an appropriate agenda for the nation. To make their case persuasive, Progressives argued that their vision emerged from, and was supported by, the authority of science in the form of evolution theory.

Moreover, the Progressive approach marks an important shift in this country's political discourse. Wilson's view of the constitutional era is instructive in this regard. It seems likely that the drafters were, as Wilson asserts, influenced by Newtonian theory. Yet the drafters did not explicitly invoke the authority of science in their campaign to convince the public to adopt the Constitution. Instead, they crafted a script based primarily on values. One measure of the success of the Progressive movement, then, is its effect on the structure of U.S. political debates. From the beginning of the twentieth century to the present, persuasive positions in politics generally, and federal land debates specifically, are ones that seem capable of basing values claims on the authority of science.

At the same time, Wilson's comments also reveal that invoking science as a foundation for political claims is more complicated than it seems. On the one hand, both Newtonian theory and evolution theory are examples of science as defined in this chapter. On the other hand, in reality government is neither a machine nor a living thing. There is a sense, then, in which we have a choice about how we connect science with politics. If we view government as a machine, then Newtonian theory represents the authoritative science. If we view government as a living thing, then evolution theory is the authoritative science.

We think it is a relatively small step from this broad discussion of government and science to the narrower area of federal land politics. As noted earlier, the conservation ethos purporting that federal land management should be guided by science became a prominent feature of the federal land policy dialogue throughout the twentieth century. For Progressives, the federal estate represented a storehouse of resources necessary to attain and maintain the material well-being of the population. In consequence, the science they invoked was consistent with their view of progress. After World War II, however, a different view of the federal estate emerged, one seemingly supported by a different science. We turn now to these developments.

SCIENCE AND THE PROCESS OF POLICY CHANGE

While Charles Darwin is widely recognized as having established the foundation for evolutionary theory, his work was a modification of the explanation offered by Jean Baptiste Lamarck in his 1809 treatise, *Zoological Philosophy*. Lamarck hypothesized that nature was in a constant state of flux, and, as such, organisms had to adapt to new conditions. Lamarck argued that the changes taking place in nature followed an underlying pattern of "increasing complexity . . . from the most imperfect to the most perfect" (1984, 107).

Darwin incorporated Lamarck's notions of a changing nature and adaptation in his explanation. He added the concepts of struggle for existence and natural selection. Although Darwin tended to portray the struggle for existence as a competitive process, he also warned his readers: "I use the term Struggle for Existence in a large and metaphorical sense, including dependence of one being on another" (Darwin 1979, 116). Thus, the play of life in Darwin's theory incorporated both competition and cooperation. And like Lamarck, Darwin believed natural selection was not a random process: "[A]s natural selection works solely by and for the good of each being, all corporal and mental endowments will tend toward progress to perfection" (1979, 459).

Although Lamarck and Darwin sought mainly to explain the process of change in the natural world, their ideas galvanized thinking about a wide array of matters in the nineteenth century. For example, Herbert Spencer demonstrated how science could be used as a foundation for understanding the social world. Like Lamarck and Darwin, Spencer viewed evolution as a progression "towards perfection" (1851, 411). In his scheme, attaining this goal required a rather complex form of society that could meet two primary conditions. First, society had to have "the best possible system of production" (1851, 411) to provide the requisite material commodities for happiness. Second, society also had to be populated by people who realized "that public interests and private ones are essentially in unison" because any one individual's "welfare and all men's welfare are inseparable" (1851, 442).

What begins to take shape here, we think, is a more textured understanding of the Progressive vision. Science suggested that evolution was a force at work in both the biological and social worlds. As such, it created a great deal of optimism about the future, as well as a new sense of purpose for government. As Wilson (1891, 366) argued, the ultimate goal of governing was to create "not administrative acts, *but happy and prosperous populations*" (original emphasis). Making the population happy and prosperous, in turn, required adopting a different approach to managing natural resources.

"The first duty of the human race," Pinchot (1967, 45) asserted, "is to control the earth it lives upon." Controlling the earth entailed adopting a utilitarian attitude toward nature (Hays 1999). National forests, for instance, were to be "tree farms" that provided timber for current and future generations. The hydrological system of the western United States, which was not particularly suitable for industrial society, could be altered, for example. Yet this also entailed paying close attention to human habits. Resource development and use needed to be guided by principles such as preventing waste and ensuring that resources served the "benefit of the many, and not merely the profit of the few" (Pinchot 1967, 20).

However, at the heart of the Progressive governing scheme was an apparent bind. The plan to steer society down the path of progress required a cadre of proactive experts. For example, Pinchot argued that the "first duty of a public officer [was] to obey the law," but he added that a "second duty, and a close second, [was] to do everything the law will let him do for the public good" (1967, 58). This view seems to suggest an image of experts given control of the governing process. Moreover, Wilson's assertion that public officials should help form public opinion "to the right ideals and purposes" and Pinchot's notion that the "ingrained habit of mind . . . had to be changed" do not conjure up images of democratic government as it is usually understood. In fact, this portion of the Progressive script seems based on the idea that experts know best and the rest of us should just do what they tell us to do.

Yet there were other edges to the Progressive script. For example, during the 1912 presidential campaign, Wilson spoke against the idea of rule by experts: "God forbid that in a democratic country we should resign the task and give the government over to experts. What are we for if we are to [be] scientifically taken care of by a small number of gentlemen who are the only men who understand the job?" (quoted in Davidson 1956, 83). And although Pinchot clearly advocated management of the nation's resources by experts, he nevertheless believed expertise was insufficient in and of itself. Commenting on the bureaucratic landscape in the late 1800s, Pinchot explained: "It was a mess. . . . The one and only way to bring order out of this chaos was to supply a common ground on which each could take its proper place, and do its proper work, in cooperation with all the others" (1974, 321). The principles of conservation, Pinchot believed, provided that necessary common ground.

It could be, of course, that the Progressives were just confused, sometimes advocating government by experts and other times recognizing the importance of democracy. We think another explanation is possible, one based on paying close attention to the distinction between science and scientific method. Science defined the broad goals of social progress and development. Attaining those goals required the kind of knowledge that could be produced by scientific method. Thus, the role played by experts in the Progressive vision was essentially that of technical advisers. Given the goal of sustaining social progress—in Pinchot's words, "The greatest good for the greatest number for the longest time" (1974, 201–202)—their task was to utilize scientific method to determine the best arrangements for achieving it.

Whatever else might be said about the Progressive vision, the first half of the twentieth century provided evidence that it was a successful approach to governing. Attention to efficiency, planning, and proactive management had shepherded the United States through two world wars and the Great Depression, allowing it to emerge as a leading world power that was experiencing a period of unprecedented material prosperity. Much the same was true of the Progressive vision regarding public lands. The unappropriated public domain had been divided up into national forests, national parks, and national grazing lands, each under the management of federal agencies—the U.S. Forest Service (USFS), National Park Service, and Bureau of Land Management—staffed with experts. The conservation philosophy did not produce the harmony Pinchot had argued it would, but it did seem to provide a way for agencies and public land users to work out their differences. But in the post–World War II era, more change began to take shape.

MOUNTAIN THINKING

The immediate post–WW II era offered good reason to question the idea of progress and the science upon which it was based. On the one hand, the atomic weapons used on Japan raised the possibility that the future might consist of a devastated planet rather than the utopia that underpinned the Progressive vision. On the other hand, the Nazi regime's horrific campaign to "purify the races" suggested that social evolution would not necessarily lead to positive results.

At a broader level, critics such as F. A. Hayek (1954, 1994) posed a troublesome challenge to the Progressive vision. Hayek's central premise was that while planning and centralization of power had been necessary components of the war effort, continuing them in the postwar effort presented a danger. In structure, the government of the United States was not substantially different from that of Nazi Germany. And although U.S. leaders assured people that such structures would be used for purposes quite different from those of Nazi Germany, Hayek suggested another possibility: the structures in place would lead the United States down a path to totalitarianism.

From our present vantage point, Hayek's clarion call might seem a bit melodramatic, even paranoid. But at the time it was not so easily dismissed by the evidence. For example, a curious organization named the Conference on the Scientific Spirit and Democratic Faith convened a meeting of nationally recognized spokespersons from universities, government, and religion to discuss the general theme "Science for Democracy." In introducing the papers presented at the conference, Jerome Nathanson offered an obvious, albeit unacknowledged, reference to Hayek: "To say that planning necessarily leads to serfdom is as ridiculous as to say that using our heads necessarily means tying our hands. . . . We can plan our national and international life intelligently and increase human freedom. The problem is how to do it. That is a problem of intelligence, of careful inquiry, of organizing knowledge, in a word, of science" (1946, viii).

Nathanson went on to suggest that future planning efforts created specific responsibilities for scientists. In particular, scientists were "obliged to see that their knowledge functions in government service, insisting wherever and whenever possible that they are not subservient employees of government officials, but their colleagues in planning policy" (1946, ix).

Paul Sears, a leading ecologist, echoed Nathanson's view of the role of scientists in the future. "We have been using the scientist as a tinker and handyman," he argued. "We must begin to use him [sic] as a consultant" (Sears 1946, 6). But Sears also suggested that the kind of consultation offered by scientists had to change. In the past, he asserted, "[w]e have underwritten the kind of science which speeds up the production of things from resources—the elaboration of consumers' goods" (Sears 1946, 4; see also Cawley and Freemuth 1993). The new emphasis had to be built on a foundation that recognized that all life on the planet was "a system by which the materials of earth and air, and the energy of the sun, are organized and put to work" (Sears 1946, 7). The system, moreover, had clear limits: "In nature such activity tends to be constructive, increasing the capacity of the earth to sustain life. . . . If this trend is interfered with, the environment is rapidly depleted, and its capacity to sustain life is lessened" (Sears 1946, 7). And in Sears's view, human activity, especially the activity associated with industrial society, had significantly interfered with nature's normal trend.

Sears's position bears a striking parallel to the argument presented by Aldo Leopold in his famous essay "The Land Ethic." Early in the essay Leopold explained: "This extension of ethics, so far studied only by philosophers, is actually a process in ecological evolution. . . . An ethic, ecologically, is a limitation on freedom of action in the struggle for existence. An ethic, philosophically, is a differentiation of social from anti-social conduct. These are two definitions of one thing" (1966, 238). It then followed that the "mechanism of operation is the same for any ethic: social approbation for right actions; social disapproval for wrong actions" (Leopold 1966, 263). And in one of the most famous passages from the essay, Leopold defined the central ecological ethic: "A thing is right when it tends to preserve the integrity, stability, and beauty of the biotic community. It is wrong when it tends otherwise" (1966, 262).

We suggest that these developments pointed to an attempt to revise the Progressive vision. Part of this revision resulted from the emergence of ecology as the dominant interpretation for change in the natural world and, through that, for change in the social world as well. Ecology altered the contours of science in two ways. First, it replaced the earlier view of change as an open-ended process that inevitably produced positive outcomes with the idea that change had limits. Second, and related, ecology dictated that failure to observe those limits carried potentially cataclysmic consequences. Taken together, these factors suggested that natural limits imposed boundaries on social development.

Embedded in ecology was the other part of the revision of the Progressive vision. Because the limits to change were often subtle and adverse consequences were not always immediately recognizable, the role of scientists-experts had to change. Rather than technicians who developed ways to accomplish goals, scientists-experts needed to become active participants in the goal-setting process. Stated differently, ecology provided the foundation for a key point of contention in the post–World War II federal land management discourse. Throughout the second half of the twentieth century, dialogue over federal land management decisions was animated by the assumption that "scientists-experts know best." This time some of the scientists themselves were making the claim.

WHEN SCIENCE CHANGED FOR PUBLIC LANDS

Although resource development was the central goal of the conservation approach, the idea that some portions of the federal estate might remain undeveloped was not really alien to that goal. After all, national parks and monuments were part of the early conservation script. Moreover, in the 1920s and 1930s, under the influence of Aldo Leopold, Bob Marshall, and Arthur Carhart, the USFS had designated sections of the national forests as wilderness and primitive areas. Yet the central justification for these early preservation efforts was human use. For example, national parks were established in part to protect special scenic and natural areas but also to provide areas for the American public to enjoy. The emergence of ecology in the post–WW II era created a new opening for revisiting the preservation issue.

More than anything else, ecology offered a seemingly scientific basis for arguing that nature could be damaged, even destroyed (Tesh 2000). The question, then, was how ecology and the older conservation approach related to each other. Leopold had sketched one possibility—ecology needed to replace conservation as the basis for land management. Federal land managers, at least initially, tended to adopt a different approach. Rather than a fundamental shift in science, they viewed ecology as a scientific method that could be grafted onto traditional conservation management approaches. Conceptually, the marriage between conservation and ecology constituted "multiple-use management."

In 1960 Congress adopted the Multiple Use / Sustained Yield Act (MUSY) drafted by the USFS. An amazingly brief act, MUSY can be read in two ways. On the one hand, it affirmed the USFS commitment to a management regime that balanced timber production with other uses, including preservation of wilderness. On the other hand, it carried a more subtle, albeit rather clear, message that Paul Hirt (1994) has labeled a "conspiracy of optimism." Land managers simply believed that if the public would merely trust their expertise and science, the federal estate could be managed in ways that benefited everyone. However, even at the time, when multiple-use management seemed to offer a source of optimism, there were signs that ecology would, of necessity, lead in different directions.

In 1962, Ashley Schiff argued that a vestige of the earlier science—which held that fire was a threat to forests—was not a supportable position in light of ecological evidence. Moreover, Schiff charged that not only had the USFS failed to incorporate this evidence, it had actively suppressed it. In his view, the explanation for this situation was that the USFS relied more on an immutable belief system than on science: "[E]vangelism subverted a scientific program, impaired professionalism, violated canons of bureaucratic responsibility, undermined the democratic faith, and threatened the piney woods with ultimate extinction" (Schiff 1962, 115). Such criticism highlighted a developing bind confronting land managers.

The hope was that multiple-use management offered a way for agencies to adapt traditional organizational imperatives and belief systems to the changing realities of scientific evidence and public demands. The bind was that ecological evidence seemed to increasingly challenge, if not contradict, the core beliefs and organizational culture of land agencies. Thus, whereas the agencies viewed the situation in terms of developing management regimes that balanced competing uses, their critics were voicing a more fundamental demand. In their view, the agencies needed to accept the authority of science in the form of ecology and transform their cultures accordingly.

Viewed in this context, the 1960s and early 1970s represent a period of realignment as important as the early conservation era. Environmentalists created an external stimulus for change by orchestrating an effective campaign through legislation and litigation that forced agencies to base their management regimes on ecology. A more subtle internal change occurred as well as new employees trained in ecology began replacing older personnel still wedded to the old conservation tradition.

By the late 1970s it seemed the agencies were well on their way to developing a new organizational culture. The change process created controversy, of course. Environmentalists criticized the agencies for moving too slowly, while commodity resource users criticized the agencies for abandoning multiple-use management in an effort to appease environmental critics. But this acrimony was viewed as simply part of the adjustment process, and public land managers believed it would subside once changes had solidified. However, events in the early 1980s suggested that the acrimony would not subside quickly. Commodity users mobilized their complaints in the so-called Sagebrush Rebellion, and in 1980 Ronald Reagan won the presidential election (Cawley 1993).

The 1980s and early 1990s were an era in which federal land agencies seemed caught between the proverbial rock and a hard place. Environmentalists and statutory requirements demanded that the agencies remain committed to the ecology agenda, but the Reagan administration, and subsequently the first Bush administration, demanded that the agencies return to the multiple-use agenda. Wanting to regain public trust, or at least escape their political maelstrom, federal agencies began searching for a new management approach. This search led them to "ecosystem management" (EM). Advocates of EM argued that the approach embraced science by making preservation of ecosystem integrity and stability the central goal of land management while still remaining sensitive to resource development. In short, EM seemed to have the potential to usher in a new period of harmony in the federal land policy arena.

We suggest, however, that the controversy over EM reveals a fundamental problem with the use of science in the post–WW II era. Consider Edward Grumbine's comments in an important 1994 article that attempted to make sense of EM. He argued that "in the academic and popular literature there is general agreement that maintaining ecosystem integrity *should take precedence* over any other management goal" (Grumbine 1994, 32 [emphasis added]). Why and how that integrity was to "take precedence" was not discussed. Those who supported the conservation movement's original goals were said to be believers in "resourcism." In an earlier article, Grumbine asserted that "we must avoid the *democratic trap* of giving equal weight to all interest groups" who would "destroy biodiversity for short-term economic gain" (Grumbine quoted in Fitzsimmons 1999, 241 [emphasis added]). Finally, ecosystem management would require a severe change, a "seismic shift" in human values (Grumbine 1994, 34).

On the face of it, Grumbine's comments are very reminiscent of the script used by the early conservationists. We confront a crisis that requires both intervention by experts and fundamental changes in our "ingrained habit of mind," to use Pinchot's phrasing. And although all this might appear to be old-fashioned elitism, it is not. These are actions dictated by science. Therein is the problem. We have seen that science at the beginning of the twentieth century had some rough edges. Indeed, it was the foundation for the very "resourcism" Grumbine criticizes.

One possibility is that we now have "better science" than was available at the beginning of the twentieth century. In consequence, contemporary scientists-experts really do know what is best. We think there might be room for skepticism regarding this explanation. And as it turns out, we are not alone.

In 1994 three prominent conservation biologists wrote a guest editorial in *Conservation Biology* in response to an earlier editorial by noted conservation biologist Reed Noss. They disagreed with Noss and his call for conservation biologists to "*link arms with activists* in efforts to reform grazing practices" (Brussard, Murphy, and Tracy 1994, 919 [emphasis added]). They cautioned that conservation biologists would damage their credibility by openly advocating and supporting political and value-laden positions. The Society for Conservation Biology, they claimed, had an applied task: to develop and implement the science needed to preserve biological diversity—a task, they argued, that required close attention to the dictates of scientific method.

These biologists' critique purports that Noss's position simply accepts the proposition "that range management must be dramatically reformed" (Brussard, Murphy, and Tracy 1994, 920). This is a form of deductive reasoning that is not true to the canons of scientific method. They asked:

> How could we continue to conduct this research and attempt to develop valid results if we worked from that premise? Our work as scientists involves recognizing patterns based on data and only then formulating a general rule. More importantly, how can we hope to advance society's mission to preserve biological diversity if our audience of policymakers assumes that we intend to "prove" a presumed conclusion instead of attempting to falsify well-framed null hypotheses? (Brussard, Murphy, and Tracy 1994, 920)

A more scientifically valid research premise would take a different approach by asking a different question: "How can livestock grazing be managed to have the fewest impacts on biodiversity and ecosystem integrity?" (Brussard, Murphy, and Tracy 1994, 920).

What the biologists are cautioning against is an approach that leads to pronouncements that do not clearly separate scientific conclusions from value judgments and assumptions. If one starts with a supposedly neutral hypothesis that asserts "grazing is bad," it is simple to "find the data" to support the hypothesis. This is the inverse of the criticism leveled against range conservation science for many years. That science often began with the presumed hypothesis that "grazing is good" and found scientific support for it. Presumably, the more appropriate null hypothesis, at least for conservation biologists, ought to be along the lines of "grazing has no effect on biological diversity." If it is falsified, then we can start to speak of reform.

There is, however, a broader issue here. Throughout the twentieth century, science was offered as a better way than politics to resolve arguments. This view was based on the belief that science emerged from scientific method. Scientific method, in turn, is a process that starts with data, looks for patterns, and then forms general principles that are subject to further testing through hypotheses development. A widely recognized violation of scientific method is to begin with predetermined principles and then collect data to support them. It seems to us that the arguments developed in this chapter raise questions about how science and scientific method have been employed in federal land management.

As noted earlier, Pinchot's predetermined principle was that humans had a duty to control the earth. He believed this principle was derived from science in the form of evolution theory. Yet such was not the case. Evolution theory in the nineteenth and early twentieth centuries defined the principles by which species change, but it contained no scientific evidence capable of supporting a proposition about which species should survive. In the post–World War II era, Sears and Leopold laid out a different predetermined principle: any human action that alters nature is by definition wrong. They believed their principle was derived from science in the form of ecology. The earlier criticism of Grumbine and Noss suggests that ecology does not necessarily support that principle.

CONCLUSION: SCIENCE, METHOD, AND PUBLIC LANDS

The foregoing discussion suggests that things have changed quite a bit since the founding of the Progressive movement. But where has the change occurred? The root question has remained fairly constant: What is the most appropriate management approach for the federal estate? Moreover, the basic answers to this question have also remained fairly constant. Some people advocate a management regime that emphasizes resource development; others support a regime that emphasizes preserving the natural character of the federal estate. And finally, today, as a century ago, virtually everyone seems to agree that management decisions need to be based on the best science available.

In this chapter we have focused on the last of these points. The Progressive vision was based on a hope that science offered a way to resolve political arguments. The Progressive hope, in turn, emerged from a belief that science defined the principles of higher law. We have tried to demonstrate that the Progressive vision contained a flaw. Science does seek to discover the underlying principles of the physical world. However, because science follows the process of scientific method, our understanding of those principles has been, and continues to be, subject to revision as new data become available. This is as it should be and in itself does not create a problem.

The flaw in the Progressive vision, then, is that rather than offering a way to *resolve* political arguments, science simply changes the way we carry out those arguments. Viewed as higher law, science gives authority to value positions masked as science. Science at the beginning of the twentieth century gave resource development a position of more authority than the preservation position in the discourse. Ecology in the post–World War II era seemed to reverse the play of authority.

Herein is a second major point developed in this chapter. The history of science over the past century provides solid evidence that our understanding of underlying principles governing the physical world has changed, and yet the same evidence also supports the possibility for more change in the future. Therefore, we think one of the most important issues in the contemporary and future federal land policy discourse is the question of whether we can move beyond the flaw in the Progressive vision. Stated differently, can we begin to develop a discourse that accepts the authority of science but also recognizes that science is subject to change?

The answer to this question, we think, lies in carefully assessing claims that invoke the authority of science. Scientists, whether they are managers or spokespersons for interest groups, need to ensure that they are employing good scientific method by not allowing their preconceived values and principles to dictate data collection efforts. At the same time, scientists and nonscientists alike need to accept that science is dynamic, not static. In consequence, "scientific truths" will be revised, necessitating changes in management decisions and policies. Such was the case with fire, and such may likely be the case with the jumping mouse.

To sharpen our point, let us conclude by returning to the story of malaria. Had we adopted a government policy to combat malaria in the late 1700s, it would have been directed at eliminating swamps. Moreover, given that swamps are breeding grounds for mosquitoes, this policy might have produced a reduction in the disease. In short, the entire situation would have provided an example of the successful application of science to public policy. After Pasteur added more data, of course, we would have had to revise our assessment of that policy.

REFERENCES

Brussard, P. F., D. D. Murphy, and C. R. Tracy. 1994. "Cows and Conservation Biology: Another View." *Conservation Biology* 8, 919–921.

Cawley, R. McGreggor. 1993. *Federal Land, Western Anger: The Sagebrush Rebellion and Environmental Politics*. Lawrence: University of Kansas Press.

———. 1998. "We May Help to Make up the General Mind Reuniting Wilson, Taylor, and Pinchot." *Administrative Theory and Praxis* 20, no. 1 (March), 55–67.

Cawley, R. McGreggor, and John Freemuth. 1993. "Tree Farms, Mother Earth, and Other Dilemmas." *Society and Natural Resources* 6, 41–53.

Darwin, Charles. 1979 (1859). *The Origin of Species*. New York: Gramercy Books.

Davidson, John Wells. 1956. *A Crossroads of Freedom: The 1912 Campaign Speeches of Woodrow Wilson*. New Haven, CT: Yale University Press. (The authors originally came across this quotation in Smith, James A. 1991. *The Idea Brokers*. New York: Free Press, 1.)

Fitzsimmons, Allan. 1999. *Defending Illusions: Federal Protection of Ecosystems*. Lanham, MD: Rowman and Littlefield.

Grumbine, Edward. 1994. "What Is Ecosystem Management?" *Conservation Biology* 8, no. 1, 27–38.

Hayek, F. A. 1954. *The Counter-Revolution of Science*. Glencoe, IL: Free Press.

———. 1994. *The Road to Serfdom*. Chicago: University of Chicago Press.

Hays, Samuel. 1999. *Conservation and the Gospel of Efficiency*. Pittsburgh: University of Pittsburgh Press.

Hirt, Paul. 1994. *A Conspiracy of Optimism*. Lincoln: University of Nebraska Press.

Lamarck, J. B. 1984 (1809). *Zoological Philosophy: An Exposition with Regard to the Natural History of Animals*. Chicago: University of Chicago Press.

Leopold, Aldo. 1966 (1949). *A Sand County Almanac*. New York: Ballantine Books.

Nathanson, Jerome. 1946. "Introduction." In Jerome Nathanson, ed., *Science for Democracy*. Freeport, NY: Books for Libraries Press.

Nelson, Robert H. 1995. *Public Lands and Private Rights: The Failure of Scientific Management*. Lanham, MD: Rowman and Littlefield.

Pinchot, Gifford. 1967 (1910). *The Fight for Conservation*. Seattle: University of Washington Press.

———. 1974. *Breaking New Ground*. Washington, DC: Island.

Schiff, Ashley. 1962. *Fire and Water*. Cambridge, MA: Harvard University Press.

Sears, Paul. 1946. "Science and Human Welfare." In Jerome Nathanson, ed., *Science for Democracy*. Freeport, NY: Books for Libraries Press.

Spencer, Herbert. 1851. *Social Statistics*. London: John Chapman.

Tesh, Sylvia. 2000. *Uncertain Hazards: Environmental Activists and Scientific Proof.* Ithaca, NY: Cornell University Press.

Waldo, Dwight. 1984. *The Administrative State*. New York: Holmes and Meier.

White House. "Protecting Our Nation's Environment." 2004 (July). At www.whitehouse.gov/infocus/environment, p. 1, site accessed August 25, 2005.

Wilson, Woodrow. 1891. "Lecture on Democracy." In Arthur Link, ed., *The Papers of Woodrow Wilson,* vol. 7. Princeton: Princeton University Press.

———. 1961 (1913). *The New Freedom*. Englewood Cliffs, NJ: Prentice-Hall.

CHAPTER FIVE

THE POLITICS OF DAM REMOVAL AND RIVER RESTORATION

Daniel McCool

Much has been written about the waste and inefficiency of traditional western water projects (Andrews and Sansone 1983; Reisner 1986; Gottlieb 1988; Bates et al. 1993; McCool 1994). Some authors have focused primarily on the negative environmental impacts of supply-centered water development (Fradkin 1981; Palmer 1986; McCully 1996; Grossman 2002). Others have specifically criticized the economic inefficiency of heavily subsidized water projects (Ferejohn 1974; Anderson 1983; Wahl 1989). In addition, innumerable critiques have been written regarding specific projects or river basins. It would not be an exaggeration to say that an entire literature has developed devoted exclusively to criticizing traditional structural water policy and demanding fundamental changes. Reform of water policy is important in every region of the country, but it is particularly critical in the arid West, where decisions regarding water are at the heart of every question concerning the region's future viability.

Given the dissatisfaction with past policy, there is great potential for a fundamental departure from traditional approaches. Thus, it is imperative to carefully examine the rate, direction, and depth of this change in policy in an effort to predict future trends involving western water. The thesis of this chapter is that western water policy is on the cusp of a new era that will focus on dam removal and river restoration. This does not mean traditional policy objectives, such as irrigation and hydropower, will be abandoned but rather that all water uses will take place within a larger framework that values intact, natural rivers; rivers will be viewed as a public commons rather than simply as a sump from which various resources can be disaggregated and distributed. As a result, a greater balance between extractive water uses and preservation of natural rivers will be achieved.

This chapter will first examine the inchoate policy of removing dams and restoring rivers and then describe two river restoration projects in the West. These projects illustrate the range and variety of factors that affect restoration.

THE POLITICS OF RESTORATION

River restoration is a function of the law of supply and demand, with a thick overlay of political tradition. For the first 200 years of this country's existence, dams were viewed as a hallmark of progress—part of the "conquest of nature." A 1950s promotional video produced by the U.S. Army Corps of Engineers to justify the Kissimmee River project claimed that the "maddened forces of nature" and the "crazed antics of the elements" had to be controlled by a massive water project (Waters of Destiny circa 1955). This image of nature as a beast, controlled through engineering, remained the dominant ethos of American society for two centuries. Its political expression found voice in two major federal agencies: the U.S. Army Corps of Engineers and the U.S. Bureau of Reclamation.

Both agencies operate in the western United States, the latter exclusively so. The Corps of Engineers has constructed 383 dams and reservoirs, 8,500 miles of levees, 10,790 miles of navigation channel with 276 locks, and 75 hydropower facilities that generate 96.1 billion kilowatt-hours of electricity (U.S. Army Corps of Engineers 2001a). The bureau has built 600 dams and provides irrigation water to 10 million acres of land, and its 58 hydropower units generate 40 billion kilowatt-hours of electricity. In addition to these dams, all built by the federal government, thousands more were built by state, local, and private entities. The Corps of Engineers has 77,000 dams in its National Inventory of Dams, which includes only dams over six feet high (U.S. Army Corps of Engineers 2004). The National Research Council estimates that there are 2.5 million dams in the United States (National Research Council 1992).

Attitudes about dams began to change as people became more aware of their significant economic and environmental costs. According to the public interest group American Rivers, 465 dams have been removed in the United States since 1912 (American Rivers 2001). In addition to dam removal, numerous river restoration projects have been implemented that range from a multiagency effort on the Lower Rio Grande (Oko 2002), to the Verde and San Pedro rivers in Arizona (American Rivers 2001b; Hanson 2001), to the formally moribund Los Angeles River (Gumprecht 2002). The corps and the bureau have recognized these new directions in policy to a limited extent, but neither agency is willing to abandon its traditional constituencies. The corps has proven sufficiently adept that it has expanded its activities to include restoration efforts; the bureau has been less responsive. Neither agency has wholeheartedly embraced dam removal as a viable river restoration tool.

The Corps of Engineers has been under tremendous political pressure to make fundamental changes. A bipartisan coalition in Congress has been pushing reform bills with titles such as the "Army Corps Reform Act of 2000" and the "Corps of Engineers Modernization and Improvement Act of 2002." The National Research Council produced a study in 1992 that recommended a host of basic changes. A 2003 report by two public interest groups, Taxpayers for Common Sense and the National Wildlife Federation, analyzed what they termed "25 of the most wasteful and environmentally damaging Corps projects . . . with a federal cost of more than $6 billion" ("Troubled Waters" 2000, 1).

The corps responded to these criticisms by developing a Progressive list of new operating principles, the first of which represented a fundamental departure from past corps philosophy: "Strive to achieve environmental sustainability. An environment maintained in a healthy, diverse and sustainable condition is necessary to support life" (U.S. Army Corps of Engineers 2002a). The corps' actual behavior, however, reflects an almost schizophrenic split between traditional priorities and its new missions. An in-depth report in *CQ Researcher* described this tendency: "In recent years [the corps' mission] has zigzagged as erratically as an untamed river prior to a Corps canalization project" (2003, 500). Thus the contemporary Corps of Engineers engages in cutting-edge river restoration on the Kissimmee River in Florida while simultaneously refusing all attempts to breach four dams on the lower Snake River to restore salmon runs. About 20 percent of the corps' budget is now allocated to river restoration and protection activities.

The Bureau of Reclamation has been more reluctant to embrace river restoration and dam removal. The agency's reluctance to change was dealt a severe blow in 1993 when President Bill Clinton appointed Daniel Beard commissioner of Reclamation. Beard developed an entirely new mission statement for the bureau and completed a major reorganization of the agency (Beard 1993). In 1995 the newly reformed agency won Harvard's "Innovations in American Government" award because of the "unprecedented" changes in the agency that went to "the very heart of the organization." Upon receiving the award, an old-time bureau employee confirmed that the agency, before Beard's reforms, had been a "New Deal agency in an e-mail age" (Harvard University 2002). Beard's reform agenda was supplemented by Secretary of the Interior Bruce Babbitt's support for selected dam removal projects.

More recently, under George W. Bush's administration, the bureau has reverted somewhat to its traditional policies. Bush's first commissioner, John Keys, a thirty-seven-year veteran of the agency, opposed dam removal: "Will we have an active program to evaluate active dams to take them out? No. We're here to make the best possible use of the existing dams" (quoted in Israelsen 2001, A1). Still, when the agency threw itself a 100-year birthday party, the official history noted that the bureau had redefined its mission to give priority to "manage, develop, and protect water and related resources in an environmentally and economically sound manner" (Bureau of Reclamation 2002). The new mission is a long way from endorsing comprehensive river restoration, but it represents a significant change from past policies.

THE LITERATURE

These changes have been reflected in both the popular and academic literature on water policy. Much of the attention has been focused on dam removal. Initially it was journalists who wrote about dam removal. In 1999, *CQ Weekly Report* ran a special report titled "Deconstructing Dams: A Watershed for Congress?" about the debate over the four dams on the lower Snake River (*CQ Weekly Report* 1999). More media attention resulted from Secretary of

Interior Bruce Babbitt's policy of participating in dam removal ceremonies. Between 1998 and 2000 he attended a dozen such ceremonies, heightening the public's awareness of the benefits of dam removal (and antagonizing proponents of dams). In writing about his efforts Babbitt noted, "In some places the case for removing a dam is so easy to make that one wonders why it took so long" (2000, 1). However, in most cases the decision is not easy and involves considerable controversy. When Oregon governor John Kitzhaber suggested in a speech before the American Fisheries Society that the four dams on the lower Snake River might be breached, he "received very severe criticism from farmers, ranchers, and shippers and other economic stakeholders for even suggesting that we consider this option" (Kitzhaber 2001, 3).

Popular periodicals soon picked up on the story. A fishing magazine ran a story in 2002 titled "Dam Removal: It's about Rebirth, Not Destruction" (Williams 2002). A widely circulated travel magazine published a feature story in 2004 with the hook "Dams: Who Needs Them?" (Sharp 2004). But apparently the editors were not ready to jump wholeheartedly into the dam removal camp, so they ran a sidebar extolling the virtues of visiting dams because the "West's Herculean dams are spectacular sights to see" (*Via* 2004, 61).

In 1996 environmental journalist Patrick McCully published *Silenced Rivers: The Ecology and Politics of Large Dams*, the first book-length study advocating the removal of dams. In 2002 journalist Elizabeth Grossman published *Watershed: The Undamming of America*, which eloquently described several dam removal projects. During the same period, public interest groups were busy publishing accounts of successful dam removals. Three groups combined their efforts to produce "Dam Removal Success Stories" in 1999 (American Rivers 1999). The following year Trout Unlimited and the River Alliance of Wisconsin produced a how-to manual titled "Dam Removal: A Citizen's Guide to Restoring Rivers" (River Alliance of Wisconsin and Trout Unlimited 2000). In 2001 Trout Unlimited published a short book called "Small Dam Removal: A Review of Potential Economic Benefits" that reviews several small dam removals in the Midwest.

A considerable scholarly literature has also developed. Much of the early work appeared in biology or ecology journals. Arthur Benke's presidential address to the North American Benthological Society (the study of the ecology of stream and lake bottoms) in 1990 focused on "vanishing streams" as a result of hydropower development (Benke 1990). In 2001 Angela Bednarek, a biologist, published the first assessment of the ecological impacts of dam removal (Bednarek 2001). The following year the journal *Bioscience* devoted nearly an entire issue to "Dam Removal and River Restoration." This issue included articles from the disciplines of ecology, biology, hydrology, geochemistry, geography, geology, fisheries and wildlife, and economics, as well as an introductory article by former interior secretary Bruce Babbitt and a concluding article by writers from American Rivers (*Bioscience* 2002).

The federal government also began publishing information on river restoration. A 1996 U.S. Geological Survey report assessed the downstream impact of dams (Collier, Webb, and Schmidt 1996). Perhaps the most ambitious report is a voluminous study titled "Stream Corridor Restoration: Principles, Processes, and Practices," produced by a multiagency team representing five federal departments and three independent agencies. The study begins by defining "restoration" as "a complex endeavor that begins by recognizing natural or human-induced disturbances that are damaging the structure and functions of the ecosystem or preventing its recovery to a sustainable condition" (Federal Interagency Stream Restoration Working Group 1998, 1–2). Significantly, the report makes a clear distinction among restoration, rehabilitation, and reclamation, noting that restoration "is a holistic process not achieved through the isolated manipulation of individual elements" (Federal Interagency Stream Restoration Working Group 1998, 1–3). Another important federal research document is the 1995 report by the National Biological Service titled *Our Living Resources: A Report to the Nation on the Distribution, Abundance, and Health of U.S. Plants, Animals, and Ecosystems.* Much of the report focuses on aquatic and riparian habitats and the species that depend on them. These two reports are significant because they represent a fundamentally different approach to viewing natural resources; both focus on the benefits of healthy ecosystems rather than on a particular product or activity.

In addition to these studies, numerous studies have been conducted by the General Accounting Office and the National Academy of Science, as well as individual agencies. And enough environmental impact statements have been written that, if stacked together, they could undoubtedly form a dam across a large river.

This burgeoning literature demonstrates clearly that dam removal and river restoration require a multidisciplinary and multiagency approach to solving scientific and technical problems. But ultimately, the fate of U.S. rivers is determined by a political process. Thus, a related literature has developed that focuses on the politics and law of river restoration. In 1995 Michael Pyle published an overview of the politics of dam removal, including a case study of the attempt to remove the dam in Hetch Hetchy Canyon (a failed effort thus far) and the successful effort to gain approval for the removal of two dams on the Elwha River (Pyle 1995). In 2002 the John Heinz Center for Science, Economics, and the Environment published two volumes on dam removal; the first was focused on "Science and Decision Making" (2002), and the second consisted of the proceedings from a workshop on dam removal research (2003). Both books included extensive discussions of the social and political dimensions of dam removal. Concurrently, Catherine Engberg published a technical analysis of the laws applicable to the removal of obsolete dams (2002). That same year the annual conference of the Association of American Geographers devoted an entire panel to dam removal (2002). But by far the most comprehensive, in-depth analysis of the politics of dam removal is William Lowry's *Dam Politics: Restoring America's Rivers*. Lowry, a political scientist, developed a policy change typology to explain political variation in different dam removal scenarios (2003). His work is the most sophisticated to date regarding the complex process of bargaining and politicking that accompanies nearly every dam removal.

CASE STUDIES

Each dam removal and river restoration project is unique. Although a few broad trends are seen in the politics of river restoration, each cases presents a unique set of political, economic, and ecological variables. This section will examine two cases that involve a diverse set of factors in river restoration: the Matilija Dam on the Ventura River and Savage Rapids Dam on the Rogue River.

Matilija Dam

The Ventura River rises in the coastal mountains of California and flows south for thirty miles to the coast. The headwaters of the Ventura encompass a federally designated wilderness area, and parts of it are designated wild and scenic. The mouth of the river disgorges at Ventura Beach, draining 228 square miles. Before the construction of Matilija Dam in 1947, sediment from the river was deposited along the shoreline and was the primary source of natural fill that created and sustained the beach.

Matilija Dam is a concrete arch dam, originally 198 feet high, situated in a narrow canyon sixteen miles from the coast.[1] It was built to "remedy continuous water supply shortages that had plagued the Ventura River watershed since the 1920s" (Bureau of Reclamation 2000, ES-2). The reservoir behind the dam was designed to store 7,000 acre-feet of water, but the dam had to be notched in 1965 because of weaknesses in the concrete; this reduced the reservoir capacity by 3,200 acre-feet. But the problems with the concrete turned out to be minor compared to the buildup of sediment behind the dam. By 1999 the reservoir bed had filled with an estimated 6 million cubic yards of sediment; the reservoir was reduced to a mere 400 acre-feet. (U.S. Army Corps of Engineers 2001b, 12; Bureau of Reclamation 2000, ES-3). In the meantime, Ventura Beach was disappearing; the boardwalk built by the city of Ventura began to calve into the ocean as waves washed away beach sand and sediment.

Another problem caused by the dam was the virtual disappearance of the Ventura River's southern steelhead run, estimated at 4,000 to 5,000 adult fish per year before the dam was built.[2] The National Marine Fisheries Service estimates the current run in the Ventura River at 200 fish. The loss of the steelhead is part of a systemic decline in riverine species: "At least 26 special status species are known from the aquatic, riparian, and wetland habitats in the study area including 13 listed species (endangered, threatened, or fully protected) and 13 California species of special concern" (U.S. Army Corps of Engineers 2001b, 12; Bureau of Reclamation 2000, ES-9).

In short, Matilija Dam no longer provided any of the benefits for which it was built but had created a host of environmental and economic problems. A report by Ventura County succinctly described the political response: "Realizing that the dam no longer serves a useful purpose, that the dam presents a significant insult to its related ecosystem, and in response to an outpouring of community interest, a multi-stakeholder effort was launched in the spring of 1999 to assess the viability of dam deconstruction and ecosystem restoration" (Ventura County Watershed Protection District n.d.).

The effort to remove the dam was given a boost in October 2000, when Secretary of the Interior Bruce Babbitt took part in a "demonstration project" at the dam and used a crane to remove a 16,000-pound chunk of concrete from its crest. The secretary told an assemblage of state, local, and federal officials: "The Matilija Dam is symbolic not only because it could become the largest dam to be taken down anywhere in the world, but also because it is a prime example of dams that are environmentally harmful as well as useless. This ceremony marks a new era in America" (Babbitt 2000, 1).

The task of removing the dam created some interesting political dynamics between the Bureau of Reclamation and the Corps of Engineers, both of which have had an active role in its removal. The bureau is popular among farmers of the region because it built Casitas Reservoir, the area's principal water supply. But the corps has more money now and is sometimes viewed as more flexible than the bureau. The bureau published the first feasibility study on the dam, but the corps—the agency that built the dam—was simultaneously working on its own reconnaissance study as mandated by Congress (U.S. House of Representatives 1999).

Early in the planning process it became clear that removal would have to involve a host of stakeholders and government agencies. The corps created a "steering committee/task force" that consisted of five federal agencies, four state agencies and districts, four cities, six public interest groups, one county, one state legislator, and one congressman's office (U.S. Army Corps of Engineers 2001b, 4). Just getting everyone into one room proved difficult. Opposition to removal was muted because the area's water supply came from Casitas Reservoir. However, part of the engineering challenge in releasing the sediment behind Matilija was to do so in a manner that did not damage or interfere with Robles Dam—the downstream intake structure for Casitas Reservoir.

Agricultural interests in the area, which grow about $1 billion worth of oranges and avocados each year and are well connected politically, have had a somewhat complex role in the debate over Matilija Dam. They have supported dam removal only if it does not come at the expense of their water supply; their rallying cry was "no oranges for fish." A larger issue for them was a requirement that fish ladders be installed at the Robles Diversion. A fish ladder requires a certain amount of water flow; in a drought, the ladder could compete with farmers for diminishing water supplies. A fish ladder at Robles Diversion was unnecessary as long as Matilija was blocking fish passage to the spawning beds. With Matilija removed, the steelhead and other species could not make a comeback without a fish ladder at Robles.

Despite opposition, the political initiative for removal quickly grew. The Ventura County Watershed Protection District took a lead role in the process, demonstrating considerable innovation and boldness. The district worked collaboratively with stakeholders that included such diverse interests as the Surfriders Foundation, the Patagonia Company, and the State Water Resources Control Board. The public interest groups that favored removal formed an umbrella group, the Matilija Coalition.

Even when widespread support for dam removal exists, significant problems can still develop. First is the engineering challenge; the nation's water development agencies have almost no experience removing large dams with massive sediment fields, and no one is quite sure how to do it. After extensive study, the Bureau of Reclamation developed several alternative removal scenarios, ranging from shaping the sediment into the existing hillside and routing the river around it to moving the sediment by truck, slurry pipeline, or natural transport (i.e., allowing the river to move the sediment as it had before the dam was built). The bureau suggested that "controlled blasting" was the best way to remove the dam itself. The corps developed a competing plan, which has since become the operative approach; it calls for "controlled blasting in 15-foot increments" and installing a five-mile-long slurry pipeline to move sediment downstream (U.S. Army Corps of Engineers 2005a).

The second problem is cost. The corps plan will cost $128.5 million (U.S. Army Corps of Engineers 2005a). The U.S. Congress appropriated $100,000 in FY 2000 for the corps' reconnaissance study—the first step in the planning process. Ventura County agreed to a 50 percent cost-share for the feasibility study. Other federal agencies have made small contributions, often as in-kind support, and the California Coastal Commission has provided significant funding. The county and its allies asked Congress for $800,000 for FY 2005.

Funding for the actual dam removal must be authorized in a separate bill. The 2005 Water Resources Development Act authorized $127 million for the "Matilija Dam Ecosystem Restoration Project," which includes dam removal and related work (Press Release 2005).

Will Matilija Dam ever be demolished, given the many challenges facing removal? "It is absolutely going to happen," according to Jeff Pratt, director of the Ventura County Watershed Protection District (Pratt 2003). The effort to remove Matilija Dam and restore the Ventura River clearly demonstrates the complexity of such an action. The length of time it takes to demolish the dam will depend on rainfall, the vagaries of federal support, and the ability of the district and the Matilija Coalition to keep the momentum and maintain a broad coalition of support. The corps' plan estimates that demolition will begin in 2008 and will take about three years "[i]f budget plans proceed as expected" (U.S. Army Corps of Engineers 2005b).

Matilija Dam was born in an age when dam builders thought they were conquering nature. In fact, they were just rearranging the resource temporarily and creating a host of unforeseen problems. In 2005 the Corps of Engineers awarded its Matilija Project Delivery Team one of the agency's highest honors, the Outstanding Planning Achievement Award, for its feasibility study, an indication of how much the corps has changed in recent years (U.S. Army Corps of Engineers 2005b).

Savage Rapids Dam

Just fifteen or twenty years ago it would have been unimaginable for an irrigation district to vote to remove its own dam, but that is what happened in January 2000, when the patrons of the Grants Pass Irrigation District voted by a 63 percent majority to remove Savage Rapids Dam on the Rogue River. The eighty-year old dam, 39 feet high and 500 feet wide, was built to divert water into irrigation canals. The politics of dam removal is always complex, even Byzantine, and the effort to remove Savage Rapids Dam has all the elements of a political roller coaster.

Savage Rapids Dam was completed in 1921, following several years of planning and construction and the passage of numerous taxes and bonds to pay for the project.[3] On November 5 of that year, "[D]edication ceremonies of the Savage Rapids Dam and the other project works were held at the dam. An immense crowd enjoyed the colorful ceremonies and all rejoiced over the culmination of their cooperative efforts which had brought to realization their dreams of a stable water supply" (General History n.d.). Eighty years later a very different kind of ceremony was held, this time to commemorate an "agreement to restore the Rogue River and modernize the Grants Pass Irrigation District's diversion system by replacing Savage Rapids Dam with pumps" (Commemorative Declaration 2001).

Thus the history of this dam began on a very positive note, at least for the farmers. However, a hopelessly inadequate fish passage was built at the dam, which dramatically reduced the number of salmon and steelhead accessing the 500 river miles of upstream habitat. The dam became, in the words of the National Marine Fisheries Service, "the biggest fish killer on the Rogue" (Hunter 1998, 29). The destroyed fishery, consisting of five runs of salmon and steelhead, was estimated by the Bureau of Reclamation to be worth $5 million a year (Bureau of Reclamation 1995).

The evolution of the Grants Pass Irrigation District, in both its thinking and its policies, is something of a microcosm of western water politics. When the dam was built, it was assumed that the future of the West would be dominated by small farmers who relied on irrigation to bring in crops. The public lands along the Rogue River were opened for settlement in the early nineteenth century, and farmers flocked to the area. They soon began discussing the need for an irrigation project to divert Rogue River water onto their fields. However, unlike those in many areas of the West, they did not go to Washington, D.C., and demand money from the government. Rather, they organized an irrigation district and imposed taxes and bonds upon themselves to finance a dam and a system of canals. These were hardy, self-reliant people. At that time very few people thought about the impact such a dam would have on fish runs; the future was with farming, not fishing. Also, the farmers wanted to minimize the cost of building a dam, and an effective fish ladder would add considerable expense.

But over time, economies and social priorities changed. Gradually, many of the farms in the Grants Pass district reduced the amount of land under cultivation and thus failed to use their full allocation of water rights. Under western water law, a state-granted water right must be diverted and used; otherwise, after a period of several years, the water right reverts back to the state.

In 1982 the state of Oregon revoked about half of the district's water right for failure to use the water. The district vehemently objected and won a temporary release from the revocation in 1990, but only if the district developed a plan to use the water efficiently and mitigate the damage the dam was doing to fish runs. This put the district in the difficult position of having to solve the problems created by its own dam. The district hired a consultant, and after four years of study the consultant concluded that the best way for the district to retain its water right was to remove the dam. This caused an instant outcry among locals and provoked a nasty split among the district's patrons. Some members of the district board who supported dam removal were subjected to recall elections and lawsuits.

Over the ensuing five years, the district experienced one setback after another as pressure built to remove the dam. In 1994 the state of Oregon ordered the district to implement its dam removal plan or risk permanently losing much of its water right. In 1997 the secretary of the interior listed the Coho salmon, which is native to the Rogue, as threatened (*Federal Register* 1997). This meant the district had to apply to the National Marine Fisheries Service for an incidental take permit. In the meantime, the district was fighting a series of court battles to regain its full water right; it appealed the cancellation order to the Oregon Court of Appeals but was dismissed (Court of Appeals of Oregon 2000). The district then petitioned the Oregon Supreme Court to review the dismissal. By then the governor of Oregon, the National Marine Fisheries Service, the Bureau of Reclamation, the U.S. Fish and

Wildlife Service, and a host of environmental groups had endorsed the idea of removing the dam and replacing it with pumps that would supply the district's canals.

In years past, it would have been political suicide to publicly oppose the wishes of a powerful and entrenched irrigation district. Such districts were part of the power structure, well organized and connected. But by the mid-1990s the political balance had begun to shift. A complex panoply of public interest groups was working to remove Savage Rapids Dam. Although the list is long, it is worth including because it starkly demonstrates the accelerating influence, number, and variety of groups advocating dam removal: American Lands Alliance, American Rivers, Association of Northwest Steelheaders, Curry Guides Association, Friends of the River, Headwaters, Klamath Siskiyou Wildlands Center, Middle Rogue Watershed Council, Northcoast Environmental Center, Northwest Sportfishing Industries Association, Oregon Council of Trout Unlimited, Oregon Guides and Packers, Oregon Natural Desert Association, Oregon Natural Resources Council, Oregon Trout, Pacific Coast Sierra Club, Rogue Valley Audubon Society, Siskiyou Regional Education Project, Trout Unlimited, WaterWatch of Oregon, The Wilderness Society, and World Wildlife Fund.

Under intense pressure, some people in the district and on its governing board began to view dam removal and the use of pumps as their best option to retain water rights to the 50 cubic feet per second (cfs) under threat of cancellation. In an internal memorandum, district leaders wrote a blunt assessment: "The bottom line: No 50 cfs = no district = no dam. Any way you look at it, the dam is going out. The only question is, will the district survive? Yes, if we have the 50 cfs supplemental water right and pumps" (Grants Pass Irrigation District n.d.). In the meantime, the district was spending several hundred thousand dollars each year on repairs to the aging dam and canals, and in just three years it had expended nearly $700,000 in legal fees (*Grants Pass Daily Courier* 2001).

On May 4, 2001, the various parties to the conflict agreed to a settlement that began with this phrase: "Whereas, continuing disputes over interim and long-term fish passage measures at the Savage Rapids Dam have resulted in this pending federal court case under the Endangered Species Act and a water right cancellation case now pending in the Supreme Court of the State or Oregon" (*USA and State of Oregon* v. *Grants Pass Irrigation District* 2001). Given that set of problems, it is fairly clear why the district chose to settle. Many people celebrated, viewing the settlement as the end of a long, divisive conflict. But not everyone was pleased. Two members of the district board resigned in protest. A local newspaper characterized the settlement as "another example of environmental terrorism winning out" (*Rogue River Press* 2001).

The settlement marked the end of one set of problems and the beginning of another: now the parties must obtain federal funds to remove the dam and install the pumps. The total cost is estimated at $20 million. The state of Oregon has already contributed $3 million. In 2003 Congress passed the Savage Rapids Dam Act, which authorized appropriations for dam removal and the installation of pumps (P.L. 108–137 2003). Congress appropriated $2.2 million in FY 2005 for dam removal and construction of pumps, and in late 2005 the bureau announced plans for the pump design (Bureau of Reclamation 2005).

Savage Rapids Dam was built at a time when people conceived of rivers not as a resource themselves but as a natural cornucopia that could be used at will. The intrepid farmers of Grants Pass were simply trying to make a living, and they tapped into the Rogue River to make that possible without conceiving of the larger impact they would have on the region's fisheries. The dam they built was part of an era when the U.S. view of rivers was narrow and myopic; it will be removed as that view undergoes a painful readjustment.

CONCLUSION

Public conceptualization of rivers and their relationship to humans is experiencing a fundamental change. This changing perception will result in a new era that will focus on rivers as a public commons. These changing priorities and values can best be understood when viewed in terms of relative scarcity. Rivers have many benefits, but they vary in regard to their relative scarcity; as public values change and the demand for river benefits rises, this relative scarcity will play a much greater role in allocating river benefits. Viewing water policy as a contest among relatively scarce zero-sum resources focuses the analysis on the most determinative decisions, that is, those that have the greatest value in predicting future trends in water policy.

Increasingly in the American West, the resource that has become the scarcest is a natural, free-flowing river with high-quality water, a healthy riparian habitat, and a high potential for recreational and aesthetic use. There will be a growing demand to (1) protect rivers that currently meet that description and (2) restore rivers in places where greater economic and social value can be obtained with a natural river, in comparison to past uses that destroyed those qualities.

The effort to restore rivers will be most successful when it combines the support of environmental groups with significant economic interests that benefit from restoration. These include the fishing industry, recreation and tourism, and some urban water interests. As river restoration becomes increasingly associated with economic well-being, it will generate greater bipartisan support. As with any widespread sociopolitical movement, it will encounter opposition; all change proceeds in fits and starts. The administration of George W. Bush is a case in point; he is attempting to stop or reverse a number of trends in natural resource management but is only delaying the inevitable. As the benefits of river restoration become more visible and widespread, resisting the trend will become more difficult. Indeed, the new era is already here.

NOTES

1. Matilija Dam is on Matilija Creek, just upstream from its confluence with the North Fork Matilija Creek; the two creeks come together to form the Ventura River. "Matilija" is a Chumash Indian term meaning divide.

2. A steelhead is an anadromous rainbow trout; anadromous means it is spawned in freshwater, then lives most of its life in the sea but returns to freshwater to spawn. The southern steelhead is a distinct species and was placed on the endangered species list in 1997.

3. The rapids, and hence the dam, was named after a family that lived nearby, not for its ferocity.

REFERENCES

American Rivers. 1999. "Dam Removal Success Stories: Restoring River through Selective Removal of Dam That Don't Make Sense." Report prepared by Friends of the Earth, American Rivers, and Trout Unlimited, Washington, D.C., December.

———. 2001. "Compilation of Removed Dams." At www.americanrivers.org, site accessed June 2005.

Anderson, Terry. 1983. *Water Crisis: Ending the Policy Drought*. Baltimore: Johns Hopkins University Press.

Andrews, Barbara, and Marie Sansone. 1983. *Who Runs the Rivers? Dams and Decisions in the New West*. Stanford, CA: Stanford Environmental Law Society.

Association of American Geographers, annual conference. 2002. Session on dam removal sponsored by the Water Resources Specialty Group and the Geomorphology Specialty Group, Los Angeles, March 22. Panel organized by Patricia Beyer, Bloomsburg University of Pennsylvania.

Babbitt, Bruce. 2000. "Secretary of the Interior Bruce Babbitt Pulls Down First Slab of 200-Foot Matilija Dam in California." Press release. Washington, DC: Office of the Secretary, October 12.

———. 2001. "A River Runs against It: America's Evolving View of Dams." *Open Spaces,* January 22, pp. 3–4.

Bates, Sarah, et al. 1993. *Searching Out the Headwaters: Change and Rediscovery in Western Water Policy*. Washington, DC: Island.

Beard, Daniel 1993. "Blueprint for Reform: The Commissioner's Plan for Reinventing Reclamation." Washington, DC: U.S. Department of the Interior, November 1, p. 2.

Bednarek, Angela. 2001. "Undamming Rivers: A Review of the Ecological Impacts of Dam Removal." *Environmental Management* 27, no. 6, 803–814.

Benke, Arthur. 1990. "A Perspective on America's Vanishing Streams." *Journal of the North American Benthological Society* 9, no. 1, 77–88.

Bioscience. 2002. Special issue on dam removal and river restoration. Vol. 52, no. 8 (August).

Bureau of Reclamation. 1995. Planning Report and Environmental Statement, Savage Rapids Dam. Boise: Pacific Northwest Region.

———. 2000. "Matilija Dam Removal Project: Executive Summary—April 2000." U.S. Department of the Interior. Sacramento, CA: Mid-Pacific Region–Division of Planning.

———. 2002. "The Bureau of Reclamation: A Brief History." Bureau of Reclamation History Program, Commissioner's Office of Policy.

———. 2005. Draft Environmental Assessment, Fish Passage Improvements, Savage Rapids Dam, Grants Pass, OR. Boise: Pacific Northwest Region, August.

Collier, M. J., R. H. Webb, and J. C. Schmidt. 1996. "Dams and Rivers: Primer on the Downstream Effects of Dams." Washington, DC: U.S. Geological Survey Circular 1126.

Commemorative Declaration. 2001. Signed October 12, 2001, by the state of Oregon, Grants Pass Irrigation District, the Northwest Sportfishing Industries Association, the National Marine Fisheries Service, Waterwatch of Oregon, and Trout Unlimited.

Court of Appeals of Oregon. 2000. "*Grants Pass Irrigation District v. Water Resources Department and Water Resources Commission*." 98-CV–0345; CA A104582. Decided May 17, 2000.

CQ Researcher. 2003. "Reforming the Corps." May 30, 497–519.

CQ Weekly Report. 1999. "Deconstructing Dams: A Watershed for Congress?" July 17, 1707.

Engberg, Catherine. 2002. "The Dam Owner's Guide to Retirement Planning: Assessing Owner Liability for Downstream Sediment Flow from Obsolete Dams." *Stanford Environmental Law Journal* 21, 177–222.

Federal Interagency Stream Restoration Working Group. 1998. "Stream Corridor Restoration: Principles, Processes, and Practices." Distributed by the National Technical Information Service, Washington, DC, October.

Federal Register. 1997. 62 Fed. Reg. 24, 588, May 6.

Ferejohn, John. 1974. *Pork Barrel Politics: Rivers and Harbors Legislation, 1947–1968*. Stanford, CA: Stanford University Press.

Fradkin, Philip. 1981. *A River No More*. New York: Alfred Knopf.

General History. N.d. "Savage Rapids Dam." Binder compiled by the Grants Pass Irrigation District.

Gottlieb, Robert. 1988. *A Life of Its Own: The Politics and Power of Water*. New York: Harcourt Brace.

Grants Pass Daily Courier. 2001. "Choice Now Down to Dam or GPID." Guest Opinion by Eric Larsen, May 14.

Grants Pass Irrigation District. N.d. "Savage Rapids Diversion Change." Internal memorandum.

Grossman, Elizabeth. 2002. *Watershed: The Undamming of America*. New York: Counterpoint.

Gumprecht, Blake. 2002. *The Los Angeles River*. Baltimore: Johns Hopkins University Press.

Hanson, Roseann. 2001. *The San Pedro: A Discovery Guide*. Tucson: University of Arizona Press.

Harvard University. 2002. "Innovations in American Government." At www.innovations.harvard.edu/winners/rrfed95.htm, site accessed July 2005.

Hunter, Robert. 1998. "Water Diversions and Salmon: Pressure Mounts to Remove Savage Rapids Dam." *Western Water Law* (December), 29–34.

Israelsen, Brent. 2001. "New U.S. Reclamation Boss Promises No Deluge of Changes." *Salt Lake Tribune*, August 13.

John Heinz Center for Science, Economics, and the Environment. 2002. *Dam Removal: Science and Decision Making*. Washington, DC: John Heinz Center for Science, Economics, and the Environment.

———. 2003. *Dam Removal Research: Status and Prospects*, ed. William L. Graf. Washington, DC: John Heinz Center for Science, Economics, and the Environment.

Kitzhaber, John. 2001. "The Politics and Policy of Dams and Dam Removals." Presentation sponsored by the Watershed Management Professional Program of the Executive Leadership Institute, Mark O. Hatfield School of Government, Portland [Oregon] State University, February 20.

Lowry, William. 2003. *Dam Politics: Restoring America's Rivers*. Washington, DC: Georgetown University Press.

McCool, Daniel. 1994. *Command of the Waters: Iron Triangles, Federal Water Development, and Indian Water*. Berkeley: University of California Press, 1987; reissued by University of Arizona Press, Tucson.

McCully, Patrick. 1996. *Silenced Rivers: The Ecology and Politics of Large Dams*. London: Zed Books.

National Biological Service. 1995. *Our Living Resources: A Report to the Nation on the Distribution, Abundance, and Health of U.S. Plants, Animals, and Ecosystems*. Washington, DC: U.S. Department of the Interior–National Biological Service.

National Research Council. 1992. "Restoration of Aquatic Ecosystems: Science, Technology, and Public Policy." Committee on Restoration of Aquatic Ecosystems. Washington, DC: National Academy Press.

Oko, Dan. 2002. "Running for Cover on the Rio Grande." *High Country News,* February 18.

Palmer, Tim. 1986. *Endangered Rivers and the Conservation Movement.* Berkeley: University of California Press.

P.L. 108–137. 2003. "Energy and Water Development Appropriations." Washington, DC, 108th Congress, Sec. 220.

Pratt, Jeff. 2003. Interview with Jeff Pratt, director, Ventura County Watershed Protection District, March 27.

Press Release. 2005. "Committee Approves $127 Million Boxer Request for Matilija Creek Restoration." Issued by Senator Barbara Boxer, April 13.

Pyle, Michael. 1995. "Beyond Fish Ladders: Dam Removal as a Strategy for Restoring America's Rivers." *Stanford Environmental Law Journal* 14, 97–143.

Reisner, Mark. 1986. *Cadillac Desert*. New York: Viking.

River Alliance of Wisconsin and Trout Unlimited. 2000. "Dam Removal: A Citizen's Guide to Restoring Rivers." Madison: River Alliance of Wisconsin and Trout Unlimited.

Rogue River Press. 2001. "Both Sides Lose in Battle over Dam." August 1.

Sharp, David. 2004. "Dam Nation." *Via* (January-February), 54–61.

"Troubled Waters: Congress, the Corps of Engineers and Wasteful Water Projects." 2000. Report by Taxpayers for Common Sense and National Wildlife Federation, Washington, DC, March.

Trout Unlimited. 2001. "Small Dam Removal: A Review of Potential Economic Benefits." October, Arlington, VA. At www.tu.org, site accessed July 2005.

U.S. Army Corps of Engineers. 2001a. "Civil Works Programs." Washington, DC: U.S. Army Corps of Engineers.

———. 2001b. "Matilija Dam Ecosystem Restoration Feasibility Study Ventura County, CA." Project Management Plan, Los Angeles District, South Pacific Division, April.

———. 2002a. "Environmental Operating Principles." Announced March 26, 2002, by Chief Engineer Lt. General Robert Flowers. At www.hq.usace.army.mil/cepa/envprinciples.htm, site accessed August 2005.

———. 2002b. "Matilija Dam Ecosystem Feasibility Study: Baseline Conditions Draft Report (F3) Milestone." Los Angeles District, August.

———. 2004. http//:crunch.tec.army.mil/nid/webpages/nidintroduction.html, site accessed March 16, 2004.

———. 2005a. Los Angeles District Office. "Matilija Dam Ecosystem Restoration Project, Ventura County, California. Project Management Plan." Design Phase, June.

———. 2005b. Los Angeles District Office. News Release. "Corps Team Wins Award for Matilija Dam Plan." August 11.

U.S. House of Representatives. 1999. Resolution of the U.S. House of Representatives Committee on Transportation and Infrastructure, docket 2593. Washington, DC, adopted April 15. *USA and State of Oregon* v. *Grants Pass Irrigation District*. 2001. Consent Decree, Civil No. 98–3034-HO. In the United States District Court for the District of Oregon, Portland.

Ventura County Watershed Protection District. N.d. "Mailija Dam Ecosystem Restoration Project." At www.matilijadam.org, site accessed June 2005.

Via. 2004. "Must-See: Dams of the West." (January-February), 61.

Wahl, Richard. 1989. *Markets for Federal Water: Subsidies, Property Rights, and the Bureau of Reclamation*. Washington, DC: Resources for the Future/Johns Hopkins University Press.

Waters of Destiny. Film on the Kissimmee River Project, produced by the U.S. Army Corps of Engineers, circa 1955.

Williams, Ted. 2002. "Dam Removal: It's about Rebirth, Not Destruction." *Fly Rod & Reel* (April), 20–26.7

CHAPTER SIX

WILDLIFE RESOURCE POLICY ISSUES IN THE WEST

William R. Mangun

Wildlife policy in the West has been shaped by competition for land and scarce water resources. This chapter examines conflicts that have occurred between the needs of wildlife and those of humans who live and work in the western United States. Political conflict and resource competition are addressed through a series of case studies collectively illustrating the consequences of policy responses to resource issues that continue to threaten wildlife populations in the western states.

Although there appears to be a growing trend toward policy collaboration on public lands (see Conley and Moote 2003; Cook 2000; Weber 1999, 2003), formulation and implementation of wildlife policy in the United States continue to be characterized by political conflict (Nie 2004). Supporters of community-based collaborative efforts argue that such efforts reduce conflicts and litigation (Wondolleck and Yaffee 2000). However, political conflicts and legal cases concerning natural resources on public lands have not diminished (Comer 2004). George Cameron Coggins (1999) has observed that collaborative approaches that vest decision-making authority over federal resources to local groups represent an abdication of federal agency legal responsibility. In a detailed legal analysis of the role of collaborative groups in federal land management, Allyson Barker and colleagues (2003) examined legal precedents associated with the Administrative Procedure Act, National Environmental Policy Act, Endangered Species Act, and various organic acts of federal land management agencies and found that such groups may provide recommendations or information, but only federal agency decision makers have the authority to make decisions regarding the use of federal resources.

Community-based collaborative efforts are further constrained in that agreements formulated through years of effort typically are not enforceable by law. Agreements established between federal agency officials and community-based collaborative groups may never be implemented if there is a change in administrations and the new administration does not support the policy. For example, the formal agreement made between the Quincy Library Group (QLG), one of a very few collaborative groups formally recognized by federal law, and the U.S. Department of Agriculture (USDA) Forest Service on logging the Sierra Nevadas in northern California was set aside by the Bush administration in 2001. The agreement had been established through negotiations with the USDA Forest Service during the Clinton administration. Following a lawsuit and congressional reauthorization of the Herger-Feinstein Quincy Library Group Forest Recovery Act, in 2003 the QLG-initiated logging program was reinstituted. But environmentalists who were not given an opportunity to participate in the negotiations sued to prevent closed-door negotiations between QLG and the Forest Service (Little 2003).

Political conflicts over natural resources appear to occur as a result of differences in values regarding how resources should be used or protected (Mangun and Henning 1999). Government action to deal with such conflict has been characterized as an "authoritative allocation of values" (Easton 1953). In this political process, governments decide who will get what and when, where, why, and how they will get it (Lasswell 1962). The history of the West has been shaped primarily by debates over who will get access to water or land resources (Stegner 1954; Worster 1985). In the past, wildlife has been inadequately represented in this political process. However, in recent decades an increasing amount of litigation has been initiated to protect wildlife at both the state and federal levels, as a result of the Endangered Species

Act of 1973, the Clean Water Act Amendments of 1972, and similar legislation. Such actions have forced state and federal agencies to develop additional innovative policy actions to reverse a pervasive pattern of species decline.

The western United States historically has provided a prime setting for large-scale human-wildlife conflicts that continue on a variety of spatial and temporal scales today. Some of the more striking and pervasive issues in wildlife policy and management in the West include a growing number of threatened, endangered, or declining wildlife populations; a related growth in human populations, leading to the destruction and fragmentation of wildlife habitat; and an increasingly scarce supply of water for both humans and wildlife in an arid environment.

First, human contamination of water and soil can kill individual wildlife directly or can indirectly affect the vigor of entire populations by altering chromosomal patterns. Second, the rapidly increasing human population in the West continues to destroy or fragment wildlife habitat in an unprecedented manner. The resulting displacement overwhelms natural adaptive capacities for wildlife to modify their breeding habits and other life-maintenance functions. Third, the growing human demand for scarce water resources spurred by uncontrolled urban growth and development is significantly impacting aquatic and terrestrial species. The water policy practices that made settlement of the arid West possible, such as prior appropriation water laws, clearly favored, at some point, unwise growth and development. Large-scale federally funded water projects continue to enable an unsustainable explosion of agricultural and urban development in an otherwise unsuited environment. Another complicating issue is the virtual nonenforcement of official Bureau of Reclamation water allocation limits that permit distribution of federal water supplies to unofficial recipients, further reducing the availability of water for endangered fish and wildlife.

The effects of these patterns are readily apparent throughout the West. California gnatcatchers, for example, are threatened by urban housing developments that destroy the coastal sage habitats in which they breed and live. San Joaquin kit foxes and blunt-nosed leopard lizards are endangered because of destruction of their essential breeding habitat by agricultural interests and urban developers in the California Central Valley. Wintering migratory waterfowl in the Kesterson Reservoir, near the California coast, are subjected to mutation-inducing chemicals in agricultural runoff from Central Valley irrigation ditches. Migratory shorebirds such as sandhill and whooping cranes that migrate across the High Plains are threatened by alterations in water flow at key staging areas on the Platte River in Nebraska. Important sandbar breeding habitat for endangered interior least terns and piping plovers, also on the High Plains, is either altered or destroyed by water management decisions made for agricultural purposes. Populations of endangered razorback suckers and Colorado topminnows (formerly squawfish) in the Colorado River are threatened by the loss of wetlands for breeding purposes, as well as by water projects that serve as barriers to migration or diminish instream flow. Over fifteen stocks of salmon and trout in the Columbia River basin have been listed as threatened or endangered as a result of high pollution levels, over-harvesting, and numerous water projects. The overall pattern is one of wildlife habitat destruction or significant reduction in habitat quality by an ever-increasing human population in the western states.

But not all news is bad; there are also notable "success" stories concerning fish and wildlife in the West. The endangered black-footed ferret was practically extirpated from the High Plains as an unintended consequence of efforts to eradicate prairie dogs. Intensive conservation efforts have brought this species back from the brink of extinction, a population low of 38 individuals. Another species almost eliminated was the California condor, a majestic bird that possesses the largest wingspan of all North American birds. Human disturbance, poisoning, and habitat destruction forced the U.S. Fish and Wildlife Service to remove the last 26 California condors from the wild in the mid-1980s. After a major cooperative restoration effort involving several federal agencies, state governments, and the Peregrine Fund, over 200 California condors have been released into the wild. These birds continue to survive, although tenuously, in two populations within California and along the Arizona-Utah border.

Not all wildlife policy "success stories" in the West have occurred as a result of management actions taken directly to conserve a particular species. Brown pelican and osprey populations along the Pacific Coast and, to some extent, bald eagle populations have recovered because of policies banning pesticides such as DDT. The banning of the infamous DDT (which promoted thinning of bird eggshells), and other lesser-known pesticides that deform or kill nontarget wildlife species, has occurred over concerns more about their effects on human health than their impacts on wildlife.

The next section of this chapter describes the evolution of wildlife policy in the United States to facilitate a better understanding of different policy actions taken to conserve wildlife in the western states. Specific human-wildlife conflicts are described to illustrate how fish and wildlife have been affected by human competition for population-limiting resources, such as land and water. Government policy responses to such conflicts are described throughout the chapter, with reference to suggestions for future policy decisions concerning interaction between wildlife and humans in the West.

EVOLUTION OF U.S. WILDLIFE POLICY

Wildlife policy formulation and implementation is a complex federal-state and public-private cooperative effort to conserve and preserve fish and wildlife resources. Early use of wildlife in the United States focused on exploitation of the resource for human survival and economic gain. Such unrestricted use resulted in severe reductions of several wildlife species, predominately game and species that had economic value (such as feathers for hats and gowns). By the early 1900s a conservation movement had emerged that promoted sustained yield through "wise use" of wildlife and other forest resources. The 1901 Lacey Act was the first federal government policy effort designed to restrict exploitation of game species by invoking "commerce clause" provisions to stop the movement of species taken in one state to another.

Concern over continued exploitation and decline of game species led to the passage of the Migratory Bird Treaty Act in 1918. This act assigned responsibility for migratory bird species to the federal government. Years later, to assist states in restoring game populations, Congress passed the Federal Aid in Wildlife Restoration Act (Pittman-Robertson Act) in 1936 and the Federal Aid in Sport Fish Restoration Act (Dingell-Johnson Act) in 1950. Each of these acts had a conservation emphasis.

In contrast to the conservationists, early preservationists such as John Muir observed that entire landscapes were disappearing and promoted efforts to set aside large areas in a relatively pristine state for future generations. This preservation movement led to the establishment of the many national parks, predominately located in the less-developed western states. However, similar preservation-oriented legislation for wildlife species was not passed for another seventy years. The growing awareness of ecological relationships, spawned by the study of ecology in the 1970s and a better-educated, more urban population, advanced wildlife preservation policies designed to protect marine mammals and endangered species. What does all this mean from a policy perspective?

In temporal terms, wildlife policy is dynamic, ever-changing. Wildlife policy is a moving target with multiple points of access. Wildlife policy can be affected at multiple levels of government and at multiple points in the policy process. As societal interests wax and wane, policy changes. New policies can be initiated or blocked in the policy initiation or agenda-setting phase, for example, at the federal level. If the policy is intergovernmental in nature, it can be altered or affected at the state level. The federal government can provide inducements or constraints that promote or retard the policy's implementation at the state or local levels of government. Since intergovernmental policies require legislative authority at the state and local levels in order to be implemented, state- and local-level actors can affect the agenda-setting and implementation processes at their levels. Ultimately, for any policy to succeed, a complex series of actions must be completed across multiple levels of government and among private citizens who respond to the policy.

INTERGOVERNMENTAL POLICY PATTERNS AND EVENTS SHAPING WILDLIFE POLICY IMPLEMENTATION IN THE WEST

National legislative and legal actions have shaped the wildlife policy milieu in the West (Mangun and Mangun 1991; see also Nie 2004). From the 1800s until approximately 1960, wildlife policy can be described as operating within a period of "game management" with an emphasis on conservation. During this period, policy was characterized by dual federalism, with the federal and state governments each maintaining their sphere of operations, with the states somewhat dominant.

In *Gibbons v. Ogden* (1824), the federal Supreme Court ruled that there were two spheres of federal and state commerce and that only the federal government could control interstate commerce. This decision provided the basis for the Lacey Act of 1901 barring interstate shipment of game species. The Migratory Bird Treaty of 1916, designed to promote conservation of waterfowl game species, led to the Migratory Bird Treaty Act of 1918, which clearly assigned responsibility for migratory species to the federal government. In *Missouri v. Holland* (1920), the Supreme Court ruled that the treaty-making powers that only the federal government possessed gave it national supremacy over policies affecting migratory species, regardless of whether the species were on federal land.

With the explosion of environmental legislation at the end of the 1960s and into the 1970s, an "environmental awareness" period occurred. Along with new legislation came federal funds for new federally legislated program activities. Much of the legislation during this period dealt with how the federal government should manage its land. Since the majority of federal landholdings were in the West, this legislation greatly impacted wildlife resources in the western states. Key federal laws that affected the West were the Multiple Use/Sustained Yield Act of 1960, the Federal Land Policy Management Act of 1976, and the National Forest Management Act of 1976. The Endangered Species Act of 1973 specifically assigned responsibility to the federal government for control of endangered and threatened species even on state and private land. Throughout this period, the federal government took a more dominant role in environmental policy.

During the 1980s a more "comprehensive management" period developed. The election of Ronald Reagan ushered in a period of "new federalism" that can be characterized as a partial return to dual federalism with the states resurgent. The Reagan administration worked with the International Association of Fish and Wildlife Agencies to formally establish dual responsibilities with regard to fish and wildlife resources. The policy was actually codified into the Federal Code of Regulations (43 CFR, Part 24) and remains in effect. The federal government has primary control of migratory and endangered species, and states have control of resident species, even on federal land. Given the ascendant role of wildlife professionals in the policy process, the Reagan administration and Congress modified federal fish and wildlife restoration policies to require state agencies to develop comprehensive wildlife management policies. Programs for nongame species (i.e., species not legally hunted) were to be added and integrated into state fish and wildlife management programs for them to continue to receive federal aid. The Fish and Wildlife Conservation Act of 1980, known as the "Non-game Bill," further promoted comprehensive state wildlife management.

From the early 1990s to 2000, federal wildlife policy operated within a "renewed environmental awareness" period characterized by more cooperative intergovernmental and public-private decision making. During this period numerous cross-jurisdictional management efforts were initiated and established for ecosystem management, watershed management, and community-based environmental protection. In 1998 Congress passed the Herger-Feinstein Quincy Library Forest Recovery Act that enabled an association of private citizens (known as the Quincy Library Group) to collaborate with the USDA Forest Service on management decisions affecting national forests in the Sierra Nevada region (Owen 2002).

Since 2000, however, federal protection of wildlife on public land has declined significantly. As the majority of U.S. public lands are located west of the 100th meridian, the greatest impact on wildlife will likely be manifested in western states. The present Bush administration is carefully taking aim at environmental laws that protect wildlife by rewriting and thereby weakening enforcement of rules designed to protect wildlife and the habitat resources upon which they depend. Several major conservation organizations have chronicled this attack and have protested the weakening of wildlife regulations to the benefit of agricultural, timber, and other commodity interests. Numerous nongovernmental organization reports describe the recent change in federal wildlife policy: *Undercutting National Forest Protections: How the Bush Administration Uses the Judicial System to Weaken Environmental Laws* (Defenders of Wildlife 2003); *Rewriting the Rules: The Bush Administration's First-Term Environmental Record* (Natural Resources Defense Council 2005); *Bush Administration Record on Public Lands: Irresponsible Management of the People's Land* (Wilderness Society 2005); and *Open Season on America's Wildlife: The Bush Administration's Attacks on Federal Wildlife Protections* (Defenders of Wildlife, Earthjustice, Endangered Species Coalition, and National Wildlife Federation 2002).

The group Environment 2004 (2004) has further identified how the Department of the Interior, under Gale Norton's leadership, failed to enforce the Endangered Species Act. For example, the U.S. Fish and Wildlife Service (USFWS) repeatedly failed to designate critical habitat for threatened and endangered species (such as the Canada lynx, the Santa Anna sucker, and the Santa Barbara tiger salamander), even though required to do so by law. Similarly, the Natural Resources Defense Council (2004) reported that the Bush administration reduced intended critical habitat designations by 69 percent less than originally proposed.

In *Sierra Club v. U.S. Fish and Wildlife Service,* the federal court ruled that critical habitat designations must be measured by their ability to promote species recovery. Environment 2004 (2004) pointed out that USFWS repealed the existing rule but did not create an acceptable new rule for more than three years. However, USFWS did use negative economic impacts on developers as a basis to exclude designation of critical habitat for several vernal pool species in California. Furthermore, after agricultural interest groups and logging companies filed lawsuits against protections for Pacific Coast salmon and the red-legged frog in California, the Bush administration simply withdrew designation of critical habitat for these species.

The future of wildlife protection on public lands in the West does not look bright. Agreements developed over many years that involved extensive collaboration among affected parties have been set aside by the present Bush administration. For example, plans to reintroduce grizzly bears into Montana and Wyoming national forests were halted. The Northwest Forest Management Plan and forest management plans for national forests in the Sierras, as required by the National Forest Management Act, are not being implemented by the Bush administration as originally intended. The administration is either failing to implement the plans or is revising them, without public input.

The Natural Resources Defense Council (Cousins, Perks, and Warren 2005) and Defenders of Wildlife (Cohn and Lerner 2003) both report that the Bush administration is rewriting the rules that cover implementation of numerous laws designed to protect natural resources and wildlife species. Although Jack Ward Thomas (2000, 12), former chief of the USDA Forest Service, has stated, "The overriding policy for the management of the national forests is the preservation of biodiversity," the Bush administration appears to be eliminating the wildlife viability requirement of the National Forest Management Act (Snape, Leahy, and Carter 2003, 14). These efforts can be expected to have significant negative impacts on threatened and endangered species such as the Northern spotted owl and the marbled murrelet of U.S. Northwest forests. The effects of such rewritten rules on wildlife populations will likely be evidenced into the distant future.

WESTERN FISH AND WILDLIFE POLICY ISSUES

This chapter provides only a sample of the many fish and wildlife policy issues in the West. The issues presented are among the more critical policy issues that must be addressed. Key western wildlife policy issues center around endangered species, urban growth and development and their associated habitat fragmentation and loss, availability of water resources, and federal public land management. In this section I examine these issues along with their individual policy implications.

Threatened and Endangered Species

Threatened and endangered species are wild populations at greatest risk and those that demand immediate attention. There are almost 1,300 federally listed endangered or threatened species currently listed in western states. From 1990 to 2007, there has been a 130 percent increase in listed species (from 559 to 1,288) under the Endangered Species Act (USFWS, 2007). Table 6.1 presents a state-by-state breakdown. Hawaii has the largest percentage increase, 488 percent, as well as the largest absolute species change. California is second with 229 percent and 215 species. The Nature Conservancy (Stein and Flack 1997) estimates that one-third of all species in the West may be at risk of extinction. B. A. Stein and S. A. Flack (1997) indicated that Hawaii may have 269 extinct species and California 48 extinct species. Without immediate policy action, many species currently listed will likely suffer a similar fate.

Mere imminence of threat does not eliminate controversy over actions that must be taken to protect such species. Is it economically worthwhile to do so? Who cares? Should we care? Should we merely accept their demise and take action to protect other declining populations? Such questions cloud policy debates over actions designed to improve the condition of threatened and endangered species.

In some cases, western states and the federal government are taking concerted action to reduce the rate of species destruction. Fish species, while particularly affected because of intense competition for scarce water resources in the West, also have benefited from cooperative restoration efforts. In the Colorado River alone, four listed endangered fish species have been negatively impacted by changes in the water regime: the razorback sucker (that reputedly has survived for 4 million years), Colorado topminnow (formerly squawfish), humpback chub, and bonytail chub (Bolin 1993). Practically all of the salmon species that migrate up the Columbia River have been listed as threatened or endangered by the National Marine Fisheries Service (*Federal Register* 62(159), 43937–43954), August 18, 1997).

Wetland alteration, water projects, and scouring dam releases destroy or significantly alter breeding habitat for fish. Along the Colorado River, state and federal agencies are attempting to restore river wetlands for species like the razorback sucker that breed in the wetlands. For species that need to migrate up the river, government agencies are building fish ladders and migration passages.

In Washington, Oregon, California, Idaho, and Montana, the millions of salmon and steelhead trout that once migrated upstream to spawning grounds have been severely reduced to mere thousands because of human activities (Commission on Life Sciences 1996; National Research Council 2004). Because over-harvest was identified as a major problem, severe harvesting restrictions have been imposed in the Northwest, with complete bans on many species. In Washington state alone, fifteen salmon and trout stocks

Table 6.1. Number of Federally Listed Endangered or Threatened Species in Western States, by State

State	*1990*[1]	*2007*[2]	*% Change*
Alaska	6	13	117
Arizona	42	55	31
Arkansas	19	31	63
California	94	309	229
Colorado	23	32	39
Hawaii	56	329	488
Idaho	8	24	200
Iowa	15	20	33
Kansas	15	17	13
Minnesota	9	16	78
Missouri	22	31	41
Montana	10	15	50
Nebraska	12	18	50
Nevada	33	38	15
New Mexico	32	46	44
North Dakota	9	9	0
Oklahoma	17	20	18
Oregon	21	57	171
South Dakota	10	12	20
Texas	59	94	59
Utah	30	43	43
Washington	14	43	207
Wyoming	8	16	100
Total	564	1,288	128

1. Source: U.S. Code of Federal Regulations, Title 50, Part 17, April 15, 1990, "Endangered and Threatened Wildlife and Plants."
2. Source: U.S. Fish and Wildlife Service, USFWS Threatened and Endangered Species System (TESS), updated April 20, 2007.

have been listed as threatened or endangered under the Endangered Species Act (Washington Department of Fish and Wildlife 2000).

In the Klamath Basin, previously altered flow regimes have been partially restored to provide water for fish. In 2001 the Bureau of Reclamation made a highly controversial decision to cut back 90 percent of the spring and summer water allocations for farmers in the Klamath Project. The action was taken to protect the survival of endangered Lost River and short-nose suckers as well as Coho salmon (Doremus and Tarlock 2003).

Unfortunately, the Klamath Project decision is an exception in allocation outcomes. In fact, fish more often suffer the consequences of a regional practice referred to as "water spreading." Poor or unfair enforcement practices allow Reclamation Project waters to be distributed or "spread" to non-project users. Water spreading in the Pacific Northwest is so widespread that the practice may further threaten endangered salmon (Tarlock 2001).

As water resources continue to diminish, especially with ongoing drought, it will be increasingly difficult to convince humans to reduce their collective demands on policy makers for more water. In contrast to the Klamath situation, past court decisions have actually ruled against fish interests. A California judge ruled that using water for irrigation purposes, for example, was a higher priority than providing minimum in-stream flows necessary for spring-run salmon on the San Joaquin River beyond the Friant Dam, built as part of the Central Valley Water Project (Robie 1990). Partially in response to such practices, in 1992 the Central Valley Project Improvement Act was enacted to better address water allocation decisions and to address the environmental legacy of irrigated agriculture in California. H. C. Dunning (1993), however, has pointed out that salmon runs are still not likely to be renewed because, at most, irrigators will lose only 15 percent of their current water allocations under the act.

Shorebirds that migrate from the Gulf of Mexico to Canadian and northern U.S. breeding grounds require appropriate habitat on the High Plains. The Central Platte River, for example, is a key staging area for sandhill and whooping cranes. Interior least tern and piping plovers require river sandbars for breeding. However, water projects on the High Plains have significantly altered or destroyed these important river habitats. The USFWS is now working with private citizens, state agencies, and others to protect threatened river habitat through the Partners for Fish and Wildlife Program in Nebraska.

Urban Growth and Development

Today, the western states are experiencing the most intensive population growth in U.S. history (Cordell and Overdevest 2001). The resulting urban sprawl and development encroaching into the interface of urban areas and wildlands has negative implications for fish and wildlife populations.

The Colorado Plateau has experienced a six-fold increase in human population growth in the past century or so. During this period, Colorado's population increased 30.6 percent, while New Mexico's and Wyoming's increased 20.1 percent and 8.9 percent, respectively. Nevada and Arizona are currently the fastest-growing states in the West. From 1990 to 2004, Nevada's population grew by 66.2 percent and Arizona's by 40 percent. In the 1990s Colorado had ten of the fifty fastest-growing counties in the United States (Riebsame, Robb, and Robb 1997). Las Vegas is the fastest-growing urban area in the country. New residents in these areas require new housing, which, in turn, leads to increasing conflict with wildlife's similar need for habitat.

Major transportation projects that alter or destroy additional habitat provide the means for citizens in these areas to sprawl over an ever-larger space, destroying and fragmenting essential wildlife habitat in the process. Similarly, such transportation projects facilitate an "exurban sprawl" involving an explosion in second-home or recreation residences and seriously altering or destroying formerly remote wildlife habitat.

Because of the rapid urban growth throughout the West, it is essential that state and local governments better integrate biodiversity goals into land-use planning. The development of Habitat Conservation Plans (HCP) since the mid-1980s is one such approach. Since the first HCP was developed for butterflies on San Bruno Mountain in 1983, the concept has been expanded to multispecies conservation plans affecting entire metropolitan areas. Multispecies plans now encompass much of Riverside and Orange counties in southern California and can be found in Arizona and Nevada as well (Cohn and Lerner 2003). An HCP permits the incidental take of endangered species through habitat destruction on private land, provided the parties to the HCP agree to set aside key habitat for the species in question and agree to maintain that habitat. Therefore, for the HCP concept to work effectively for endangered wildlife, each plan must be based on sound science.

In 1999, the Washington Forest Practices HCP (aka "Forests and Fish Forever") was approved by the state of Washington. The plan applies to 9.1 million acres and is the largest HCP in the West. Although scientists in the Clinton administration criticized the agreement as "voodoo science" with inadequate safeguards for threatened species, the Bush administration supports the plan and has approved it (McClure and Stiffler 2005). In return for maintaining vegetated buffers along streams, abiding by timber harvest constraints, and taking other protection measures, the Washington timber industry would be guaranteed fifty years of protection against prosecution for "incidental take" of threatened or endangered species. However, critics of the plan point out that almost half of affected stream miles would not be covered by the buffer requirements and that the Washington Department of Natural Resources lacks sufficient personnel to monitor timber harvest practices adequately (McClure and Stiffler 2005). The American Fisheries Society and the Society for Ecological Restoration concurred (2000) and found the report used to set the rules for HCP forest practices deficient because it inadequately addressed erosion and landslide considerations, application of pesticides, and streamside buffers.

Similar large-scale HCPs have been developed in California (Pacific Lumber HCP) and Oregon (Elliott State Forest HCP) to protect Northern spotted owls, marbled murrelets, and salmon while addressing timber and local economic development needs. In return for maintaining an adjacent tree farm as a potential dispersal area for the birds, among other provisions, under the terms of the latter HCP, Weyerhauser would gain access to a sixty-year incidental take permit for Northern spotted owls and a six-year permit for marbled murrelets requested by the Oregon Department of Forestry (ODOF) (Oregon Department of Forestry 1995). The ODOF HCP indicates that habitat protection during the sixty-year period would probably support twenty-six spotted owls, yet timber harvesting could result in the incidental take of sixty owls (Oregon Department of Forestry 1995, IV-14). The final Elliott State Forest plan was completed in 2005 and submitted for public comment.

The Pacific Lumber HCP would allow incidental take of 36 species of wildlife in the Northern California Headwaters Forest area, including threatened Northern spotted owls, marbled murrelets, and Coho salmon. After a review of the HCP, the Environmental Protection Information Center (EPIC) (EPIC 2005) questioned the adequacy of Pacific Lumber's data collection procedures used to obtain information for the establishment of baselines for affected species. For example, EPIC pointed out that the poor baseline data could result in an incidental take of over 700 marbled murrelets (roughly half of the resident population) rather than the 251 to 340 identified in the HCP because increased amounts of habitat harvesting would occur. In light of reduced federal oversight and the long-term influence of HCPs, such faulty plans could have serious ramifications for numerous species throughout the West.

Habitat Fragmentation and Loss

Habitat is defined as "the physical and biological setting in which organisms live and in which the other components of the environment are encountered" and is an essential element for all species (National Research Council 1995, 71). In a review of the status of wildlife species in the United States, David S. Wilcove and colleagues (1998) determined that habitat destruction and fragmentation are the main threats to species survival.

Habitat fragmentation occurs when a large, fairly contiguous tract of vegetation is subdivided and converted to other land-use regimens such that only scattered "fragments" or patches of the original habitat remain (Faaborg et al. 1993). The magnitude of habitat loss and fragmentation in the United States grows daily. In a major report on endangered ecosystems in the United States, Reed Noss and colleagues (1995) reported that 98 percent of Great Plains tallgrass prairie has been destroyed. Wetlands loss between 1780 and 1980 in the West was extensive as well. Colorado lost over half of its wetlands, while Idaho lost 56 percent, Wyoming 38 percent, and Montana 27 percent. Southern California lost 70–90 percent of its coastal sage scrub habitat, principally to housing and urban development. In addition, New Mexico and Arizona lost about 90 percent of their riparian ecosystems. The loss of such habitat has had major ramifications for fish and wildlife.

Wildlife habitat requirements often conflict with human needs or desires. In the natural world, species partition habitat and other resources by occupying different niches. Bird species such as the golden-crowned kinglet are "crown" species that tend to feed and nest in the highest parts of spruces and conifers. A similarly sized species such as the Connecticut warbler can utilize the same habitat by preferentially feeding and nesting near the ground. Natural niches are confounded by human actions that rarely acknowledge or accommodate other species. For example, housing development, row-crop agriculture, and transportation projects fragment wildlife habitat and interfere with important wildlife transportation corridors. Wetlands that are essential fish and avian breeding grounds are altered permanently for water projects or marinas or are filled in for urban development.

Growing urban populations demand more and more housing, leading to urban sprawl that encroaches on the wildland-urban interface. Such actions increase the likelihood for direct conflict between humans and wildlife when the latter attempt to reestablish former territories. Undesired direct contact can result in the further destruction of wildlife, as when mountain lions are shot after negative interactions with humans.

Conversion of land for industry, urban, and, especially, agricultural development in central California provides a good example of how land conversion has negative implications for wildlife. Species such as the blunt-nosed leopard lizard and the San Joaquin kit fox are threatened with extinction as a result of such conversions (USFWS 1998). So many species in this area have been affected by habitat loss, resulting in their listing as endangered, that the Metropolitan Bakersfield HCP was approved in 1994. This plan was the first municipal multiple-species HCP. Urban development was allowed to proceed with "incidental take" of species permitted during development, but specific conservation actions were required to protect listed species.

Controversial wildlife policy decisions often involve the input of scientists and judges, in addition to environmental advocates and agency bureaucrats. Interior forest species such as the Northern spotted owl and marbled murrelet require extensive areas of old-growth forest relatively undisturbed by humans for 200 or more years. Environmentalists and many biologists believe the loss and fragmentation of old-growth forests from logging in the Northwest threaten these species' long-term viability (Swedlow 2003). However, high demand for timber and the need for jobs in the Northwest challenge decision makers in development and implementation of conservation strategies designed to preserve the spotted owl (Yaffee 1994). A long and highly contentious legal battle has occurred in which the courts have been asked to balance society's economic and development needs against the need to protect endangered species. Brandon Swedlow (2003) provides a detailed account of the lengthy policy and legal debates over the spotted owl.

A very important recent development in the endangered species policy debate was a move away from large-scale management decisions based on a single indicator species to an ecosystem-based perspective. In 1993 the Clinton administration formed the Forest Ecosystem Management Assessment Team, which recommended that 24 million acres of federal lands be placed under ecosystem management to address the needs of multiple species within an ecosystem. Instead of reducing conflict, however, this controversial management strategy, when applied to old-growth forest, effectively reduced timber harvests on federal lands by 75 percent. The net result was an energized timber industry that pursued support from the courts (Swedlow 2003).

Water Availability

Water-use conflicts among humans have a long history in the western states (see Reisner 1987; Worster 1985). The new urban West puts extreme demands on scarce water resources, demands that lead to increasing conflicts with wildlife, particularly aquatic species. It is no longer possible to ignore the fact that close relationships exist among water, urban population growth, and endangered species and that new policies have to be devised to "confront difficult choices between competing human uses of land and water" in the West (Doremus 2001, 381).

Water scarcity has intensified in the West because of increased demand compounded by reduced supplies. After numerous years of drought—probably associated with global climate change and reduced snowpack—and more projected years of drought to come, western state and local governments are scrambling to address water needs. Unlimited urban growth in the West can no longer be supported given available water supplies. In the arid West, water policies must be better coordinated with urban growth strategies that integrate land-use decision making with water allocation decisions and take biodiversity into consideration (Lucero and Tarlock 2003). On October 6, 1999, Governor Gary Johnson issued an executive order for environmental and natural resource agencies in New Mexico to work with citizens, businesses, and communities to promote balance and stewardship of water resources. He directed them to employ the "Enlibra" environmental management principles adopted by the Western Governors' Association (Western Governors' Association 1999).

The previous pattern of large federal water projects in the arid and semiarid western states is slowly being replaced with policies that place greater emphasis on conservation and aquatic ecosystem restoration (Tarlock 2001). This shift in water policy has been plagued by contentious debates over water-use reallocation, especially when decisions are made that favor wildlife, as occurred in 2001 with the Klamath Project. Debates have occurred over funding proposals for the construction of fish ladders as well, but such debates are far less contentious than reallocation of water releases that provide greater in-stream flows for endangered fish species or protect endangered shorebirds.

Federal Public Lands

Another defining feature of the West is the overwhelming presence of the federal government, which owns more than half the land area of many western states. In addition to extensive landholdings on military bases, there are national parks, national forests, and national wildlife refuges, as well as Bureau of Land Management and Bureau of Reclamation lands.

Almost half of listed threatened and endangered species exist in federal lands in the West, yet highly subsidized private activities on those federal lands pose substantial threats to endangered wildlife. Lobbyists for cattle and sheep associations, logging companies, and mining industries get laws and policies formulated and implemented that can negatively impact fish and wildlife habitat on public lands. Congressional lobbyists have succeeded in having legislation enacted that permits below-fair-market sales of timber and coal on public lands, thereby increasing demand for the resource. Grazing policies that set fees below the fair-market value further encourage overuse and degradation of grasslands. Exemptions to the National Environmental Policy Act's environmental impact assessment requirements, for example, in the Salvage Timber Harvesting bill (attached as a rider to a budget reconciliation bill) and in amendments to the General Mining Law of 1872 permit private companies to harvest timber and to mine on federal lands without consideration of the environmental consequences. These practices can result in increased release of sediment and toxic substances into streams and have negatively affected aquatic species such as salmon and snails, as well as terrestrial wildlife such as endangered southwestern willow flycatchers and Sonoran pronghorn.

Collaborative Resource Management

As political conflict has become more intense in recent years with regard to resource use on public lands and other shared resources such as watersheds, there has been a concurrent growth in innovative collaborative resource management initiatives (Cestero 1999; Wondolleck and Yaffee 2000). Sydney F. Cook (2000) has described the emergence of collaborative decision making as a possible revival of Jeffersonian democracy, giving power back to the people closest to and most affected by the resources. Cook also described such developments as a possible result of the resurgence of western anger previously visible in the Sagebrush Rebellion of the 1980s. Whatever the case, collaborative initiatives do represent a move from centralization in decision making about federal public lands to collaborative decision making at the local level among diverse interests. Despite its potential, George Cameron Coggins (1999), a leading scholar on public lands law and policy, condemns collaborative decision making as an abdication of responsibility by federal officials, especially with regard to complex and difficult decisions fraught with political overtones.

Although Edward Weber (1999), a grassroots democracy scholar, acknowledges that collaborative decision making may be limited to select cross-jurisdictional, contentious policy issues, he suggests it is a desirable alternative to constant policy gridlock. Weber believes the American political system, with its numerous checks and balances, provides losers in policy conflicts with multiple avenues to effectively block policy action. In this sense, collaborative decision making allows for a more equitable solution to natural resource policy debates. However, as Denise Fort (1998) observes in an article on watershed management of the Rio Grande, local collaborative efforts may require the stimulus of federal legislation such as the Endangered Species Act or the Clean Water Act, which mandate protection of ecological values.

CONCLUSION

This chapter illustrates that human activities and demand for resources shape wildlife policy as much as politics and personal values. As with natural resource policy in general, wildlife policy is concerned with the use and exploitation of resources. Fish and wildlife are classic common-pool resources, which means they are owned by everyone and by no one. Hence, they are subject to overuse and degradation, with insufficient consideration of their value to society. There are conflicts and tradeoffs in wildlife policy. Policy debates occur over the mere taking of wildlife, over how much, when, and where it can be harvested, as well as over the manner of taking. Conflicts also occur over the use of public and private resources, such as land and water, that affect wildlife populations.

Water and land use are probably the two resource areas of greatest policy conflict in the West. Politicians create laws and policies that favor their constituents' use of scarce water supplies. Prior appropriation water-use policies that fostered much of the growth in the West and the unsustainable water allocation decisions that followed serve as examples. Unwise land-use decisions that allowed unrestricted growth patterns were based, in part, on frontier ethics that assumed unlimited resources. Utilitarian resource policies predicated on unlimited resource availability are now challenged by actual resource limitations. Increasing numbers of threatened or endangered wildlife species are a consequence of poorly constructed, wasteful policies of the past. Future policies must better integrate growth planning with biodiversity considerations.

Specific policy changes needed to improve the status of fish and wildlife populations in the West include:

1. Better integration of fish, wildlife, and other biodiversity considerations into land-use planning and management

2. Revision of water-use and allocation policies to conserve water better and increase allocations for fish, wildlife, and other ecosystem processes
3. Revision of federal mining, forest management, and grazing policies to price natural resources obtained on federal lands more in line with prices in the private sector
4. More stringent controls on the importation and use of species that could become invasive threats

Wildlife resources in the West face an uncertain future. Only a concerted effort to create ecologically enlightened policies will reconcile human actions and the needs of wildlife populations in western states.

REFERENCES

American Fisheries Society (Western Division) and Society for Ecological Restoration (Northwest Chapter). 2000. "Professional Organizations Find Forests and Fish Report Lacking." At www.sernw.org/for_fish/ff_pr.htm.

Barker, A., et al. 2003. "The Rise of Collaborative Groups in Federal Land and Resource Management: A Legal Analysis." *Journal of Land Resources and Environmental Law* 23, 67–141.

Bolin, J. H. 1993. "Of Razorbacks and Reservoirs: The Endangered Species Act's Protection of Endangered Colorado River Basin Fish." *Pace Environmental Law Review* 11 (Fall), 35–79.

Cestero, B. 1999. *Beyond the Hundredth Meeting: A Field Guide to Collaborative Conservation on the West's Public Lands*. Tucson, AZ: Sonoran Institute.

Coggins, G. C. 1999. "Regulating Federal Natural Resources: A Summary Case against Devolved Collaboration." *Ecology Law Quarterly* 25, 602–610.

Cohn, J. P., and J. A. Lerner. 2003. *Integrating Land Use Planning and Biodiversity*. Washington, DC: Defenders of Wildlife.

Comer, R. D. 2004. "Cooperative Conservation: The Federalism Underpinnings to Public Involvement in the Management of Public Lands." *University of Colorado Law Review* 75, 1133–1157.

Commission on Life Sciences. 1996. *Upstream: Salmon and Society in the Pacific Northwest*. Washington, DC: National Academies Press.

Conley, A., and M. A. Moote. 2003. "Evaluating Collaborative Natural Resource Management." *Society and Natural Resources* 16, 371–386.

Cook, S. F. 2000. "Revival of Jeffersonian Democracy or Resurgence of Western Anger? The Emergence of Collaborative Decision Making." *Utah Law Review* 2000, 575–600.

Cordell, H. K., and C. Overdevest. 2001. *Footprints on the Land: An Assessment of Demographic Trends and the Future of Natural Resources in the United States*. Champaign, IL: Sagamore.

Cousins, E., R. Perks, and W. Warren. 2005. *Rewriting the Rules: The Bush Administration's First-Term Environmental Record*. Washington, DC: Natural Resources Defense Council.

Defenders of Wildlife, Earthjustice, Endangered Species Coalition, and National Wildlife Federation. 2002. *Open Season on America's Wildlife: The Bush Administration's Attacks on Federal Wildlife Protections*. Washington, DC: Defenders of Wildlife.

Doremus, H. 2001. "Water, Population Growth, and Endangered Species in the West." *University of Colorado Law Review* 72 (Spring), 361–413.

Doremus, H., and A. D. Tarlock. 2003. "Fish, Farms, and the Clash of Cultures in the Klamath Basin." *Ecology Law Quarterly* 30, 279–350.

Dunning, H. C. 1993. "Confronting the Environmental Legacy of Irrigated Agriculture in the West: The Case of the Central Valley Project." *Environmental Law* 23, 943–969.

Easton, D. 1953. *The Political System*. Chicago: University of Chicago Press.

Environment 2004. 2004. *Putting Polluters First: The Bush Administration's Environmental Record*. Washington, DC: Environment 2004, June 24. At www.environment2004.org, site accessed July 2004.

Environmental Protection Information Center (EPIC). 2005. *EPIC's Summary and Critique of the Pacific Lumber Habitat Conservation Plan and Sustained Yield Plan*. Garberville, CA: EPIC.

Faaborg, J., M. Brittingham, T. Donovan, and J. Blake. 1993. "Effects of Land Use Practices on Neotropical Migratory Birds in Bottomland Hardwood Forests." In D. M. Finch and P. W. Stangel, eds., *Status and Management of Neotropical Migratory Birds*. USDA Forest Service General Technical Report RM 229. Fort Collins, CO: Rocky Mountain Forest and Range Exp. Station.

Federal Register. 1997. 62(159), 43937–43954, August 18.

Fort, D. D. 1998. "Restoring the Rio Grande: A Case Study in Environmental Federalism." *Environmental Law* 28, 15–52.

Lasswell, H. R. 1962. *American Politics: Who Gets What, When, Where, Why, and How*. Chicago: University of Chicago Press.

Little, J. B. 2003. "Quincy Library Group." At www.redlodgeclearinghouse.org/stories/quincy.html, site accessed August 2004.

Lucero, L., and A. D. Tarlock. 2003. "Water Supply and Urban Growth in New Mexico: Same Old, Same Old or a New Era?" *Natural Resources Journal* 43, no. 3, 803–836.

Mangun, W. R., and D. H. Henning. 1999. *Managing the Environmental Crisis: Incorporating Values into Natural Resource Administration*. Durham, NC: Duke University Press.

Mangun, W. R., and J. C. Mangun. 1991. "Implementing Wildlife Policy across Political Jurisdictions." *Policy Studies Journal* 19, nos. 3–4, 519–526.

McClure, R., and L. Stiffler. 2005. "Scientists Fault State Habitat Plan." *Seattle Post-Intelligencer*, May 5.

National Research Council. 1995. *Science and the Endangered Species Act*. Washington, DC: National Academies Press.

———. 2004. *Endangered and Threatened Fishes in the Klamath River Basin*. Washington, DC: National Academies Press.

Natural Resources Defense Council. 2004. www.nrdc.org/bushword/wildlife_species, site accessed September 2004.

Nie, M. 2004. "State Wildlife Policy and Management: The Scope and Bias of Political Conflict." *Public Administration Review* 64, no. 2, 221–233.

Noss, R. F., E. T. LaRoe, and J. M. Scott. 1995. *Endangered Ecosystems of the United States: A Preliminary Assessment of Loss and Degradation*. National Biological Service Report 28. Washington, DC: National Biological Service.

Oregon Department of Forestry. 1995. *Elliott State Forest Habitat Conservation Plan*. Eugene: Oregon Department of Forestry.

Owen, D. 2002. "Prescriptive Laws, Uncertain Science, and Political Stories: Forest Management in the Sierra Nevada." *Ecology Law Quarterly* 29, 747–804.

Reisner, M. P. 1987. *Cadillac Desert: The American West and Its Disappearing Water*. New York: Penguin.

Reisner, M. P., and S. F. Bates. 1990. *Overtapped Oasis: Reform or Revolution for Western Water*. Washington, DC: Island.

Riebsame, W. E., J. J. Robb, and J. Robb, eds. 1997. *Atlas of the New West: Portrait of a Changing Region*. New York: W. W. Norton.

Robie, R. B. 1990. "An Update on Legal Issues." *Transactions of the Fifty-fifth North American Wildlife and Natural Resources Conference* 55, 255.

Snape III, W., M. T. Leahy, and J. M. Carter II. 2003. *Undercutting National Forest Protections: How the Bush Administration Uses the Judicial System to Weaken Environmental Laws*. Washington, DC: Defenders of Wildlife.

Stegner, W. E. 1954. *Beyond the Hundredth Meridian: John Wesley Powell and the Second Opening of the West*. New York: Houghton-Mifflin.

Stein, B. A., and S. A. Flack, eds. 1997. *1997 Species Report Card: The State of U.S. Plants and Animals*. Arlington, VA: The Nature Conservancy.

Swedlow, B. 2003. "Scientists, Judges and Spotted Owls." *Duke Environmental Law and Policy Forum* 13 (Spring), 187–278.

Tarlock, A. D. 2001. "The Future of Prior Appropriation in the New West." *Natural Resources Journal* 41, no. 4, 769–794.

Thomas, J. W. 2000. "What Now? From a Former Chief of the Forest Service." In R. J. Sedjo, ed., *A Vision for the U.S. Forest Service: Goals for the Next Century*. Washington, DC: Resources for the Future.

United States Fish and Wildlife Service (USFWS). 1998. *Recovery Plan for Upland Species of the San Joaquin Valley, California*. Portland, OR: USFWS California/Nevada Operations Office.

Washington Department of Fish and Wildlife. 2000. *Partnerships in Science: A New Era in Salmon Recovery*. Olympia: Washington Department of Fish and Wildlife.

Weber, E. P. 1999. *Pluralism by the Rules: Conflict and Cooperation in Environmental Regulation*. Washington, DC: Georgetown University Press.

———. 2003. *Bringing Society Back In: Grassroots Ecosystem Management, Accountability, and Sustainable Communities*. Cambridge, MA: MIT Press.

Western Governors' Association. 1999. "New Mexico's First Water Summit Encourages Communities to Use Enlibra, Make Water-Planning Decisions." Press Release, October 20. At www.westgov.org/wga/press/watersum.htm, site accessed September 2004.

Wilcove, D. S., D. Rothstein, J. Dubow, A. Philips, and E. Losos. 1998. "Quantifying Threats to Imperiled Species in the United States." *Bioscience* 48, 607–615.

The Wilderness Society. 2005. *Bush Administration Record on Public Lands: Irresponsible Management of the People's Land*. Washington, DC: The Wilderness Society.

Wondolleck, J., and S. L. Yaffee. 2000. *Making Collaboration Work: Lessons from Innovation in Natural Resource Management*. Washington, DC: Island.

Worster, D. 1985. *Rivers of Empire: Water, Aridity, and the Growth of the American West*. New York: Pantheon.

Yaffee, S. L., ed. 1994. *The Wisdom of the Spotted Owl: Policy Lessons for a New Century*. Washington, DC: Island.

CHAPTER SEVEN

THE POLITICS OF HARD-ROCK MINING IN THE AMERICAN WEST

Charles Davis and Sandra Davis

The symbol of the miner seeking gold or silver has survived for well over a century, the rugged individual replete with hard hat, a pickax, and a mule who dreams of finding mineral wealth through a combination of hard work and luck. The dream remains alive on U.S. federal land because the Mining Law of 1872 continues to offer easy access to mineral-rich land sites in the West and limits government interference in the form of regulations or royalties. The law's primary goal was to remove legal impediments to the development of mineral resources on federally owned lands in the late nineteenth century, an act that also contributed to a congressional desire to promote settlement in the West. This was accomplished by giving miners the legal right to stake a claim or obtain title to the land through patenting. While the central features of the Mining Law have remained largely intact for over a century because of a lack of controversy and the emergence of a protective subgovernment, it was inevitable that the principle of free access would eventually clash with the imperatives of the environmental movement (Klyza 1996).

To date, congressional efforts to reform the Mining Law have largely fallen short. Our goal in this chapter is to analyze the politics associated with attempts to alter or defend the policy since the mid-1960s. Have environmentalists made any political headway in changing policy by promoting an alternative, less favorable image of mining-related impacts? Have alternative policy-making venues been more receptive to reform proposals? How can we explain mining companies' ability to defend favorable program benefits despite less than optimal trends in the production of mineral resources since the mid-1980s?

We begin by providing a brief overview of the legal, social, economic, cultural, and political contexts of the Mining Law, along with a description of environmental impacts linked to mining operations. Next, we chronicle efforts by members of Congress to make the law more responsive to demands for both economic and environmental reform. Third, we examine the attainment of de facto changes through the application of other environmental laws. Finally, we look at the use of policy and planning tools at state and local levels aimed at inducing mining companies to operate in a more environmentally responsible manner.

ECONOMIC AND CULTURAL CONTEXTS

Although early federal mining policy was largely adopted from the practices and rules miners used on a day-to-day basis, the prevalent ideology, legal and institutional structure, and level of economic development affected both daily practices and the adoption of policy. Much of American mining policy was codified from 1848 to 1872, a time when economic liberalism defined public land decisions. During this era, the government encouraged mineral development as a means to bring settlers into western territories for a number of reasons. Government support for and subsidization of mining was based on the belief that society benefited from mining activity because it stimulated economic growth and protected national security by freeing the nation from dependence on minerals from foreign countries (Klyza 1996, 31 and 39; Leshy 1987, 89). Mineral production stimulated industrial development, as it provided materials for manufacturing. Furthermore, gold had a special role in an economy based on the gold standard (Power and Barrett 2001, 52). Thus, mineral production provided a livelihood and brought welcome capital investment into territories and newly admitted states.

Over time, mining and other natural resource jobs were important contributors to the economies of western states, especially to the well-being of isolated rural areas in which mining often occurred. Today western states are more economically dependent on tourism, second-home residents, and service jobs than they were before (Power and Barrett 2001, 120). However, mining jobs pay very well, particularly in comparison to many other jobs in the area (McClure and Schneider 2001c). And mining continues to constitute a major economic activity in the West (Humphries 2005, CRS1). The gross value of hard-rock mineral production on public lands amounts to approximately $600 million a year, according to recent estimates by the Congressional Budget Office (2005).

THE POLITICAL CONTEXT

Mining's privileged status is guarded by a powerful policy subsystem consisting of the Bureau of Land Management (BLM), mining companies, and western legislators, among others. Individual mining companies and the National Mining Association seek support from and provide campaign contributions and votes to pro-development members of the U.S. Congress, especially those from western states. Although this monopoly has had little impact on the passage of environmental laws, it has succeeded in protecting the beneficial components of the 1872 Mining Law that allow companies to mine without paying royalties to the federal treasury and to patent (purchase) federal land for five dollars an acre. The House Resources Committee and the Senate Energy and Natural Resources Committee have been especially supportive of mining interests. This is a predictable outcome because since the mid-1960s, on average, more than half the seats on each committee have been held by legislators representing western states.

The policy subsystem operates with the assistance (and sometimes the opposition) of a fragmented executive branch. Federal agencies such as the BLM and the Forest Service have most of the authority over mining on public lands, but a vast array of other departments and agencies can be involved in mining policy making and implementation (Klyza 2001, 115–117). A fragmented system, of course, provides multiple venues in which political interests can seek program benefits. State and local officials may also be active in mining policy. Western governors, state-level legislators, and state agencies often lend support to mining operations, although some states have environmental laws that are more protective of the environment than others (U.S.

Environmental Protection Agency 1997, 9). Traditionally, state officials have prized mining as an important catalyst for economic development.

Despite the dominance of mining interests, arguments for environmental protection are made by environmental interest groups and officials at various levels of government. The most influential environmental group within the hard-rock mining policy arena is Earthworks (formerly the Mineral Policy Center). Earthworks, in collaboration with other environmental groups, has brought lawsuits; used the initiative process; lobbied the legislative branch at the national, state, and local levels; and, most recently, reached an agreement with eight of the largest jewelry companies in the world to restrict their purchase of minerals to companies using sustainable mining practices (Earthworks 2006). In fact, grassroots efforts have sometimes been successful in reforming state mining laws and decisions. Since the advent of federal and state environmental laws, the mining policy monopoly is no longer invincible, but it is also not inconsequential.

ENVIRONMENTAL EFFECTS OF MINING

Just as context shapes policy, mining policy affects the environment, usually in a negative manner. Although mining may benefit wildlife (i.e., tunnels become homes for bats and reclaimed mining sites serve as habitat), it more often has harsh effects on the environment. For example, in the Environmental Protection Agency's (EPA's) 2000 Toxics Release Inventory, the mining industry was the country's largest toxic polluter (U.S. Environmental Protection Agency 2003, 2–3). Similarly, it is estimated that 40 percent of western watersheds and 10,000 miles of streams are polluted by mining activity (Klyza 2001, 130; McClure and Schneider 2001c).

Mining can cause air pollution, land subsidence, changes in the paths of waterways (for placer mining), large-scale changes in the landscape, hazardous waste contamination of land, and water pollution (Klyza 2001, 129). Water pollution, the most serious risk posed by mining, can occur in a number of ways (U.S. Environmental Protection Agency 1997, 3). First, there is the danger of a cyanide spill if mining operations use the heap leaching process (U.S. Environmental Protection Agency 1997, 3), in which cyanide and water are applied to huge piles of crushed ore to extract a mineral such as gold. Cyanide spills can have devastating effects on rivers. In addition, a long-term potential problem occurs when tailings and waste rock left after mining is completed are exposed to the weather. The rocks may oxidize, forming sulfuric acid and ferric hydroxide that pollute surface water. Unfortunately, acid mine drainage is both costly and extremely difficult to clean up (U.S. Environmental Protection Agency 2003; McClure and Schneider 2001b).

Abandoned mines are a major source of water pollution. A mining engineer working for environmental groups estimated that the total cost of cleanup at existing mines in ten western states would be between $254 million and $1,037 million if certain companies entered into bankruptcy (McClure and Schneider 2001a). This is a major concern to policy makers and citizens alike. If EPA officials are unable to locate pollution-generating firms that are able or willing to contribute their share of cleanup costs, a possible result is the designation of contaminated areas as Superfund sites (Wilkinson 1992). While it is unlikely that all affected companies would go into bankruptcy, the number of abandoned mines in western states is substantial: between a quarter million and half a million mines (McClure and Schneider 2001c). Of these, eighty-seven abandoned mine sites were on the Superfund National Priorities List as of January 2003 (U.S. Environmental Protection Agency 2003, 2).

THE LEGAL CONTEXT

The Mining Law of 1872 is the dominant statute that controls mining activities on federal lands for a number of minerals including copper, silver, gold, lead, zinc, molybdenum, and uranium. Unlike coal miners and petroleum companies, hard-rock mining companies do not pay royalties on the minerals they extract (Leshy 1987). The Mining Act neither limits the number of claims a company can file nor requires that the land be mined (Humphries 2005, CRS2). In fact, land may be sold as soon as it is patented (U.S. Environmental Protection Agency 1997, 7). In a recent example, BLM sold 155 acres of land near the resort community of Crested Butte, Colorado, to Phelps Dodge for less than $1,000. Local opponents, who have fought to prevent mining in this locale for more than thirty years, complained that the transaction will allow the company to open a mine or simply sell the land for profit. Crested Butte mayor Jim Schmidt recently noted that a one-tenth-acre lot in the area typically sells for $100,000 (Lipsher 2004, 1A).

Mining can proceed by two methods. First, a mining claim can be patented (i.e., purchased), allowing the company to obtain title to the surface and mineral rights for $2.50 an acre (for placer claims) and $5.00 an acre (for lode claims). Once patented, mining activity is brought under state law and supervision (U.S. Environmental Protection Agency 1997, 8). Second, a company can stake a claim and mine it under federal supervision. In this method, the federal government retains title to the land. The company pays a $25 location fee and an annual maintenance fee of $100 per claim (Humphries 2005, CRS-2). When the federal government retains ownership and management of the land, greater environmental protection is likely to be provided (U.S. Environmental Protection Agency 1997, 8).

A substantial proportion of hard-rock mining—30 percent of all gold and 29 percent of all silver resources mined in the United States—occurs on federal lands through this second method (U.S. Environmental Protection Agency 2003, 4). The federal agency that manages the land (often the Forest Service or the Bureau of Land Management) has the responsibility to regulate the mining process and provide necessary cleanup. Although the 1872 Mining Law indicates that these agencies should supervise mining activities, both have historically been reluctant to regulate on the basis of what they thought was an overly vague source of authority (Klyza 2001, 131). More recently, however, the Forest Service and BLM have taken steps to limit the impacts of mining activities on other surface land uses, such as grazing and timber cutting (National Research Council 1999, 37–39 and 40), as a result of changes in regulatory authority and the enactment of federal environmental laws since the mid-1960s.

CONGRESS AND MINING POLICY ISSUES

Members of Congress have attempted to address a number of challenges associated with the Mining Law. The first political test occurred during congressional debates over the Wilderness Act in the early 1960s. The bill's main purpose was to require that federal land management agency administrators identify lands deemed suitable for designation as wilderness and then recommend a shift from multiple-use to single-use management. A predictable outcry arose from constituencies who lost access to the resource base and Forest Service officials miffed about the prospective loss of decision-making autonomy to Congress. A host of industry officials and their chief organizational voice, the American Mining Congress, complained that the withdrawal of lands would "lock up" important mineral deposits unless an exemption was granted for mining claims. After various wilderness bills were passed by the House of Representatives and the Senate, Representative Wayne Aspinall (D-

CO) and Senator Clinton Anderson (D-NM) led an effort to negotiate a statutory exemption for mining companies in conference committee. The result was a clause in the final bill allowing mining companies to explore for minerals in wilderness areas for a nineteen-year period ending December 31, 1983, and a continuation of mining on valid claims after that date (Allin 1982).

While mining groups and their congressional allies succeeded in incorporating a statutory exemption allowing mineral exploration in wilderness areas, it proved a symbolic victory. Between 1964 and 1983, no companies entered wilderness areas for exploration purposes, a de facto policy accepted by interior secretaries serving under Presidents Johnson, Nixon, Ford, and Carter. The amount of land set aside as wilderness increased gradually, and in 1976 Congress gave BLM the authority to recommend new additions to the National Wilderness Preservation System under a provision of the Federal Land Policy Management Act (FLPMA) of 1976. That same year, mining activities were further restricted under a new law that prohibited mining operations in national parks (Klyza 1996).

But members of the mining policy subgovernment were cheered by the election of President Ronald Reagan in 1980 and his subsequent appointment of James Watt as interior secretary. One of Secretary Watt's initial acts was to encourage mining firms to find new mineral deposits in wilderness areas, a decision that fit within the mining exemption clause in the Wilderness Act. However, this suggestion triggered an immediate and negative outcry from Congress, and Watt eventually decided not to push the issue further (Wilkinson 1992). On a related front, legislators representing mining states, notably Senator James Santini (D-NV), attempted to use a cold war rationale to further open public lands for the extraction of strategic minerals. Despite support from industry and the Reagan administration, the enactment of policies such as the National Security Minerals Act of 1984 did little to increase public land access (Klyza 1996).

The most serious threats to the Mining Law began to emerge in the late 1980s, caused by a combination of environmental and economic factors. A new group dedicated to mining reform, the Mineral Policy Center (MPC), was established through the efforts of former interior secretary Stewart Udall (Wilkinson 1992). The MPC lobbied Congress for changes in the Mining Law and found a pair of important allies within the key committees. Representative Nick Rahall (D-WV) and Senator Dale Bumpers (D-AR) attempted to push reform legislation that would achieve three objectives: (1) to require royalty payments from companies that profit from mining operations on federal lands, (2) to end the practice of ceding ownership of federal lands to mining companies or individuals through the issuance of patents for as little as $2.50 to $5.00 per acre, and (3) to develop reclamation standards to restore the land as much as possible to pre-mining conditions.

Several bills came close to passage between 1990 and 1992, including a proposed moratorium on patenting. Reform advocates used research to demonstrate abuses of the existing policy, such as the acquisition of prime real estate near scenic mountain resorts for rock-bottom prices using the pretext of mineral development plans. Reform advocates also emphasized the need for royalties on the grounds of fairness to taxpayers and for increased attention to pollution control measures to protect air and water quality. Proponents of the status quo directed attention to the economic importance of high-paying mining jobs in rural areas with few alternative employment opportunities.

Finally, in 1993 the timing seemed right for a major overhaul of the Mining Law. Interior Secretary Babbitt strongly backed proposed changes in policy, as did George Miller (D-CA), chair of the House Natural Resources Committee, and, to a lesser degree, Senator J. Bennett Johnston (D-LA), chair of the Senate Energy and Natural Resources Committee. Bills passed both chambers but died in conference committee in the summer of 1994 despite extensive efforts by Senator Johnston to produce a workable compromise. This was perhaps the best chance to achieve major reforms of the Mining Law in Congress.

Both advocates and proponents of the Mining Law have continued to introduce legislation, to little effect. Industry officials have pushed for legislation designed to provide them with additional incentives to jumpstart domestic mineral production and address the declining number of surety companies willing to offer bonds to cover mining operations, a direct consequence of post-9/11 financial losses (*Public Lands News* 2003a).

Likewise, environmentalists and fiscal conservatives have been unsuccessful in their efforts to eliminate patenting, require reclamation practices, and reduce tax breaks for mining companies. In short, each coalition has ample clout to prevent the passage of unwanted policies in Congress but not enough influence to enact new laws. Consequently, mining policy activists in both camps have attempted to achieve their goals within alternative venues—state and local political institutions, federal courts, political action committee funding to elect "like-minded legislators," and the implementation of other federal policies that affect the feasibility of mining activities.

REGULATORY DEVELOPMENTS

Advocates of change face a particularly difficult challenge in overcoming political resistance to well-entrenched policies such as the Mining Law. Given the prospect of continuing gridlock within the legislative arena, they have increasingly turned to the administrative branch or the courts. Agency officials have sometimes sought changes to restore management flexibility in the implementation of policies that compromise the attainment of other policy goals. This has been more relevant for public land administrators within the Forest Service and the BLM, whose land-use decision-making priorities have occasionally been trumped by mining claims that require adjudication or financial settlement.

In 1974, Forest Service officials promulgated regulations that required the industry to give notice to the agency prior to the onset of mining activities and to submit a plan of operations if these activities adversely affected subsequent surface land uses. Mining companies were also expected to minimize environmental impacts and to undertake reclamation of affected lands after mining operations had ceased. Similar but weaker regulations were issued by BLM in 1981 that were more ambiguous on the issue of environmental mitigation and on mined land reclamation requirements. In neither case did agency rules specify penalties for noncompliance (Wilkinson 1992).

From the late 1990s to the present, both proponents and opponents of mining reform have attempted to utilize administrative procedures to bring about significant changes in the Mining Law. The chief advocate for a regulatory overhaul was Bruce Babbitt, who served as secretary of the interior under President Bill Clinton from 1993 to 2001. After the mining reform legislation supported by the Clinton administration stalled in a congressional conference committee in 1994, he turned to administrative action—that is, revising the "section 3809 surface regulations"—to achieve similar policy goals.

An especially contentious decision dealt with mill-site limitations. A key justification for change was advanced in a 1997 legal opinion by Department of the Interior (DOI) solicitor John Leshy, who ruled that each mining claim was restricted to a maximum of five acres for mill sites. Environmentalists hailed this interpretation of the Mining Law, since it effectively precluded industry use of environmentally damaging technologies such as heap leach mining that require large amounts of land per claim. Administration officials argued that other approaches, such as land exchanges or leasing arrangements, could be deployed to guide mining operations in a more environmentally sensitive manner (Humphries 2005).

Not surprisingly, the DOI decision was roundly condemned by industry officials as an effort to shut down domestic mining operations. As Senator Harry Reid (D-NV) later stated, "It doesn't make sense that only five acres of land should be allocated to provide facilities for every 20 acres of ore. That's like trying to pour a gallon of milk into a ten ounce glass—it can't be done" (*Public Lands News* 2003a, 1). Things heated up in 1999 when Solicitor Leshy used the ruling to deny permission to the Battle Mountain Gold Mining Company's request to commence work at a mining site in Washington state (Humphries 2005). The 106th Congress enacted legislation that forbade the application of the mill-site limitations to mining projects already under way or previously approved. When the Bush administration took office in 2001, Interior Secretary Gale Norton made it clear early on that her department would adopt a new approach more conducive to the development of mineral resources. In October 2003, DOI formally announced a new interpretation of the mill-site clause within the Mining Law that effectively restored the policy framework in place prior to the 1997 opinion (*Public Lands News* 2003a).

Other decisions from the Clinton administration to alter the 3809 surface management regulations included new regulations involving performance standards designed to prevent "unnecessary or undue degradation" of public land resources under the authority of the Federal Land Policy and Management Act of 1976. This rule not only provided another legal means by which DOI or Forest Service officials could say no to mining operations that posed a threat to cultural, scenic, or environmental resources but also required companies to undertake reclamation work and to post bonds equal to the total cost of site recovery efforts (Humphries 2005).

The Bush administration chose to retain the latter part of the regulation mandating industry responsibility for full-cost reclamation bonds. However, in October 2001 DOI officials decided to restore the historical "right to mine" by putting forward a new rule that disallowed prospective vetoes of mining plans on the basis of negative resource impacts. This rule was immediately challenged in a U.S. district court by the Mineral Policy Center. In November 2003, Judge Henry Kennedy issued a ruling that offered comfort to both sides. Industry and DOI officials were cheered by his decision that the regulation, as stated, did not violate the law. On the other hand, the door was left open for future litigation by affirming the legality of the FLPMA mandate requiring BLM officials to prevent undue degradation of public land resources (*Public Lands News* 2003b).

FEDERAL ENVIRONMENTAL REGULATION

A number of federal environmental statutes impinge upon hard-rock mining that occurs on public and private land. The Wilderness Act (1964) was the first major challenge to the Mining Act. While it did not affect mining activities until 1984, it prohibited most new mining claims in wilderness areas after that time whereas earlier valid claims were honored. The Wilderness Act also required reclamation, allowed patents for the minerals but not the land, and required that mining activities be compatible with restrictions customarily made on wilderness areas (for example, access to a mining claim cannot be made by vehicles because roads are not allowed in wilderness areas). Although mining is still allowed in wilderness areas, the wilderness designation has effectively discouraged this activity (Leshy 1987, 232).

Another federal statute, the National Environmental Protection Act, enacted in 1969, requires that the EPA assess the impacts of mining. The agency must prepare an environmental impact statement (EIS) for the proposed mining operation. A comment period allows environmental groups, mining interests, and other federal and state agencies the opportunity to review and provide their evaluation of the proposed mining project (U.S. Environmental Protection Agency 1997, 9). The EIS provides the framework around which decisions are made and other federal and state permitting is integrated. It must disclose alternatives and their impacts (National Research Council 1999, 42).

The Clean Water Act (1972) is part of the regulatory matrix because of the National Pollutant Discharge Elimination System (NPDES) permits required when water drains through tailings and is discharged as pollution into surface water. Under primacy, the federal government has delegated authority to many western states to implement the NPDES permits. Christopher Klyza has noted that NPDES restrictions have "helped reduced acid mine drainage by a third since the early 1970s" (2001, 130). Primacy states (or the EPA if a state does not have primacy) set the limits on pollution discharges and are also responsible for enforcement of the permit system (U.S. Environmental Protection Agency 2003, 13; Klyza 2001, 130). The EPA has formal oversight authority of the permit system, but the agency has been criticized for failing to provide adequate supervision of some states

(U.S. Environmental Protection Agency 1997, 17). Also affected is the supply of scarce groundwater resources. Companies may pump out groundwater to keep the mine dry enough to operate. It is estimated that the current mineral extraction in Nevada will reduce the groundwater supply by 1 million acre-feet over the life of the mines, reducing water available for other needs such as ranching and domestic consumption (Klyza 1996, 130).

Like the Clean Water Act, the Clean Air Act (CAA) of 1965 regulates mining activities. It restricts pollution from smelting, blasting, or moving ore (Cubbage, O'Laughlin, and Bullock 1993; Leshy 1987, 187). A provision of the CAA, prevention of significant deterioration, was first interpreted by the courts (and later ratified in the 1977 amendments to the CAA) to protect *and* enhance air quality on public lands (Leshy 1987, 279). The mining industry, however, has succeeded in limiting the effects of federal regulation in the area of hazardous waste. Wastes from extraction and beneficiation (a process that makes mineral matter richer or more concentrated) are exempt from the Resource Conservation and Recovery Act (RCRA, 1976) (National Research Council 1999, 51). Since the industry produces billions of tons of waste each year, this is a major victory for mining companies (Klyza 2001, 130).

The EPA had announced it would develop hazardous waste regulations for mines in 1986 under the authority of the RCRA and the 1984 Hazardous and Solid Waste Amendments but failed to follow through on its intentions under pressure from mining state legislators (U.S. Environmental Protection Agency 1997, 15). A direct consequence of the failure to act is the increased risk of pollution that can occur when a mine is abandoned. Heavy metals, arsenic, and mercury from mining wastes may contaminate rivers and soil. In this situation, the Comprehensive Environmental Response, Compensation, and Liability Act (1980, called Superfund) may require the potentially responsible parties to clean up the site; failing to find those responsible, the EPA may take over the job of cleaning up the abandoned mine (Klyza 2001, 130).

Other federal statutes also affect mining. The Endangered Species Act (1973) requires that the federal management agency consult with the U.S. Fish and Wildlife Service when mining operations might harm a threatened species. If a mine threatens Indians' protected resources, the National Historic Preservation Act (1966) and the American Indian Religious Freedom Act (1976) also require that the federal manager consult with other agencies and tribes. These consultations are usually integrated into the National Environmental Policy Act (NEPA) review. Since 1997, the Emergency Planning and

Community Right-to-Know Act has required that mines report releases of 650 chemicals in the Toxic Release Inventory (National Research Council 1999, 43–44, 52).

THE STATES' ROLE IN MINING POLICY

States also play a role in mining regulation. States have the authority to regulate mining activities on private land (which includes former federal land that has been patented). State laws and agencies interact with federal laws and agencies, often in a complex manner that can make implementation difficult. This can result a layer of negotiated decisions made by a variety of officials based on multiple federal and state laws and regulations (National Research Council 1999, 54). This complex system also provides an opportunity for one level of government to cover gaps in regulatory coverage in another government's program. For example, gaps in federal authority such as groundwater quality can be filled by state programs. Or, states often have weak financial assurance requirements, but federal agencies have authority to require adequate bonds when mining operations occur on federal land (National Research Council 1999, 53). We will describe the interactions of state and federal laws and agency interaction.

First, state governments have enacted an array of mining laws that are not preempted by federal statutes (National Research Council 1999, 45; Leshy 1987, 214). States have passed laws pertaining to reclamation, surface and groundwater quality, water rights, fish and wildlife, and air quality that have been upheld by federal and state courts (National Research Council 1999, 45–51). Most laws are relatively recent, since states did not become serious about environmental protection until the federal government began passing the environmental statutes discussed earlier (Leshy 1987, 213). Beginning in the mid-1980s, state regulation evolved to become "more pervasive and more technically prescriptive" (McElfish et al. 1996, 351).

An example of how state mining policy can constrain industry operations recently occurred in a California case involving federal land, state policy actors, and tribal religious concerns. A mining company submitted a controversial proposal to mine gold on federal land in the Mohave Desert, using heap leach technology, that would have created a pit 800 feet deep and a mile wide. The proposed site was located in an area sacred to the Quechan Indian tribe. Tribal leaders successfully appealed to then-interior secretary Babbitt to deny the permit request on religious grounds.

With the advent of the Bush administration, the mining company again applied for a permit, and Interior Secretary Gale Norton reacted favorably. Quechan leaders responded by persuading the California state government to create more stringent reclamation standards: if the land on which an open pit mine is located is sacred to Indians, it must be returned to its natural state. The compliance costs required to achieve these reclamation standards are sufficiently high that the new regulations are expected to be a major disincentive for mining operations (Krist 2003).

However, there is agreement that states' regulations vary tremendously in their depth and stringency. Furthermore, state mining regulations do not provide comprehensive protection from the impacts of mining operations (McElfish et al. 1996, 6 and 351). An EPA evaluation of eight western states in the mid-1990s concluded that some state laws provide less environmental protection than others. Six of the states failed to provide adequate financial assurance to correct potential contamination problems. Unlike federal agencies, Nevada did not require that contaminants be removed from a site before closure of the mine. Failures such as these could result in contaminated mining sites that states do not have adequate resources to clean up (U.S. Environmental Protection Agency 1997, 9–10). An example of this, the Summitville Mine, will be discussed later in this chapter.

Second, states can establish their own NEPA laws that require state agencies to evaluate a mine's environmental impact. States often integrate their evaluation process with federal NEPA procedures to simplify the process. These states may perform as a "cooperating agency" or a co-lead agency. States that do not have their own NEPA laws can also become a cooperating agency in the federal NEPA process (National Research Council 1999, 43).

Third, planning processes offer states an opportunity to influence mining decisions made on federal land. The Federal Land Policy and Management Act requires that BLM management decisions be consistent with state and local land-use laws (as long as state and local requirements are consistent with federal laws and regulations). The FLPMA's consistency requirement enhances the ability of subnational governments to limit mining activities, but this provision also gives states and local governments the opportunity to facilitate mining at the cost of environmental protection (Leshy 1987, 219–220).

Fourth, state managers are sometimes drawn into the federal planning and management process when issues of endangered species or historic preservation are of concern. Like federal managers, state officials are required to consult with tribes, U.S. Fish and Wildlife, and other appropriate agencies when a mine threatens endangered species or historical artifacts. States use memoranda of understanding (MOUs) to define their participation. The MOUs are diverse. They may pertain to a single issue, or they may be concerned with a broad array of management decisions; similarly, they may involve two or many agencies. MOUs often stipulate which parties have authority to make decisions and discuss how inspections, monitoring, and bonding will proceed. States use MOUs much as they rely on NEPA to avoid redundancy and simplify the process (National Research Council 1999, 43–44).

Finally, the federal government takes responsibility for some of the worst mining contamination under the auspices of the Comprehensive Environmental Response, Compensation, and Liability Act (Superfund). Superfund calls upon the EPA to provide emergency response and long-term cleanup for badly polluted mining sites that have been placed on the National Priority List (U.S. Environmental Protection Agency 2003, 14). The Summitville Mine fiasco provides an example of how this process works.

The Summitville gold mine is located in a mountainous region of southern Colorado. The mine was discovered in the 1870s and sporadically mined until 1944, leaving a legacy of land and water contamination (Warhurst and Mitchell 2000, 93; Davis 1994). The contamination problem, however, only became worse. In 1984 a Canadian firm, Summitville Consolidated Mining Company, Inc. (SCMCI), leased the site and sought a permit to mine under a weak Colorado law, the Colorado Mined Land Reclamation Act of 1976 (Warhurst and Mitchell 2000). Armed with a state permit, SCMCI began cyanide leach mining in 1986. Almost immediately, cyanide spills occurred.

An unfortunate by-product was increasing environmental damage within the immediate watershed. By 1990 Summitville contamination was responsible for decimating trout stocks in a seventeen-mile stretch of the Alamosa River (Hunter 2000; U.S. Department of Justice 2000; U.S. Environmental Protection Agency 1995; U.S. Geological Survey 1995). Despite the effects of contamination, mining continued until SCMCI filed for bankruptcy in December 1992. At that time there were 150 to 200 million gallons of cyanide solution in a containment basin. The immediate requirement was to keep the mine's water treatment plant online and prevent the containment basin from overflowing. At the request of the state of Colorado, the EPA took responsibility for the mine, avoiding a catastrophic overflow of contaminated water. The cleanup is estimated to have cost between $150 million (Ring 1998) and $200 million (McClure and Schneider 2001c).

In the aftermath of the Summitville threat, Colorado strengthened its reclamation law, although questions remain about its efficacy. Four years after SCMCI's bankruptcy, the EPA told the state to increase the stringency of regulations on another gold mine or the federal agency would take over its regulation (Emery 1996). Thus, a consequence of the Summitville case has been increased EPA attention to mining pollution issues.

INTEREST GROUPS AND MINING POLICY

Both industry and environmental interest groups have been actively involved in efforts to preserve or alter hard-rock mining laws. The National Mining Association has been quite influential in maintaining the status quo, collaborating with pro-development members of the House Resources Committee and the Senate Energy and Natural Resources Committee to prevent major changes to the 1872 Mining Law. Some temporary reform measures have been adopted, such as the decade-long moratorium on the issuance of mining patents. And in 1976, Congress banned the issuance of new permits to mines within national parks. But efforts by pro-environmental legislators to do away with key provisions of the Mining Law, such as patenting (acquiring federal land at absurdly low rates), or to require that royalty payments be paid to the federal government for mineral production have fallen by the wayside.

Environmental groups such as Earthworks, the Wilderness Society, the Sierra Club, and others have pushed for change in multiple venues. At the state level, these groups have utilized the initiative process to achieve policy goals following the failure of reform bills within state legislatures. Perhaps the best example of this tactic is the successful attempt of Montana environmentalists, ranchers, and fly-fishermen in 1998 to persuade state voters to approve a ban on the use of cyanide-based heap leach mining in new or expanded mines (Mineral Policy Center 2003, 5; Raabe 2000, 1C). To date, the policy has survived court challenges from the mining industry. However, later efforts to replicate the Montana initiative in Oregon and Colorado were unsuccessful.

A second example involves efforts by environmentalists to increase the scope of conflict by enlisting former President Bill Clinton's help in working against the start-up of mining near the northern border of Yellowstone

National Park. The bid to open the New World Gold Mine in 1996 raised the ire of preservationists because of the possibility that mining might contaminate the upper fork of the Yellowstone River. With Clinton's support, a negotiated settlement was reached among the National Park Service, the mining company, and environmentalists. All parties agreed that the mine would not be developed and that the company would pay $22.5 million to clean up hazardous pollution from past mining operations. In return, company officials received a substantial payment in the form of federal land with comparable mineral development potential at another location (Barker 1996).

Third, environmental groups have occasionally engaged in different forms of collaborative decision making with other parties to allow mining to occur in a more environmentally sensitive manner. One particularly useful example is the resolution of land-use and legal concerns in a rural area of Montana between the Stillwater Mining Company (SMC) and the Northern Plains Resource Council (NPRC), a conservationist group. In 1986 the SMC began mining operations for palladium (a hard-rock mineral) with a permit capping production at 1,000 tons per day on 550 acres of land. By the late 1990s the company had changed ownership and sought to expand the permit area to include over 2,200 acres and mineral production to exceed 2,000 tons per day. An environmental impact statement supported the changes company officials wanted to make (Clayton 2001).

Nearby ranchers and NPRC members were alarmed by the proposed changes and the seeming lack of concern about impacts to the landscape, wildlife, and water quality. Company officials were fearful of the expense and delay associated with potential lawsuits. Rising tensions led to an invitation for a meeting between a prominent local resident and SMC officials, eventually resulting in a series of more formal negotiations involving SMC and NPRC representatives in the summer of 1999. Following a brief dispute in December 1999 over legal liability issues, the parties reconvened, and in May 2000 they signed a "good neighbor agreement."

The agreement was clearly a win-win proposition for both parties. SMC officials were able to plan for expanded production without the aggravation of a lawsuit from the affected parties. NPRC representatives promised not to contest the issuance of a water discharge permit for the mine. In return, the company promised to utilize best environmental management practices and to allow a committee of NPRC members to periodically monitor mining operations. SMC officials also donated conservation easements on ranch properties with assurances that no subdivisions would be developed (Johnson

2004). The good neighbor agreement is not collaborative decision making in the traditional sense because of the absence of public officials at the bargaining table. But it did produce a legally defensible contract with an understanding on both sides that subsequent concerns would be addressed through communication and negotiation rather than litigation (Clayton 2001).

CONCLUSION

The mining policy regime is a complex set of federal and state laws, regulations, and management practices. The foundation of this regime is the 1872 Mining Act, which greatly benefits mining interests. For many decades a dominant policy subsystem consisting of mining companies, congressional committees, BLM, the Forest Service, and state government officials subscribed to a laissez faire policy of facilitating and subsidizing mining. Miners received support from natural resource committees in Congress, U.S. representatives and senators (especially those from western states), western governors, and federal and state agencies. Geographic decentralization of mining policies has been politically useful, allowing group leaders to emphasize issue containment arguments such as the importance of jobs, community, and a way of life. Mining companies could (and still can) mine on federal public land without paying royalties on the minerals they extracted; furthermore, they could (and still can) patent valuable public land at bargain prices, to make a profit from mining or from selling the property. Under this regime, mining operations were free to pollute land, water, and air.

With the advent of the environmental movement in the late 1960s and early 1970s, the federal government passed a series of regulatory laws that withdrew some lands from mining activities and limited the amount of pollution mines were allowed to produce. The net effect of these policies was to restrict the conditions under which mining operations could occur under the 1872 Mining Act. An important exception was the decision by Congress to exempt mines from the RCRA, an action financially important for mining companies. The mining interests were also able to prevent the imposition of royalties and protect the lucrative patenting system. Thus, mining interests remain influential but are no longer completely dominant.

As the federal government began passing environmental laws, states participated by accepting primacy of some of these programs. States also have authority to regulate reclamation, bonding requirements, and other mining practices on private land. As is typical with a federal system, the strength of these programs varies from state to state. Today, states routinely enforce their own laws, implement federal programs, participate in the NEPA planning process, and negotiate memoranda of understanding to define their policy role relative to the federal role.

Environmental forces have not been successful in reforming the 1872 Mining Act, but grassroots organizations, in conjunction with state and federal officials, have had some successes in increasing the stringency of environmental protection and banning heap leach mining. Some groups have also achieved their policy goals by operating in a more collaborative fashion with industry officials. At present, it appears that successful reform is more likely to occur through actions taken privately or at the state and local levels of government than at the federal level. Until a trigger event such as a mining disaster occurs, state and local governments hold the keys to mining reforms.

REFERENCES

Allin, Craig. 1982. *The Politics of Wilderness Preservation*. Westport, CT: Greenwood.

Barker, Rocky. 1996. Grassroots Grit Beat "the Mine from Hell." *High Country News*, September 2. At http://www.hcn.org/servlets/hcn.PrintableArticle? article_id=2764, site accessed September 2005.

Clayton, John. 2001. *The Stillwater Mine Good Neighbor Agreement*. Red Lodge, MT: Workshop on Collaborative Resource Management in the Interior West, October 18–22.

Congressional Budget Office. 2005. *Reauthorize Holding and Location Fees and Charge Royalties for Hardrock Mining on Federal Lands*. Washington, DC: Congressional Budget Office, February.

Cubbage, Frederick, Jay O'Laughlin, and Charles Bullock III. 1993. *Forest Resource Policy*. New York: John Wiley & Sons.

Davis, Alexandra L. 1994. "Policy in the Wake of Summitville." Boulder: Conflict Research Consortium.

Earthworks. 2006. "Eight of the World's Leading Jewelry Retailers Urge Mining Industry to Clean up 'Dirty' Gold." News release, February 13.

Emery, Jenny. 1996. "EPA Tells Colorado to Get Tough on Mine." *High Country News*, March 18. At http://www.hcn.org/servlets/hcn.PrintableArticle?articlee_id=1726.

Humphries, Marc. 2005. *Mining on Federal Lands*. CRS Issue Brief for Congress, updated February 28. Washington, DC: Congressional Research Service, Library of Congress.

Hunter, Mark H. 2000. "Colorado Considers a Mining Ban." *High Country News* 32, June 19. At http://www.hcn.org/serlets/hcn.PrintableArticle?article_id=5786.

Johnson, Clair. 2004. "Conservationists, Stillwater Make Deal to Preserve Land." *Billings Gazette,* October 6.

Klyza, Christopher McGrory. 1996. *Who Controls Public Lands?* Chapel Hill: University of North Carolina Press.

———. 2001. "Reform at a Geological Pace: Mining Policy on Federal Lands." In Charles Davis, ed., *Western Public Lands and Environmental Politics*. Boulder: Westview.

Krist, John. 2003. "California Trades Gold Mining for Mixing Cement." Writers on the Range. At http://hcn.org/servlets/hcn.WOTRArticle?article_id=14123.

Leshy, John D. 1987. *The Mining Law*. Washington, DC: Resources for the Future.

Lipsher, Steve. 2004. "Feds' Sale of Mining Rights Roils Locals." *Denver Post*, April 6, 1A.

McClure, Robert, and Andrew Schneider. 2001a. "New, Righter Regulation Irks Miners." *Seattle Post-Intelligencer*, June 14. At http://seattlepi.nwsource.com/specials/mining26875_mine11.?searchpagefrom=1&sea, site accessed March 2, 2004.

———. 2001b. "More Than a Century of Mining Has Left the West Deeply Scarred." *Seattle Post-Intelligencer*, June 12. At http://seattlepi.nwsource.com/specials/mining26875_mine11.?searchpagefrom=1&sea, site accessed March 2, 2004.

———. 2001c. "The General Mining Act of 1872 Has Left a Legacy of Riches and Ruin." *Seattle Post-Intelligencer*, June 11. At http://seattlepi.nwsource.com/specials/mining26875_mine11.?searchpagefrom=1&sea, site accessed March 2, 2004.

McElfish, James M., Jr., Robie Bernstein, Susan P. Bass, and Elizabeth Sheldon. 1996. *Hard Rock Mining: State Approaches to Environmental Protection*. Washington, DC: Environmental Law Institute.

Mineral Policy Center. 2003. "Montana: Cyanide Ban Intact." *MPC News* (Summer), 5.

National Research Council. 1999. *Hardrock Mining on Federal Lands*. Washington, DC: National Academy Press.

Power, Thomas Michael, and Richard N. Barrett. 2001. *Post-cowboy Economics*. Washington, DC: Island.

Public Lands News. 2003a. "DoI: Mining Law Doesn't Limit Number of Mill Sites." October 17, 1–3.

———. 2003b. "Judge Upholds BLM's 3809 Regs, But Leaves Room for Attack." November 28, 5–6.

Raabe, Steve. 2000. "Gold-Mining Firm Sues Mont. over Cyanide Ban." *The Denver Post*, April 12, 1C.

Ring, Ray. 1998. "Summitville: An Expensive Lesson." *High Country News,* January 19. At http://www.hcn.org/serlets.thm, site accessed March 2005.

U.S. Department of Justice. 2000. News release. At http://www.usdoj.gov/enrd/summitville. htm.

U.S. Environmental Protection Agency. 1995. "NPL Site Narrative for Summitville Mine." At http://www.epa.gov/superfund/sites/npl/nar1366.htm.

———. 1997. "EPA Can Do More to Help Minimize Hardrock Mining Liabilities." Washington, DC: EPA Office of Inspector General Audit Report EIDMF6-08-0016-7100223, June 11.

———. 2003. "Implementation, Information and Statutory Obstacles Impede Achievement of Environmental Results from EPA's National Hardrock Mining Framework." Washington, DC: EPA Office of Inspector General's Evaluation Report, #2003-p-00010, August 7.

U.S. Geological Survey. 1995. "The Summitville Mine and Its Downstream Effects." At http://pubs.usgs,gov/of/1995/ofr-95-0023/summit.htm.

Warhurst, Alyson, and Paul Mitchell. 2000. "Corporate Social Responsibility and the Case of Summitville Mine." *Resources Policy* 26, 91–102.

Wilkinson, Charles. 1992. *Crossing the Next Meridian*. Washington, DC: Island.

CHAPTER EIGHT

SUBURBAN SPRAWL AND SMART GROWTH IN THE WEST

Matt Lindstrom and Hugh Bartling

The Prosperi family has lived and farmed on nearly 600 acres of land in Madera, California, for the past century, but as the suburbs slowly creep closer to their land, they may be forced out of their home. Between 1998 and 2002 Madera's population jumped by 50 percent, and permits for single-family homes doubled. These circumstances have pushed the suburbs closer to the Prosperis' land and made it more difficult for them to grow substantial crops. Not only are the Prosperis losing money because of weak crops, but they also face the possibility of losing close farming friends as well.

As suburban sprawl in Madera continued, the Prosperi family was offered a good deal of money to sell 40 acres of their land to be developed. Their neighbors, and fellow farmers, became enraged and sent around a petition to get developers to stop the sprawl in Madera. They, along with the Prosperis, also set up 440 acres in easements, which cost $4.5 million, to secure a buffer against suburban sprawl. The farmers of Madera hope this buffer will be enough to secure their fate and help them stay on their land for many years to come (Garvin 2002).

The Prosperi family, and the other farming families in Madera, are just one example of the ever-expanding crisis of suburban sprawl. In this chapter we examine the causes and consequences of suburban sprawl in the West and analyze the components and politics of smart growth. After introducing the primary debates over western land use, we discuss western demographic changes and their influences on land-use planning. The federal government's catalytic role in encouraging low-density, auto-centric suburban development in the West is also examined. Similar to other western environmental issues such as water, energy, and endangered species, federal policy makers and bureaucrats have an enormous influence on the direction and nature of land-use policy and planning in the West. Specifically, we emphasize federal transportation and housing policies. In conclusion, we review several recent state and local political decisions regarding smart growth and land-use planning in the West.

Contrary to the stereotypical positioning of the "environment versus jobs" in western environmental discourse, the issue of metropolitan growth has avoided conventional political and policy-making framing. On the local level, fast-growing metropolises such as Phoenix, Denver, and Salt Lake City have exhibited unique and innovative policy prescriptions for managing the challenges and opportunities that have accompanied population gains. The particular nature of metropolitan growth and its governance offers little in the way of generalizable explanations for its patterns of emergence and development given the West's variegated social and political geography. Fragmented governing structures that respond to different interests and constituencies, local political cultures, and the severity and character of a metropolitan region's growth will all affect the ways responses to growth emerge and are articulated.

The challenge of managing growth in the West is colored by the somewhat incompatible nature of the region's individualist culture—which exhibits a strong regard for maintaining the sanctity of private property rights—and the social value of the region's attractive and dramatic landscape. While recent population growth in cities of the West has undeniably been guided by the relatively low cost of living and the perceived abundance of economic opportunities, the quality of life and attractive environment of many western cities have also drawn population to the region. Maintaining western metropolitan regions' attractiveness both environmentally and economically provides the backdrop for the growing concern over the consequences of growth in the West. With this in mind, one can begin to understand how active government policies have been embraced in traditionally libertarian locales. As will be discussed, smart growth planning alternatives have attracted support across the political spectrum and throughout the so-called red states of the Rocky Mountain West and Southwest. In keeping with metropolitan growth's anomalous political character, activist government approaches have not been universal, however. For instance, in 2004 traditionally Democratic states such as Oregon voted to effectively nullify growth restrictions in place for over thirty years.

Because the issues of sprawl, metropolitan expansion, and smart growth are complex, articulated in numerous ways, and inherently contextual, it is difficult in a single chapter to capture all of the political and policy approaches in the contemporary West that are trying to address these phenomena. For clarity, we first discuss suburbanization in the West, with an emphasis on the environmental aspects of metropolitan expansion that have gained greater prominence in the region's political agenda since the mid-1990s. Next, we look at some political and policy-making responses to metropolitan expansion and suburban sprawl, beginning with the numerous referenda and ballot initiatives since the mid-1990s to preserve open space and encourage smart growth practices. These modes of direct democracy are important to acknowledge, given their long-standing history in the western context (Lascher, Hagen, and Rochlin 1996) and the fact that they can offer insight into public values relating to the nexus between issues of environmental concern and metropolitan growth. Then we discuss innovative private-public partnerships designed to stem sprawl and encourage smart growth in the region.

Because many environmental policy problems associated with massive metropolitan expansion are related to changes in land use proposed by private landowners, the various ways of negotiating the adversarial relationship between private and public interests are noteworthy. Both private developers and local and state governments are finding that taking a more cooperative approach to managing metropolitan development can minimize costs and help create more livable communities. We conclude with an assessment of smart growth strategies in an economic and ecological context in which greater scrutiny is placed on traditional patterns of development and a yearning to develop more sustainable metropolitan regions throughout the West.

FROM URBAN TO SUBURBAN: THE RISE OF THE ASPHALT NATION

In the 1890s, Frederick Jackson Turner declared the American frontier officially closed. The drive for western expansion, Turner contended, was part of an American identity of rugged individualism and entrepreneurship (Turner 1920). If the myth of the western frontier characterized the nineteenth century, the myth of the metropolis characterized the twentieth century. The city became a symbol of prosperity and hope, as well as the site of rampant poverty and ecological malaise. With industrialization and the spatial commingling of extreme wealth and extreme destitution came a host of urban environmental problems. Poor air quality, contaminated water supplies, and overburdened sewage systems cultivated an urban environment rife with multiple threats to human health. Within this context suburbanization expanded in earnest whereby, according to the historian Sam Bass Warner (1972), a process of metropolitan bifurcation was emerging that separated largely clean, salubrious, modern suburbs linked to central cities by expanding transit systems from overcrowded urban slums.

Much of this early suburban impetus evident in the late nineteenth century occurred in cities in the East and the Midwest because western cities were relatively small. During the first decades of the twentieth century, however, the closing of the western frontier declared by Turner gave way to an opening of a new "suburban frontier" in western cities.

The emergence of the suburban frontier in western American cities has interesting ecological origins. At the turn of the twentieth century, of the twelve largest cities in the United States, only one—San Francisco—was in the West (Weber 1899). While many of the West's larger urban centers developed industrial manufacturing as an economic linchpin during the twentieth century, emergent cities such as Denver, San Francisco, and Los Angeles grew because they were either sites of natural resource production or extraction or important for transporting natural resources to distant markets (Soja and Scott 1996).

As the twentieth century progressed and the prominence of resource extraction declined, the West continued to gain population at a greater rate than most other parts of the country. With population growth and technological transformations in mobility and habitation emerging concomitantly, many considered the western metropolis to typify a new type of metropolitan form. This new urban form was marked by a predilection toward low-density development, zoning schemes mandating the separation of land-use functions, and planning around the automobile as the primary technology of mobility. As Richard Weinstein (1997) discussed in an essay on Los Angeles, the new western town looked to architectural models like Frank Lloyd Wright's anti-urban Broadacre City as a model for twentieth-century metropolitan development.

The model of low-density inhabitation that spawned post–World War II suburban growth is dependent on numerous ecological processes whose sustainability is now being called into question. At the most basic level of mobility, the decentralized nature of western metropolitan regions has made their functionality dependent on massive consumption of petroleum to power automobiles. In many states in the West, the penchant for low-density metropolitan expansion coupled with high levels of population growth has resulted in longer distances traveled by private automobile. Todd Goldman (2001) found that in California between 1980 and 2000, the number of vehicle miles traveled per capita grew twice as much as the population. The combination of more people and lower density requires more fuel use. Similarly, the development of the West's metropolitan areas has been built upon the dispersed delivery of scarce water resources. Southern California and central Arizona, for instance, have relied on extensive surface water diversion projects to support the high levels of population growth each region has experienced since the 1950s (Fogelson 1993; Wehmeier 1980).

With increasing population and stagnant or declining natural resources to sustain growth, issues involving metropolitan expansion and suburban sprawl are gaining considerable attention in the West. According to a Brookings Institution study, from 1982 to 1997 the amount of urbanized land grew by 47 percent while the national population only grew by 17 percent (Fulton et al. 2003). When land conversion rates outpace population growth rates, landscapes turn into streetscapes characterized by vast parking lots, new strip malls, abandoned strip malls and box stores, more off-ramps and on-ramps, and tract housing—all spread in the wake of urban sprawl.

Sprawl and urban development in the West are not isolated to the traditional pattern of a metropolis expanding evermore outward. The trend is developing toward high rates of population growth in the West's rural tourist towns as well. Places like Eagle County, Colorado, Washington County, Utah, and Nye County, Nevada, are among the fastest-growing counties in the country. They are all a significant distance from urban centers with substantial coverage by interstate highway systems. The towns in these largely rural counties tend to be small and have developed infrastructures to accommodate transitory, seasonal visitors.

Since the mid-1990s, however, with baby boomers reaching retirement and the surge in telecommuting professions, individuals who can "live anywhere" have been attracted by the West's natural environment and recreational opportunities, giving these largely transitory towns and counties an influx of permanent residents. More permanent residents attract more development and the emergence of a host of public policy challenges normally associated with urban and suburban settings. In some sense, debates over the impending presence of a rural variant of suburban sprawl are more pronounced in these settings because of heightened awareness of the natural environment's role in defining a particular place's identity. Perceptions of a pristine natural environment are often what draw people to these smaller communities in the West, making challenges to those perceptions urgent for residents and policy makers.

DEMOGRAPHIC AND POLITICAL CHANGE IN THE WEST

The rise of sprawl and metropolitan expansion as a major policy issue since the mid-1990s has resulted largely from the high rates of growth experienced in the region. The 2000 census counted 281.4 million people in the United States—an increase of 32.7 million from 1990 to 2000, the largest increase in census history (Perry and Mackun 2001, 1). According to the U.S. Census Bureau, the West, with a 19.7 percent increase, grew the fastest of any U.S. region. Its population increased by 10.4 million, bringing the region's total population to 63.2 million. State population growth in Nevada—66 percent—was the largest of any western state over those ten years, followed by Arizona with 40 percent, Colorado with 31 percent, Utah with 30 percent, and Idaho with 29 percent (Perry and Mackun 2001, 3). Las Vegas was the fastest-growing metropolitan area, with 83 percent growth over the decade (Perry and Mackun 2001, 6). Each state in the West either remained in its same U.S. ranking according to resident population or moved up on the list.

As with demographics, the politics of the West are anything but static; rather, it is a dynamic region in which political views are becoming less distinct and a wide range of ideas are converging into what could be called the "political purple"—from the mixing of "blue" and "red" states. As we shall see, states that voted Republican in the 2004 presidential election also supported greater government intervention at the state and local levels through the passage of various initiatives involving open space protection, mass transit, renewable fuels, and other measures related to smart growth.

Rocky Mountain states are among the fastest growing in the West. Colorado provides an example of the dramatic sociopolitical changes occurring in this region. In addition to the migration of residents from California, new residents are also coming from places like Texas (Tilove 1999). Many of the newcomers are registered Republicans, and while they may greatly outnumber Democrats, these individuals are fiscally conservative and socially liberal (Thurman 1999). Many westerners have been drawn to the area because of open space and the pristine environment, something they are wary of losing (Milligan 2004). Because suburban sprawl and land-use decisions are complex and ever-changing, there is no absolute political consensus among voters in the West, especially among the urban and rural populations (Sneider 1996). Many people are concentrated in cities and towns as a result, creating a cultural divide between those in the urban West and those in the rural West. The divisions revolve around property, as many traditional western industries such as mining and farming are losing favor to more modern industries (Elliott and McGuire 1995).

Rural populations may consistently vote for Republican candidates at the national level, but western communities facing growing pressures from suburban sprawl are also using government policies to protect ranch and farmland, as well as their long-standing cultural traditions. Traditional environmental organizations are joining forces with farm groups as well as hunting and fishing advocates all across the West in an effort to protect ranch land, streams, and big-game habitat from condos, highways, and suburbanization.

The flood of newcomers makes land an especially valuable resource in the West. A vast majority of that land is under the control of the federal government, so much so that it can be said that "the interior West is a colony of the federal government" (Marston 2005). With the vast majority of national forests, Bureau of Land Management lands, national parks, and so forth located in the West, many municipalities' growth options are significantly limited. In addition, natural barriers such as oceans, mountains, deserts, and water sources affect western local land use in unique ways.

The West is anything but homogeneous, as reflected in the changing demographics of suburbia. Much like metropolitan areas in other parts of the country, the suburbs of the West no longer fit the stereotypical image of exclusively Caucasian spaces. The "Wonder Bread" stereotype of the suburbs no longer applies. The Brookings Institution recently reported that between 1980 and 2000, the black population of suburban areas in the West increased by 11 percent (from 27 to 38 percent of the total black population) and the Hispanic population by 9 percent (from 40 to 49 percent of that population) (Armas 2001).

STATE AND LOCAL LAND-USE POLICIES IN THE WEST

Because many of the main policies affecting metropolitan land use and suburban sprawl in U.S. cities are under local, regional, or state authority, it is important to be aware of the distinct differences in political expression that emerge in this subfield of environmental politics. While noncoastal western states voted mainly Republican at the federal level in recent elections, the political climate pertaining to issues of suburban sprawl is more complicated. The propensity to utilize the initiative and referendum process at the state and local levels in western states highlights this complexity.

The reasons for utilizing initiatives and referenda to institute policy change are complex and are related to factors such as the responsiveness (or lack thereof) of political leadership, legal requirements to justify tapping into new revenue streams, grassroots political mobilization, and special interest advocacy. While understanding the political context surrounding the emergence of, and campaigns around, specific referenda is important for assessing their role within particular issue areas pertaining to environmental politics and suburban sprawl, in this chapter we take an aggregate-level view of the referendum and initiative phenomenon to assert its growing primacy as a political tool for addressing suburban sprawl.

Referenda and initiatives are most often utilized at either the state or municipal level and can be advisory or legally binding. While the substantive scope of referenda and initiatives has few formal limits, in the domain of the environmental politics of sprawl they can be discussed in two main categories: (1) referenda and initiatives pertaining to land acquisition in the form of open space preservation, park expansion, and other attempts to protect "green spaces" on the exurban fringes of western metropolises, as well as more proactive efforts in smaller cities and counties; and (2) referenda and initiatives relating to higher-density development and mass transportation efforts. If, as argued earlier, the type of suburbanization dominant in the West is marked by low-density land use, little regulation of the transfer of land from agricultural and wilderness uses to urban uses, and a transporta-

Table 8.1. Land Protection Referenda, Western United States, Municipal, County, and State Levels, 1996–2005

State	*Total*	*Municipal*	*County*	*State*
Alaska	5	5	0	0
Arizona	20	15	4	1
California	46	28	11	7
Colorado	98	65	32	1
Hawaii	2	0	2	0
Idaho	3	1	2	0
Montana	4	2	2	0
New Mexico	13	3	8	2
Nevada	6	1	4	1
Oregon	17	16	0	1
Utah	9	6	2	1
Washington	28	21	7	0
Wyoming	2	0	2	0
Total	253	163	76	14

Source: Trust for Public Land, Land Vote. 2006. At www.tpl.org, site accessed May 2006.

tion "monoculture" based on the automobile, then referenda that fit these categories can arguably be said to address sprawl.

The nonprofit Trust for Public Land maintains a database that tracks local and state referenda placed on ballots each year that deal with land preservation and conservation. Between 1996 and 2005, as Table 8.1 delineates, 253 referenda dealing with land preservation were brought before western voters with 173 passing, a 68 percent success rate. The vast majority of these initiatives have been presented and contested at the local level and—not surprisingly—in states with large urban centers.

As Table 8.1 suggests, the referendum process has been employed throughout the region, with some states—particularly Colorado—showing higher utilization. Colorado provides an interesting example of the political complexity inherent in the referendum process. While a significant number of referenda have been put forth in nominally rural parts of the state, where there has been less sprawling development compared with larger urban areas, the heavily urbanized Front Range has seen the bulk of open space referenda. As mentioned earlier, it is difficult to make generalizations as to why certain referenda pass and others fail. They are generally not covered intensively in the media, particularly when they take place at the same time as a prominent national or statewide election. Levels of turnout, mechanisms of political socialization, and historical patterns of grassroots participation differ in various settings, making it impossible to develop a grand theory. However, an exploration of particular regions can be useful for understanding the dynamics of popular political responses to confronting urban sprawl.

In greater Denver, open space referenda are relatively popular among the region's municipalities, both north and south of the Interstate 25 corridor. This pattern is similar with regard to county-level referenda.

Occasionally, the results of referenda conflict with established preconceptions about political behavior. For example, suburban Golden, Colorado, is in the reliably Republican Jefferson County. During the closely contested 2000 presidential contest, George W. Bush won 51 percent of the vote in Jefferson County, while 62 percent of voters in Golden voted to expand the city's debt by $26.4 million to expand parks and protect open space (Campaign 2000).

On the surface, the electorate's impulses may seem contradictory. On the one hand, voters endorsed a presidential candidate from a party commonly associated with limited government and fiscal conservatism, yet they heartily endorsed increasing local government spending to protect open space. However, to conclude that the electorate was acting inconsistently ignores the fact that most government policies relating to sprawl and its mitigation are understood within a localized context. The changing urban and suburban environment in fast-growing communities in western states is something people experience and witness directly on a daily basis, as opposed to the more distant policies of the federal government.

The second trend in popular political participation through the referendum process—voting on issues relating to mass transportation—clearly reflects this emerging appreciation of the unsustainable nature of a sprawling environment. One of the least anticipated by-products of the low-density, automobile-dependent form of suburban sprawl dominant in western states has been the problem of congestion. Most western metropolitan areas experienced growth in the years following World War II. During the same time, the automobile was becoming the country's primary means of mobility. This simultaneous development caused transportation systems (and the land-use planning regimes that influence them) to elevate the car to a position of primacy while excluding other forms of transportation. As a result, western metropolitan areas dominate the lists of the nation's most congested places. For instance, in the Texas Transportation Institute's 2005 Urban Mobility Study, in the category of urban areas between 1 million and 3 million inhabitants, six of the country's top ten most congested metropolitan areas were in western states (Table 8.2) (Schrank and Lomax 2005).

Table 8.2. Transportation Referenda, Western United States, Municipal, County, and State Levels, 2000–2005

State	*Total*	*Municipal*	*County*	*State*
Alaska	4	3	0	1
Arizona	5	5	0	0
California	22	4	16	2
Colorado	8	6	1	1
Hawaii	0	0	0	0
Idaho	0	0	0	0
Montana	1	0	1	0
New Mexico	0	0	0	0
Nevada	2	2	0	0
Oregon	2	2	0	0
Utah	1	0	1	0
Washington	11	6	3	2
Wyoming	0	0	0	0
Total	56	28	22	6

Source: Center for Transportation Excellence. 2005. At www.cfte.org.

There have been multiple responses to mitigating increasing congestion in western metropolises. Some urban and suburban areas, such as those in the Los Angeles, San Francisco, and Portland regions, have had long-standing viable mass transportation systems. While those systems have not necessarily expanded in line with areas of intense population growth, these metropolitan areas are important places in which costly infrastructure exists.

In other metropolitan areas with a less established history of mass transit, significant public works projects have been targeted to change patterns of mobility. Cities and counties in metropolitan areas such as Salt Lake City, Denver, Phoenix, and San Diego have had popular referenda to establish or expand public transit options since the mid-1980s. Light rail proposals appear to be the most attractive option for many of these municipalities, but generating political support has not necessarily been contestation-free.

In Salt Lake City, efforts in the early 1990s to fund a start-up light rail program were roundly defeated by voters, leaving the local transit agency with the option of developing a small-scale project utilizing existing funds. Building on the city's initial success with the project, Salt Lake County voters approved a sales tax expansion for public transit by a 54 percent to 46 percent margin in the same 2000 election in which 55 percent of county residents embraced the conservative presidential candidate George W. Bush.

Similarly, in the sprawling Arizona county of Maricopa, in 2004 voters chose to expand the region's bus and rail system by approving a dedicated sales tax by a margin of 58 percent; simultaneously, 57 percent voted for Bush. Unlike Salt Lake County, Maricopa County has yet to open its light rail service, demonstrating significant faith in the viability of a future plan (Werbel and Haas 2001).

Mass transit referenda in the West do not always result in policy changes that mitigate against sprawl. Seattle voters, for instance, have gone to the polls repeatedly since the mid-1990s to consider both expansions and closures of the city's monorail system while at the same time voting for competing light rail plans. In the case of Seattle's monorail, voters have supported creating a monorail authority but have had greater difficulty mandating mechanisms for financing its operation and construction.

While public transit projects in western metropolises have received support in recent years, their efficacy in combating sprawl and reducing the environmental costs associated with mobility remains unresolved. Because of the fragmented nature of policy making and the framing of issues related to sprawl, the challenges for addressing the systemic dynamics that fuel sprawl have yet to be coherently approached. The emergence of the various referenda relating to transit and open space does tell us, however, that significant latent political support for new initiatives likely exists if political leaders can find creative ways to frame policy.

It is important, however, not to accept optimistic assessments of the electorate's political support uncritically. Not all of the initiatives passed in 2004 had a positive effect on the environment. In Oregon, a state that supported John Kerry, voters also passed Measure 37. The measure says that "if governments change land use regulations so that properties cannot be developed as lucratively as before, owners who can prove a drop in fair market value either must be compensated by the government for their loss or allowed to develop their land to the level allowed when they acquired the property" (Bjornstad 2004).

Further, landowners can force the government to compensate them if their land has been negatively affected by environmental policies, zoning laws, or both. If governments do not provide compensation, the land-use ordinance is considered null and void. Environmentalists say this measure "will 'wreck the policies that have succeeded in preserving Oregon's rural charms,' opening the door to 'urban sprawl,' residential development of farm and forest land, and the desecration of fish and wildlife habitat" (Bjornstad 2004). For fear of having to pay landowners, local governments may be less willing to support environmental and restrictive zoning policies. This measure is currently in the court system and will take several years to be adjudicated. But given the fact that the measure received rather wide support throughout the state, future attempts to erode the power of statewide growth management policies have the potential for success. Although regional differences exist in the level of support for the measure, the fact that such a significant change to Oregon's much-trumpeted land-use policy could pass so overwhelmingly will undoubtedly cause smart growth advocates in the West and throughout the country to take notice. In the state of Washington, private property advocates hope to introduce a similar measure to voters in the near future, so a backlash related to sprawl mitigation should not be prematurely discounted.

SMART GROWTH IN THE WEST

Because so much of metropolitan development in the West is influenced by the decisions of developers and choices made in the private market, it is important to mention instances in which local governments are encouraging private development around smart growth dictates. Smart growth is an amorphous planning movement that emerged in earnest during the 1990s as a response to popular conceptions that environmental protections and restrictions on development were somehow antagonistic to economic growth. Advocates of smart growth responded to these critiques by saying that environmental protection and growth management were not inimical to economic health; rather, it was important to guide and manage growth in particular ways to maximize the likelihood of sustained environmental and economic prosperity. In 1996, the U.S. Environmental Protection Agency, in partnership with a variety of nongovernmental institutions and professional groups, established the Smart Growth Network and Smart Growth America to share strategies that would support sustainable development at the local level.

Western cities have made many attempts to establish smart growth projects. A project is generally accepted as indicative of smart growth if it accommodates some or all elements of mixed-use development, combines single-family and multifamily housing choices, provides multiple transportation options, accommodates pedestrians by having dynamic public spaces, and establishes a process of developing planning priorities for a community that engages with its residents, developers, and business owners. Because of the high-density and mixed-use nature of such projects, smart growth advocates argue that they contribute to lessening the community's environmental footprint while encouraging civic interaction, which is essential to a vibrant community. While grand claims of improving community can be nebulous and self-promoting, the market demand for neo-traditional housing and mixed-use development will be a true test of their success.

Because redevelopment and smart growth occur in localized spaces—such as Hercules' plan to develop its town center or Oakland's attempt to revitalize the neglected Fruitvale neighborhood around a rapid transit station—regional problems relating to such issues as commuting patterns and water quality are often beyond the scope of many smart growth efforts. Nonetheless, their increasing prevalence offers evidence that a new awareness is emerging that can appeal to both environmental concerns and market imperatives.

In response to consumers' desire to live in the suburbs, Joel Kotkin and the Planning Center in Costa Mesa, California, argue for a "new suburbanism" model of land-use planning. Incorporating elements of smart growth's higher-density and mixed-use models, Kotkin argues that suburbs should be developed in an older village style, with detached, single-family homes and lawns but also with downtown centers that are walkable and vibrant. Kotkin argues that smart growth is too urban-centric and as a result ignores market demands for better suburban housing (Kotkin 2005). He explains, "We reject the notion of the continued primary of the city center by many urbanists, and the widespread assertion that suburban life is, on principle, unaesthetic and wasteful" (2005, 5).

While smart growth tends to focus on developing buildings, another element of western land-use politics concerns land preservation and conservation. All across the West, groups such as the Nature Conservancy and American Farmland Trust are working with local ranchers, farmers, and timber companies to conserve land by purchasing development rights, building conservation easements, and creating land trusts. The loss of fertile farmland is particularly a concern in California's Central Valley, where the population is expected to double in the next twenty years. In Madera, California, the American Farmland Trust has worked with several farm families, along with the California Farmland Conservancy Program and the federal Farmland Protection Program, to preserve 440 acres as a "farmland security perimeter" (Garvin 2002).

Despite the growing interest in land trusts, skeptics suggest that the agreements are made on an ad hoc basis and thereby create a checkerboard of preserved land rather than a comprehensive ecosystem approach. Moreover, the pressure to develop on the suburban fringe is so strong that land trusts face an uphill battle. Madera County's planning director, Dave Herb, explained, "It's like going onto a medieval battlefield with a cardboard shield" (quoted in Garvin 2002).

CONCLUSION

This chapter does not capture every aspect of sprawl and environmental politics as they pertain to the western United States. It is evident, however, that suburban sprawl occupies an important position in the present and future landscape of environmental political contestation in the West. As with environmental struggles at the global and national levels, there is a gradual awakening to an understanding that issues relating to the environment are connected to a host of disparate issues. In the case of suburban sprawl, this complex dynamic becomes most pronounced when diverse factors such as school funding, water use, air pollution, property tax rates, zoning laws, and cultural norms influence habitation and developmental patterns. These patterns, in turn, are the substance of policies and behaviors that impact the environment.

Many communities in the West are increasingly recognizing that existing patterns of development are unsustainable in the long term. The promise of the suburbs as the West's new frontier has to contend with growing concerns about water quality, energy affordability, and air pollution. While these challenges are becoming evident, the approaches to addressing them remain unsettled. As the discussion in this chapter suggests, conflicting sentiments exist regarding different policy plans to address sprawl. Perhaps this conflict is a result, in part, of the complex and interrelated nature of the problems associated with urbanization, which single-issue fixes—such as public transit or land protection—are ill equipped to resolve; or perhaps there is a recognition that the traditional mechanisms of political expression, policy making, and political institutions are not structurally able to serve as arenas for substantive change. Regardless, suburban areas in the West continue to grow (at least in the near term), and evidence suggests that there are social and ecological limits to their present trajectories of growth. Given these realities, the nature of human settlements in the West will continue to receive scrutiny and critical assessment.

REFERENCES

Armas, G. 2001. "Racial Diversity Grows in the Suburbs." *Associated Press*. June 25. At Lexis-Nexis database, accessed July 28, 2005.

Bjornstad, R. 2004. "Measure 37 Rules Effective Today." *The Register Guard* [Eugene, OR]. December 2. At http://www.registerguard.com/news/2004/12/02/c3.cr.measure3871202.html, site accessed July 28, 2005.

Campaign 2000. 2000. "Metro Roundup." *Rocky Mountain News*, November 8, 34A.

Elliott, M., and S. McGuire. 1995. "The West at War." *Newsweek*, July 17, 24.

Fogelson, R. 1993. *The Fragmented Metropolis: Los Angeles, 1850–1930*. Berkeley: University of California Press.

Fulton, W., R. Pendall, M. Nguyen, and A. Harrison. 2003. *Who Sprawls Most: How Growth Patterns Differ across the U.S.* Washington, DC: Brookings Institution.

Garvin, C. 2002. "Farmers Band Together to Stave off Sprawl." HighCountryNews.org. December 9. At http://www.hcn.org/servlets/hcn.Article?article_id=13581, site accessed April 26, 2006.

Goldman, T. 2001. *Consequences of Sprawl: Threats to California's Natural Environment and Human Health*. Berkeley: University of California Institute of Urban and Regional Development.

Kotkin, J. 2005. *The New Suburbanism: A Realist's Guide to the American Future*. Costa Mesa, CA: The Planning Center, November.

Lascher, E., M. Hagen, and S. Rochlin. 1996. "Gun behind the Door? Ballot Initiatives, State Policies, and Public Opinion." *Journal of Politics* 58, no. 3, 760–775.

Marston, E. 2005. "It's the West's Turn to Call the Shots." HighCountryNews.org. January 24. At http://www.hcn.org/servlets/hcn.Article?article_id=15241, site accessed July 28, 2005.

Milligan, S. 2004. "To Boost Party Support, Strategists Tell Democrats to Look West." *The Boston Globe*, December 30. At http://www.boston.com/news/politics/president/articles/2004/12/30/to_boost_party_support_strategists_tell_democrats_to_look_west/, site accessed July 28, 2005.

Perry, M., and P. Mackun. 2001. *Population Change and Distribution 1990–2000*. Washington, DC: U.S. Census Bureau.

Schrank, D., and T. Lomax. 2005. *The 2005 Urban Mobility Report*. College Station: Texas Transportation Institute.

Sneider, D. 1996. "Stampede of Newcomers Alters How West Is Won." *Christian Science Monitor*, October 28, 1.

Soja, E., and A. Scott. 1996. "Introduction to Los Angeles: City and Region." In A. Scott and E. Soja, eds., *The City: Los Angeles and Urban Theory at the End of the Twentieth Century*. Berkeley: University of California Press.

Thurman, J. 1999. "New Republican Politics of the Old West." *Christian Science Monitor*, April 20, 2.

Tilove, J. 1999. "The New Map of American Politics." *American Prospect* 10, no. 44, 34.

Turner, F. J. 1920. *The Frontier in American History*. New York: Henry Holt.

Warner, S. B. 1972. *The Urban Wilderness*. New York: Harper and Row.

Weber, A. F. 1899. *The Growth of Cities in the Nineteenth Century: A Study in Statistics*. New York: Macmillan.

Wehmeier, E. 1980. "The Salt River Project (SRP), Central Arizona and the Area of Greater Phoenix—A Study in Urbanization and Trends of Water Consumption." *Geoforum* 11, no. 2, 107–121.

Weinstein, Richard. 1997. "Wright's Vision of 'Broadacre' City." *The Los Angeles Times,* August 31, M1.

Werbel, R., and P. Haas. 2001. *Factors Influencing Voting Results of Local Transportation Funding Initiatives with a Substantial Transit Component: Case Studies of Ballot Measures in Eleven Communities*. San Jose, CA: San Jose State University Mineta Transportation Institute.

CHAPTER NINE

WATER POLICY IN THE WESTERN UNITED STATES: HISTORICAL AND CONTEXTUAL PERSPECTIVES

Jaina L. Moan and Zachary A. Smith

Every morning at ten o'clock a spray of water shoots 560 feet above the Sonoran desert. Located in the upscale neighborhood of Fountain Hills, Arizona, the highest-shooting manmade fountain in the world emits 7,000 gallons of water per second and operates for fifteen minutes every hour, seven days a week (Gelt 2004). This occurs in one of the most arid regions in the world, a place that receives an average of 7.66 inches of annual precipitation and where summer temperatures regularly exceed 100 degrees Fahrenheit (Smith and Thomassey 2002, 104). Similarly, across the sprawl of the Phoenix metropolitan area, green lawns flourish, residential pools sparkle in the sun, and hundreds of golf courses provide a lush green landscape. Although very little natural water is found in this arid region, a metropolitan area of 3.2 million people has flourished because of the efforts of over 100 years of water diversion and manipulation.

The history of western water policy and management is complex and wrought with conflict. It has been riddled with bad decisions and incomplete policies that do not serve the needs of the public or of ecosystems. Four important factors need to be considered in this history: (1) societal, economic, and political change, (2) federalism issues, (3) federal water agencies, and (4) the impact of scientific management. This chapter will discuss important people and events throughout the history of western water policy in the context of these four factors.

SOCIETAL, ECONOMIC, AND POLITICAL CHANGE

The values and beliefs that govern our way of life are often thought of as our dominant social paradigm (DSP) (Smith 2004a, 7). Manifest destiny and the Jeffersonian era, the Industrial Age, and themes of conservation, preservation, and environmentalism are dominant social paradigms that have driven policy. In addition to these paradigms, events such as the discovery of gold in the West, the Great Depression, World War II, scientific discoveries in the 1960s, the energy crisis in the 1970s, and the Sagebrush Rebellion of the 1980s have also facilitated changes in water policy. This section will discuss the ways these paradigms and events have shaped western water policy.

Manifest Destiny and the Jeffersonian Ideal

In the nineteenth century the expansion of U.S. territory allowed for seemingly infinite growth of the nation. As the United States began to acquire more land, exploration and surveys became important for the future settlement of these lands. Survey expeditions, such as John Wesley Powell's famous 1869 journey along the Colorado River, were subsidized by the federal government to understand the constraints of the arid western region.

In the late 1800s the dominant social paradigm regarding land and water development in the West was focused on the Jeffersonian notion of an agrarian society, under which every family in America would be able to own and operate a farm. The federal government reflected this DSP with policies supporting western expansion. The Homestead Act of 1862 (authorizing that citizens could settle 160-acre tracts of land), the Timber Culture Act of 1873 (granting land to settlers who planted trees on their property), and the Desert Lands Act of 1877 (offering land grants to settlers provided they irrigate the arid land they settled) are three examples of policy enacted to promote western settlement (Laitos and Tomain 1992, 83; Smith and Thomassey 2002,

47). Similarly, the Hard Rock Mining Act of 1872 gave miners the rights to land and water when they staked claims for the purpose of mining hard rock and minerals. The miners' attitude of "first-in-time, first-in-right," reflected in legislation, established the basis for prior appropriation, the doctrine that largely governs western water law (Wilkinson 1992, 231–235).

To further support western expansion, the federal government was interested in ways water could be captured and stored for the use of yeoman farmers. The Carey Act of 1894 was enacted to help states gain revenue for reclamation. Under this mandate, the United States ceded millions of acres of federal lands to the states with the notion that the sale of the land would help states fund reclamation projects (McCool 1987, 15–16; Moreell 1972, 37). The next hundred years would be wrought with efforts to tame the West's aridity.

The Industrial Age, Reclamation, and the Progressive Era

As the nation became increasingly industrialized, the use of natural resources expanded and western settlement accelerated. The thrust of rapid growth caused concern about the availability of water resources. Two schools of thought arose regarding how the nation's natural resources could be utilized: the respectful view of nature held by preservationists and the utilitarian view of conservationists.

The preservationist philosophy promoted the belief that land should not be developed for the benefit of humans. Rather, nature had an inherent beauty, and it would be better to preserve land for the enjoyment of future generations (Cortner and Moote 1999, 15). The preservationist movement helped establish the National Park Service in 1916. This philosophy was also reflected in the 1912 Supreme Court decision *Winters v. the United States,* which found that with the establishment of reserved lands, the federal government would reserve water rights on federal lands (*Winters v. the United States* 1912). This included reservation lands established for Native Americans (Smith and Thomassey 2002, 52).

On the other side of the spectrum, the Progressive movement held a strong faith in science and technology. Proponents of this movement embraced the utilitarian theme of "the greatest good for the greatest number of people." The notion that nature was subservient to humans was a prevailing view, a philosophy that drove its supporters to champion all aspects of development (Cortner and Moote 1999, 13–19).

The conservationist philosophies of the Progressive movement were prevalent in the DSP in the early 1900s. During this time, dam building along navigable rivers became rampant. In 1902 Congress passed the Reclamation Act, establishing the Reclamation Service (later the Bureau of Reclamation). The act allowed the federal government to implement large water projects for irrigation in the West. Under this legislation, loans for construction of reclamation projects were interest free, and repayment needed to occur within ten years. The payments contributed to a revolving fund established for future reclamation projects (McCool 1987, 67).

The act had several problems. The federal government quickly realized that loan repayment was not feasible within the time frame specified. The act bankrupted the farmers it was established to benefit. Additionally, the high rate of project approval resulted in a lack of funding for existing projects. Congress responded by extending the repayment deadline several times and revising the structure for approval of water projects. For example, the 1928 Boulder Canyon Act used funds from the general treasury instead of the revolving fund to construct Boulder Canyon Dam in Colorado, and the Reclamation Act of 1939 (a revision of the 1902 act) relieved farmers of debt if they could not make the payments (McCool 1987, 67). Over a nineteen-period (from 1910 to 1939), eighteen similar statutes were passed, relieving debt owed to the Federal Treasury from the reclamation fund while still providing funding for reclamation projects.

Economic and political factors also contributed to social attitudes toward water resources. World Wars I and II stimulated the mining and defense industries, requiring more resources for weapons production. The Great Depression of the 1930s led to New Deal programs that created jobs and provided cheap, federally subsidized electricity to impoverished communities.

The potential for hydropower increased the pace of dam building in the West. The construction of Hoover Dam in 1928 by the Bureau of Reclamation was approved because of its promise of hydroelectric power, making it the first large western river used for multiple purposes, reclamation, and power (Moreell 1972, 42). The 1938 Bonneville Dam Project along the Columbia River included federal control over hydroelectric power in an effort to bring electricity to the Northwest. Throughout the 1950s the Bureau of Reclamation expanded its dam-building programs by selecting eighty-one sites for dam construction (Moreell 1972, 42).

By the end of the 1950s, federal control over water resources included recreation as well as irrigation, flood control, and hydropower production.

The Reclamation Project Act of 1939 authorized multiple uses for water projects. The Flood Control Act of 1954 expanded multiple use to include recreation on flood-control reservoirs, and in 1958 the National Boating Act authorized recreational uses for all reservoirs. Also in 1958 urban and industrial water supplies were included as additional needs multiple-purpose water projects could provide (Smith and Thomassey 2002, 54).

Despite this rampant development, the preservationist movement had not died. The Sierra Club and the Wilderness Society were influential forces that fought for the preservation of land. These organizations helped establish a movement that would eventually play an important role at the end of the reclamation era.

The Environmental Movement

The "new conservationism" that emerged in the 1950s and 1960s was born from the preservationist notions of the early 1900s. During this time, two events stimulated U.S. citizens to take a more holistic view toward the use of natural resources. The first major event arose with opposition to the proposed construction of Echo Park Dam, a reservoir that would inundate a portion of Dinosaur National Monument (a unit of the National Park System). Conservation groups initiated a public campaign to save the monument from being destroyed. In the end, a large public outcry halted construction of the dam.

The second event was the widespread distribution of Rachel Carson's *Silent Spring.* Published in 1962, the book caused concern about the effects the use of synthetic chemical pesticides and herbicides in agriculture posed to public health (Rothman 1997, 84–90). Carson explained that these chemicals contaminated streams, rivers, and drinking water as nonpoint source runoff from agricultural and industrial practices. From such events, U.S. society became aware of the consequences of the Industrial Age, which motivated a new movement—environmentalism.

Protection of the environment became a national priority. In 1969 President Richard Nixon signed the National Environmental Policy Act (NEPA), establishing the federal government's firm commitment to combat environmental degradation. The Environmental Protection Agency (EPA) was established in 1970, centralizing the different parts of the federal bureaucracy that handled environmental agendas (Lindstrom and Smith 2001, 117–118).

Water quality was a top concern for the EPA. Prior to the environmental movement, federal regulation of water quality was limited and scattered among many different interests. Section 13 of the 1899 Rivers and Harbors Act, also known as the Refuse Act (prohibiting the dumping of debris and waste into rivers), the 1912 establishment of the Public Health Service (the agency authorized to study stream pollution), and the 1924 Oil Pollution Act (prohibiting the discharge of oil into navigable waters along the coast) are three examples of early water quality policies (Gerlak 1996, 30; Howe 1991; Smith and Thomassey 2002, 71).

In 1972 the Clean Water Act made water pollution a federal responsibility and established the EPA as the agency to regulate its provisions (Smith 2004a, 128). This legislation mandated that standards be applied to all treatment of municipal sewage and industrial waste facilities and required permits for the discharge of defined pollutants (Deason, Schad, and Sherk 2001, 175; Smith and Thomassey 2002, 86). It also addressed the issue of wetland degradation by mandating that permits be issued for dredging or filling navigable waters (Gerlak 1996, 30). However, the nonpoint sources of pollution about which Rachel Carson warned were not addressed. Additionally, the 1974 Safe Drinking Water Act required strict regulation of the quality of drinking water in municipal water systems and the designation of maximum contaminant level goals for contaminants already found in the water system (Deason, Schad, and Sherk 2001, 175).

Water diversions and structural manipulations also had negative effects on stream ecosystems. In the Northwest, severe declines in salmon populations were observed. In the Southwest, the alteration of stream habitat caused many native fish species of the Colorado River to become threatened. Several pieces of legislation were passed to protect the survival of those species. The 1965 Anadromous and Great Lakes Fish Act supported protection of fish resources, and in 1968 the National Wild and Scenic Rivers Act prohibited the construction of dams on any designated wild and scenic river (Smith and Thomassey 2002, 25).

Shifting Attitudes toward Environmental Concerns

Environmental concerns continued throughout the 1970s, but by the end of the decade the movement was in decline. The 1973–1974 OPEC oil embargo, inflation, and distrust brought on by the Vietnam War and the Watergate scandal had created a feeling of disillusionment among American citizens (Rothman 1997, 132–134). A new movement, the fourth Sagebrush Rebellion, spurred animosity against the federal government and the environmental regulations it imposed on western lands. Ranchers and landowners revitalized states rights sentiments and declared their right to independence from environmental regulation. The 1980 elections proved decisive for the Sagebrush Rebellion with the election of Ronald Reagan (Rothman 1997, 178).

Reagan's election marked a shift away from water quality protection and toward support for agribusiness. In 1982 the Reclamation Reform Act increased the amount of farm property eligible to receive federally subsidized water for irrigation to 960 acres (Smith and Thomassey 2002, 57). Reagan also supported giving more control to the states, relaxing many federal environmental regulations. The 1981 changes to the Clean Water Act reduced federal funding for water pollution control facilities to 50 percent of construction costs, and the 1986 Water Resources Development Act required greater state involvement in water management (Smith and Thomassey 2002, 57). Also in 1986, Reagan vetoed the reauthorization of the Clean Water Act (CWA). Congress overrode the veto in 1987, but it clearly demonstrated a new approach toward water quality protection (Smith 2004a, 130).

The 1987 revision of the CWA also followed the trend of increasing the states' role, mandating that states be responsible for identifying insufficient pollution control in rivers and lakes. Although provided with a State Revolving Loan fund, this legislation was insufficient for preventing nonpoint source pollution, largely because implementation was the responsibility of the states (Lovejoy and Hyde 1997, 100).

In the 1990s environmental concerns began to resurge. A decline in Northwest salmon populations and declines in water quality across the nation were still pressing problems. The election of President Bill Clinton led to some reforms during the 1990s. The reauthorization of the Safe Drinking Water Act in 1996 gave the EPA flexibility to consider any number of contaminants for regulation. The 1996 Federal Agricultural Improvement and Reform Act authorized $2.2 billion in additional funding for conservation and nonpoint source pollution reduction programs. In 1998 the Clinton administration introduced a Clean Water Action Plan, which sought to unify and coordinate problems affecting common watersheds, further reduce pollution, and coordinate government efforts in watershed management (Raloff 1998, 159).

In 2000 political attitudes toward environmental stewardship and water quality changed once again with the election of George W. Bush. Public concern for environmental protection was replaced by concern for national security in 2001, when terrorists attacked the World Trade Center in New York City and the Pentagon in Arlington, Virginia. In the absence of strong public opposition, the Bush administration undermined many of the environmental laws Clinton had established. Bush administration proposals sought to give more power to the states. In 2002 the Bush administration announced a plan that reduced federal oversight of state Total Maximum Daily Load programs designed to target nonpoint sources of pollution (Grunwald 2002). In 2003 the administration proposed removing 20 million acres of wetlands from federal jurisdiction (Jehl 2003). The Bush administration has also affected stream wildlife protection by removing sixteen species of salmon and steelhead fish from "critical habitat" protection in the rivers of the Northwest (Kamieniecki 2003).

The recent trends in social paradigms have shifted between concern for water quality protection and deregulation of water policies. The Bush and Reagan policies that sought to give power to the states highlight another important aspect in the history of water policy and management—the role of federalism. The next section will discuss how federalism has shaped the history of water policy in the United States.

FEDERALISM

Federalism is the broad term used to define relations between the federal and state governments (Henry 2004, 379). As society has grown, jurisdictional debates have arisen over the development of water resources. The lines of this jurisdiction are blurred because water flows across state lines. Western states historically have opposed federal government involvement in public affairs, and the level of the federal contribution to management of waterways has been disputed. This section discusses the intergovernmental relationships important to western water development. In particular, it focuses on the tension between state and federal governments and the associations between states in water allocation decisions.

Initial State Control, Increasing Federal Involvement

Throughout the nation, funding and management of water development was initially the responsibility of states and local entities. In the eastern states, devastating floods and problems with navigation along waterways highlighted a greater desire for federal intervention. In 1824 the Supreme Court cemented the federal role in *Gibbons v. Ogden*, in which it established that development along navigable rivers was the federal government's responsibility under the Commerce Clause of the U.S. Constitution (*Gibbons v. Ogden* 1824). This decision was especially important for eastern river development where federal management was welcomed. Pursuant to this verdict, Congress passed a series of flood control acts that authorized the U.S. Army Corps of Engineers (USACE) to develop and maintain water projects along navigable waterways in the East.

In the West, where allocation and distribution of water (as opposed to flood control) were primary concerns for water users, attitudes toward the role of the federal government were vastly different. The doctrine of prior appropriation established from miners' resource needs in the early days of settlement gave water rights to those who first extracted and continually used the water (i.e., if you did not use it, you lost the claim to the waters) (Wilkinson 1992, 234–235). When state governments were established, this doctrine of water law was adopted into the administrative structures, and state water agencies carried out the duties of issuing and enforcing water rights. Funding for water development came from private enterprise and irrigation districts (cooperative associations of water users). However, as the West expanded, the need for large water diversions and reservoirs became apparent and the role of the federal government more necessary.

Because of the established water code, the federal government, although supportive of western settlement, was hesitant to interfere with local and state administration of water development. In the West, early irrigation policies, such as the Carey Act of 1894, were designed to retain state control of water resources. Federal involvement began when state funding was insufficient to construct water projects. Most important, the Bureau of Reclamation was created in 1902 to develop western rivers. Despite the federal control exerted by the agency, the Bureau of Reclamation was careful to limit its extension of federal water rights to western waters (McCool 1987, 67–72). The federal government subsidized large water projects, but allocation and distribution were left up to the states. As a result, the dominant water law of prior appropriation implemented by state governments remained the foundation for water policies.

The management of hydropower is an interesting exception to the western state–federal relationship. The federal government has always maintained administrative control over the sale and distribution of hydropower from large water projects it has subsidized. In 1884 Congress authorized dams along the Missouri River for the purpose of private power development (Smith and Thomassey 2002, 48 and 69). The late 1800s and early 1900s witnessed many similar congressional authorizations. By 1920 the federal government recognized that revenue generated from hydropower could pay for large water projects. The 1920 Federal Water Power Act established the Federal Power Commission, an agency to regulate the sale of electricity from federally funded dams (Moreell 1972, 41).

Attitudes toward federal aid during the Great Depression enhanced hydropower development. The industry flourished under federal direction, with little input from the states. The 1935 Public Utility Act gave the Federal Power Commission the responsibility of "regulating interstate electric utility rates of investor-owned power producers" (Moreell 1972, 43). In the 1940s and 1950s hydropower became an important justification for federal subsidization of large dams in the West. Large projects along the Columbia River, such as the Grand Coulee and Bonneville dams, accelerated northwestern settlement. In the Southwest, hydropower was an important benefit of the Hoover Dam and other portions of the Colorado River Storage Project.

Federal involvement in western water allocation became more important during the environmental movement. With the passage of NEPA and the Endangered Species Act, the federal government adopted the responsibility of ensuring that its public projects did not diminish environmental quality. As a result, large water projects requested by states were scrutinized to a greater degree. Jimmy Carter's "hit list" was an example of the greater consideration given to the necessity of water development. Since then, the construction of large dams has been curtailed. Additionally, diversions from streams have been challenged and in some cases limited for the protection of wildlife. These changes have created a backlash among some western water users (visible in the Sagebrush Rebellion in the late 1970s and early 1980s), as they have challenged the long-held notion of state and local control of water use.

Cooperation between States

To resolve differences within watersheds that cross state lines without federal intervention, many western states have implemented interstate water compacts that outline water sharing agreements between their jurisdictions.

Allocation of water in many large western rivers, including the Arkansas, Colorado, Colombia, Rio Grande, and Snake rivers, has been determined by river compacts. For the most part, they have been successful in determining water allocation between states.

The Colorado River Compact (CRC) is an exception to this record of success, and conflicts over Colorado River rights are still being debated. The CRC, developed in 1922, divided an estimated annual 16.5 million acre-feet of Colorado River water between the upper basin states (Colorado, Utah, Wyoming, and New Mexico) and the lower basin states (California, Nevada, and Arizona), with each basin receiving 7.5 million acre-feet annually and Mexico receiving the remaining 1.5 million acre-feet. Although all states signed the compact in 1922, Arizona did not ratify the agreement until 1963 because of a conflict over its share with California, during which time California constructed major diversions from the Colorado River. The compact's main problem was that the amount of water outlined in the first agreement was overestimated; 16.5 million acre-feet of water was not an annual average of river flows.

Intergovernmental relationships over time are complex, and much of the conflict that shaped water development remains today. An important aspect of the federal-state relationship involves the agencies that have implemented the water policies set forth by the federal government. The next section discusses how these water bureaucracies have established their role in the history of water development.

FEDERAL WATER AGENCIES

The Bureau of Reclamation and the U.S. Army Corps of Engineers are the two federal bureaucracies that have been essential to the development of western water resources. Their role in western water history is important because they were responsible for engineering and constructing the major water projects in the West. Although the two agencies were devoted to different purposes, competition between them accelerated the pace of water development. This section discusses the roles of the water agencies in the development of the West and how their missions have change over time.

The USACE was established in 1802, initially as a unit in charge of training new federal engineers. The agency grew to be the principal federal bureaucracy in charge of public works projects. In the area of water resources, it was responsible for flood and navigation control. Many of the water projects constructed and managed by USACE are east of the Mississippi River. However, USACE also worked on western water projects in which the primary reason for development was associated with flood control and hydropower.

The Bureau of Reclamation was established as the Reclamation Service in 1902 with the passage of the Reclamation Act. Its original mission was to facilitate irrigation in the western states (McCool 1987, 80). The bureau worked with local government agencies, establishing irrigation districts for the operation and maintenance of its water projects. By working with local governments, the Bureau of Reclamation constructed 236 reservoirs for irrigation and hydropower generation (Cech 2003, 235–236).

The USACE opposed the establishment of the Reclamation Service. The new agency encroached upon the jurisdiction of water engineering held by USACE and competed with USACE for funding (McCool 1987, 24). This rivalry spurred both agencies to build bigger and better dams at a faster rate, resulting in wasted resources and the construction of unnecessary water projects (Wilkinson 1992, 248; Reisner 1993, 171). Although the Bureau of Reclamation was established to be the primary agency involved in western water development, USACE managed to develop the Kings and Kern rivers in California. Additionally, USACE constructed many of the large water projects along northwestern rivers that were primarily developed for purposes of flood control, navigation, and hydropower (Reisner 1993, 165).

Problems of poor engineering associated with the increased pace of development became apparent in the 1970s. The Grand Teton Dam, constructed in Idaho in 1975, collapsed in 1976—killing eleven people, drowning major towns, and causing $1 billion in damage (Smith and Thomassey 2002, 56). The fault of the collapse resided with the Bureau of Reclamation, which because of faulty engineering and poor planning had built an unsafe dam (Reisner 1993, 379–410). By the late 1970s dam building had become publicly and politically unpopular. Funding for the Bureau of Reclamation was cut in 1977 when President Jimmy Carter announced his "hit list" of water projects (Cech 2003, 236). By 1987, one-third of USACE dams and one-fifth of Bureau of Reclamation dams were classified as unsafe (Smith and Thomassey 2002, 56). The decline in popularity of large water projects and the surge in environmentalism forced the water agencies to adapt to changing times.

During the 1990s the Bureau of Reclamation's mission changed to include an environmental focus. Announcing in 1993 that its goal of enhancing western settlement had been accomplished, the agency established a new mission "to manage, develop, and protect water and related resources in an environmentally and economically sound manner in the interest of the American public" (Cech 2003, 236–237; U.S. Bureau of Reclamation 1993). The bureau implemented water management programs that included habitat restoration, wildlife protection, and water conservation. The Stream Corridor Restoration program, implemented in 1993, involved the cooperation of fifteen federal agencies, including the bureau, to restore natural biological integrity to the nation's stream corridors (U.S. Department of Agriculture 1993). In 1997 the agency implemented the Water Conservation and Field Services Program designed to promote and assist in the development of water conservation programs through water management planning and education (U.S. Bureau of Reclamation 2005). In 2000 the bureau made a commitment to keep enough water in the Rio Grande to protect the silvery minnow, and in 2001 the bureau shut off a large portion of water used for irrigation by farmers in the Northwest to protect Coho salmon and suckers residing in the Klamath River and Upper Klamath Lake (Smith and Thomassey 2002, 61–62).

The mission of USACE also changed during this time. The USACE conducted extensive studies on stream bank erosion and wildlife conservation (U.S. Army Corps of Engineers 1998). In 1989 the agency participated in the Environmental Compliance Program established by the Department of Defense to ensure that the operation of all USACE facilities complied with federal, state, and local environmental laws and regulations (U.S. Army Corps of Engineers 1989). In 1991 the USACE implemented a Wetland Research Program to combine both environmental and engineering responsibilities to promote restoration and sustainable management of wetlands (Williams 1993, 127).

The development of these two primary water agencies over time has been important to the way western water resources have developed. The Bureau of Reclamation was forced to adapt more drastically to the decline in construction of large water projects, but both agencies changed their missions to adopt a more environmentally friendly approach to water management. Engineering and technical expertise provided the fundamental role these agencies played in western water development. The agencies embraced scientific management as a discipline in their efforts. Because of its importance to western water development, the role of science and technology is the topic of the last section of this chapter.

Our focus in this section has been on the federal role in western water development. As important as that role is, we should not overlook a central fact involving western water: most water is regulated and distributed on the local level by cities, towns, and regional water agencies. Although many of these water entities receive their water from one of the federal projects (and agencies that manage them) described earlier, the actual distribution occurs on the local level. This is particularly true of the water that reaches homes and factories in the West. Fragmentation and decentralization characterize environmental policy in the United States generally, but they are quite pronounced in the area of water policy. Although the federal role in water pollution control has expanded significantly, states and localities still have primary responsibility for implementation of water pollution policy. At least 27 federal agencies are involved in water policy in some capacity. Over 59,000 water supply utilities, thousands of state and local governments, as well as water districts, improvement districts, and other special districts are involved in water quality and supply delivery in some way (Rogers 1986, 32).

SCIENCE AND WATER DEVELOPMENT

Society's trust of science and technology has played a large role in the development of water policy. The practical applications of scientific rigor in the field of engineering have allowed for the large water projects that make up such an integral part of the western landscape. Although the government has often heralded this ingenious employment of science and technology in the development of public works, scientific uncertainty has also impacted water policies. This section examines the faith in science and technology that have comprised a large part of the philosophy of scientific management and demonstrates how that faith in engineering has outshone alternative development possibilities for the West.

Scientific management has been an important part of water development's mission. Essentially, this philosophy heralds the scientific method as a rational tool for managing society's needs. Engineers and scientists are experts specialized in this mode of thought, and they are looked upon as objective agents who help society construct what it needs to grow and survive. Embodied in this notion is the view that societal growth equals progress and that objective, rational actions are the most efficient way to achieve this goal. This faith in science and technology has been especially important in the West, where agriculture and resource extraction have proved difficult without an abundance of water. The design and construction of water delivery systems and large dams demonstrate faith in the scientific method. The importance of this theme as an underlying driver of western water policy is evidenced in everything from the historical denial of alternatives to water resource planning. The management suggestions of John Wesley Powell and the use of watershed management in planning are two examples.

The most famous of the early survey expeditions funded by the federal government was conducted by Major John Wesley Powell in 1869 along the Green and Colorado rivers. Through these expeditions, Major Powell developed a proposal for water management in the western United States. The *Report on the Lands of the Arid Region, with a More Detailed Account of Utah,* was presented to Congress in 1879, calling for planning western settlement within the boundaries of regional watersheds. The report advocated that cooperative management should drive the region's settlement practices and that settlement should be defined within the region's environmental constraints (Wilkinson 1992, 244–245). Despite the popularity of, and interest in, Powell's survey work, Congress rejected his management recommendations in favor of a more settler-friendly approach. The government needed to find a fast solution for the water shortage, one that would appease states rights advocates. This was not feasible under Powell's plan for development. Powell's suggestions were disregarded because of the time frame involved in basin-wide development (Wilkinson 1992, 236–237).

The fate of watershed management in planning provides another example of the power of the scientific management philosophy. In 1965 the Water Resources Planning Act created the Water Resources Council. The council conducted two National Water Assessments that gathered a broad range of water resource data from river basins across the nation and created commissions to produce plans for managing those basins (Platt 1993, 40). In accordance with its mandate, the National Water Commission released a report in 1973 that emphasized a need for water resources planning that enhanced water quality, environmental protection, and conservation. The Water Resources Council became politically unpopular in the late 1970s because President Carter used much of the data it gathered to suspend several water projects as part of his hit-list plan for budget restructuring. In 1982 President Reagan "zero-budgeted" the council, and the project ended (Platt 1993, 40–41). Watershed management was not revisited again until the 1990s, when President Clinton introduced the Clean Water Action Plan; however, this plan did not result in a restructuring of water management.

CONTEMPORARY ISSUES

Although the bulk of this chapter is devoted to western water policy history, the water world has changed significantly since the mid-1980s. The realization among water professionals that the era of large dam construction was over was just the beginning of many new ideas and innovations in water management. The orientation of municipal water managers has undergone important shifts. Once, in many western cities, water was considered very abundant and nearly free. Fresno and Sacramento, California, were among the many cities that did not meter water delivered to homes. Running a sprinkler all afternoon was not unusual during the hot summer months. Most westerners over age forty can remember letting the hose run continuously while washing your car without thinking about it. Today, however, a new era of conservation has taken hold in households and in efficiency of water management. Municipal water agencies all over the West admonish customers to conserve water. Some local government water utilities pay the cost of installing water reduction devices in showers and toilets in residents' homes. The state of Colorado has created an Office of Water Conservation and Drought to oversee and implement conservation programs in the state.

Water management has changed in other ways as well. With the growth and development of the West, water laws of the past—notably prior appropriation—have come into question. Why should a farmer who has a legal right to enough water to serve 1,000 new homes instead use that water to grow alfalfa worth only a few thousand dollars? Why should a cattle rancher who has a state-issued permit to take water from a stream to water cattle be allowed to continually renew his or her permit when people who want to protect the fish in the stream (or the vegetation on the stream banks) have no right to any water in the stream? In a wet year (when there is abundant water for everyone on a river), why should the law prohibit a state from storing some of the water it cannot use that year in underground reservoirs for use in future years when the river runs low? Each of these situations has been a part of western water management in the past. And although many states have worked to change their laws to address the poor management these situations represent, many others have not. In the case of the farmer who grows alfalfa, limits on water transfers and sales that may have prevented him or her from selling water to the new-home development have been modified in many places to allow for such transfers.

Water marketing in some states, particularly Colorado, allows water to be sold on open markets, sometimes through competitive bidding, and then transferred to other (higher economic) uses. At one time, few western states recognized in-stream uses (or water uses for aesthetic purposes) as beneficial. Because they were not recognized by the state as beneficial, no right to use water and no in-stream or environmental uses could be claimed for water. Although Arizona still does not recognize in-stream uses as beneficial, most western states now do so that people who want to protect the aesthetic value of rivers and streams are on the same legal footing as those who want to use the water for raising cattle or cotton. Finally, most western states have rewritten their state laws (and sometimes entered into compacts with other states) so they can manage water conjunctively—drawing water from one source when it is abundant and "banking" it for future use in a physical location or retaining a reserved right to some future use of water not used today. Water "banks" have been created all over the West (see Clifford, Landry, and Larsen-Hayden 2004 for a list) and involve state, local, special district, tribal, and federal government entities banking surface and groundwater for trade, market price, or fixed price sale.

These are all issues that have changed the way we think about and use water in the West.

CONCLUSION

This chapter has provided a brief overview of water policy in the United States. This history was framed in the context of four factors—changes in the dominant social paradigm, federalism, the role of water management agencies, and the role of scientific management. These themes illuminate how and why western water development and management have progressed in a complex and conflicting manner. We have also provided an overview of issues in western water management, focusing on some of the changes that have taken place in our assumptions and in the legal framework for water management. We conclude with an examination of the politics and economics of water and some observations about future water management.

Water Politics and Economics

The water future of most metropolitan areas in the urban West is assured. Although the water economy in each area is different and generalizations can hence be problematic, for the most part, large-scale surface storage and distribution systems have guaranteed that central Utah, Phoenix, southern

California, Las Vegas, and other metropolitan areas will enjoy many more years of suburban road and home construction. A close examination of the political economy of water development (i.e., the politics, history, and economics of water project authorization and construction) reveals that most projects were built at the behest of people with a large economic stake in their development. Although this is not surprising to people who study economic history or political science, it is interesting that most of these projects were promoted to the public as a way to "protect the future" and to guarantee that we will be able to water our lawns and otherwise live happy, comfortable, and healthy suburban lives. Stated another way, large surface water delivery projects have been conceived by and for relatively narrow economic interests and then pushed—usually by federal bureaucrats, politicians, and large landowners and speculators—as a benefit and a "need" for the general public (a need they heretofore did not know they had).

One of the earliest examples of this water sleight of hand occurred in the development of the Owens Valley Project in California (see Kahrl 1981; Walton 1992). The Owens Valley Project brought water from the Eastern Sierra in California down to the city of Los Angeles. In that instance, shortly after the turn of the twentieth century, water boosters falsified information about a "water shortage" in Los Angeles to coincide with voter approval of bonds that would fund construction of the Owens Valley Project. The voters of Los Angeles, thinking they were securing a source of water so faucets in their homes would not run dry, did not know that the primary beneficiaries of the new water would be land speculators in the San Fernando Valley. These speculators were largely members of Los Angeles's business elite, and the new water made them fabulously rich. To varying degrees, the pattern is similar when one examines the development of water projects throughout the West.

In more contemporary times, California voters were asked to approve a huge water delivery project—the California State Water Project—under similar conditions. Shortly before the election to approve bonds to finance the first phase of construction for the project, the *San Diego Union* ran a front-page story that proclaimed "millions of gallons wasted to sea" in an article bemoaning the fact that rivers do have a tendency to end up in the ocean and encouraging people to support the State Water Project. Newspapers throughout southern California provided similar support for the project. At the same time, through a vigorous campaign—underwritten primarily by the largest landholders in California, including the Southern Pacific Railroad Company and several land cooperatives—voters in southern California were being told that the State Water Project was necessary to secure their own water security. What the voters were not being told was that the primary beneficiaries of the new project would be landowners in the southern Central Valley whose property—heretofore with no water—values would multiply by tenfold as soon as the State Water Project was approved (Smith 2004b).

In Arizona the Central Arizona Project (CAP), conceived in the 1920s, was promoted until recently as a water distribution system to "save agriculture" in the state. Interestingly, throughout most of the CAP's promotional period, farmers actually had very little interest in the project. Only when told that they would be given an almost unlimited amount of water at virtually no cost (something no one seriously anticipated) did some Arizona farmers become CAP boosters. When the real costs became apparent, which occurred when the water started to be delivered, most farmers did not want it—it was too expensive. The earliest promoters of CAP water were not farmers but rather land developers, bankers, and other Phoenix businesspeople (Johnson 1977).

In Utah the Central Utah Project (CUP) was initially promoted as a project with widespread public benefits. As Utah senator Arthur Watkins argued, "[M]any young [people] are forced to leave the state because of economic reasons. The [CUP] could double the population of the state and create jobs which would keep young people in the state" (quoted in Ashley and Jones 2002, 276). Perhaps he was correct for the long term, but most of the water would initially be delivered to heretofore unirrigated land, making the owners of that land the primary beneficiaries of the CUP at the expense of federal taxpayers. Like the CAP, the CUP would evolve into primarily a municipal and industrial water project. Also as with the CAP, to repay the CUP obligation it became necessary to levy property taxes on property owners in central Utah. Many of those property owners will never receive any of the water they are now paying for.

These are not isolated instances. This is the politics of water project construction. Politicians cannot get support to approve large water projects if the general public knows that a handful of large landowners will be the primary beneficiaries, so the projects must be sold as a way to help the individual.

But that is all history. The plumbing is in place, and for many major metropolitan areas the future is secure, or at least the water will be delivered.

On the local level the process is little different. Almost without exception, localities sell water bonds and develop water acquisition, distribution, and treatment plants because they are good for the "community," not bothering to tell voters that the community in question has not yet been built. Voters, wanting to do the right thing and knowing that water is essential to life, approve these bonds. Business leaders and others who pay close attention to local government often know that the "community" in question is future development, but since population growth promises increased business activity, no one is anxious to make that distinction clear. Occasionally the system breaks down, and not enough water is developed for projected construction; hence, to ensure their economic future, citizens are urged to "conserve." Wanting to be good citizens (and most people want to think that they care about protecting the environment), people dutifully install low-flow showerheads, low-flow toilets, and rock gardens—not knowing that they are providing a very inexpensive and direct subsidy to future development (Smith 2004b).

What Water Will the Future Hold?

The future of water management in the West promises to be very similar to the past. The major projects have been built. On the local level, the "need" for more water is almost always a given. Conflict, politics, and some deception will be a part of decisions over which local projects are built and where. Contrary to what chambers of commerce, politicians, and even well-intentioned but misguided environmentalists will say, for the most part, most major metropolitan areas in the West have no shortage of water. Of course, there is always a shortage of "cheap" water. Not everyone can have all the inexpensive water they want. The conflicts over water will be over its distribution and use. Farmers are still by far the largest users of water, which in a way is good news for developers. Water politics in this context involves simply finding the most efficient means of subsidizing agriculture to obtain water to which it is legally entitled so that water can be converted to a "higher" (read: more profitable) use. This is what water marketing and, to a lesser extent, water banking are all about. In other words, the water politics of the West in the future will be not about scarcity (although, as in the past, the public is likely to be told that scarcity is the issue) but about distribution or who gets what.

Adding to this interesting mix is a huge unknown quantity—Indian water. Native American tribes in the Southwest have potential water rights that equal, and in some cases exceed, current water users in several tributaries in the West. These Native American water rights, which have not been secured and often not even quantified, create a huge question mark for water planners in parts of the West.

We conclude on a happy note. Unless we need to flood irrigate cotton or increase the rice harvest, plenty of water will be available for urban uses and limited agricultural uses in the future. Certainly, agricultural users will continue to convert to less water-intensive crops and more efficient means of irrigation as their heretofore cheap water becomes more expensive. And homeowners will dutifully conserve, thereby making more water available. Big dams will no longer exist. Desalinization will be a part of the future. As of this writing, we are very close to being able to desalinate water for domestic use at little more cost to homeowners than what they currently pay for cable television. For the most part, the water that is here is the water we have to work with. So, as in the past, much of water politics will be about distribution—who pays, how much they pay, and for what use.

REFERENCES

Ashley, Jeffrey, and Robert L. Jones. 2002. "The Central Utah Project." *Journal of Land, Resources, and Environmental Law* 22, no. 2, 273–307.

Cech, Thomas V. 2003. *Principles of Water Resources: History, Development, Management and Policy.* New York: John Wiley & Sons.

Clifford, Peggy, Clay Landry, and Andrea Larsen-Hayden. 2004. *Analysis of Water Banks in the Western States*. Seattle: State Department of Ecology, Publication 04-11-011. At http://www.ecy.wa.gov/biblio/0411011.html, site accessed July 2005.

Cortner, Hanna J., and Margaret A. Moote. 1999 *The Politics of Ecosystem Management*. Washington, DC: Island.

Deason, Jonathan P., Theodore M. Schad, and George William Sherk. 2001. "Water Policy in the United States: A Perspective." *Water Policy* 3, no. 3, 175–192.

Gelt, Joe. 2004. "Fountains: Water Wasters or Works of Art?" University of Arizona, Water Resources Research Center. At http://ag.arizona.edu/AZWATER/arroyo/073fount.html, site accessed August 2005.

Gerlak, Andrea K. 1996 "Federal Wetlands Policy: Is This Policy All Wet?" In Dennis L. Soden, ed., *At the Nexus: Science Policy.* Commack, NY: Nova Science.

Gibbons v. Ogden. 1824. 22 U.S. 1.

Grunwald, Michael. 2002. "White House Relaxes Rules on Protection of Wetlands: Two Agencies Criticized Revision of Permit Laws." *Washington Post,* January 15.

———. 2003. "Washed Away." *New Republic* 229, no. 17, October 27, 16–18.

Henry, Nicholas. 2004. *Public Administration and Public Affairs* (9th ed). Upper Saddle River, NJ: Pearson Prentice-Hall.

Howe, Charles W. 1991. "An Evaluation of U.S. Air and Water Policies." *Environment* 33, no. 7 (September), 10–19.

Jehl, Douglas. 2003. "U.S. Plan Could Ease Limits on Wetlands Development." *New York Times,* January 11.

Johnson, Rich. 1977. *The Central Arizona Project: 1918–1968.* Tucson: University of Arizona Press.

Kahrl, W. L. 1981. *Water and Power: The Conflict over Los Angeles' Water Supply in the Owens Valley.* Berkeley: University of California Press.

Kamieniecki, Sheldon. 2003. "The George W. Bush Environmental Record." *Step Ahead: The American Political Science Association* 1, no. 1 (Summer), 3–4.

Laitos, Jan G., and Joseph P. Tomain. 1992. *Energy and Natural Resources Law in a Nutshell.* St. Paul: West Group.

Lindstrom, Matthew J., and Zachary A. Smith. 2001. *The National Environmental Policy Act: Judicial Misconstruction, Legislative Indifference, and Executive Neglect.* College Station: Texas A&M University Press.

Lovejoy, Stephen B., and Jeffrey Hyde. 1997. "Non-point Source Pollution Defies U.S. Water Policy." *Forum for Applied Research and Public Policy* 12, no. 4, 100–159.

McCool, Daniel. 1987. *Command of the Waters: Iron Triangles, Federal Water Development, and Indian Water.* Berkeley: University of California Press.

Moreell, Ben. 1972. *Our Nation's Water Resources—Policies and Politics.* New York: Arno.

Platt, Rutherford H. 1993. "Geographers and Water Resource Policy." In Martin Reuss, ed., *Water Resources Administration in the United States: Policy, Practice, and Emerging Issues.* East Lansing: American Water Association / Michigan State University Press.

Powell, John Wesley, et al. *Report on the Lands of the Arid Region, with a More Detailed Account of Utah.* Washington, DC: GPO, 1879.

Raloff, Janet. 1998. "Fine-Tuning Federal Water Policies." *Science News* 53, no. 9, 159.

Reisner, Marc. 1993. *Cadillac Desert: The American West and Its Disappearing Water.* New York: Penguin Books.

Rogers, Peter. 1986. "Water: Not as Cheap as You Think." *Technology Review* 89, no. 8, 32.

Rothman, Hal. 1997. *The Greening of a Nation: Environmentalism in the United States Since 1945.* New York: Wadsworth.

Smith, Zachary A. 2004a. *The Environmental Policy Paradox* (4th ed.). Upper Saddle River, NJ: Prentice-Hall.

———. 2004b. "Water Development in the West." *Water Resources Impact* 6, no. 2, 10–13.

Smith, Zachary A., and Grenetta Thomassey. 2002. *Freshwater Issues: A Reference Handbook*. Santa Barbara, CA: ABC-CLIO.

U.S. Army Corps of Engineers. 1989. "Environmental Operating Principles." For more information about the Environmental Compliance Program, see a description of environmental compliance history at http://corpslakes.usace.army.mil/employees/envcomp/pback.html and a specific fact sheet for environmental compliance programs for USACE at http://corpslakes.usace.army.mil/employees/envcomp/pdfs/ec-facts.pdf, sites accessed September 2005.

———. 1998. "A History of the Army Corps of Engineers." At http://www.usace.army.mil/inet/usace-docs/eng-pamphlets/ep870-1-45/entire.pdf, site accessed May 2005.

U.S. Bureau of Reclamation. 1993. "Mission Statement." At http://www.usbr.gov/main/about/mission.html, site accessed September 2005.

———. 2005. "Water Conservation." At http://www.usbr.gov/waterconservation/index.html, site accessed September 2005.

U.S. Department of Agriculture. 1998. "Stream Corridor Restoration." At http://www.usda.gov/agency/stream_restoration/, site accessed September 2005.

Walton, John. 1992. *Western Times and Water Wars: State Culture and Rebellion in California*. Berkeley: University of California Press.

Wilkinson, Charles. 1992. *Crossing the Next Meridian: Land, Water, and the Future of the West*. Washington, DC: Island.

Williams, Arthur E. 1993. "The Role of Technology in Sustainable Development." In Martin Reuss, ed., *Water Resources Administration in the United States: Policy, Practice, and Emerging Issues*. East Lansing: American Water Association/Michigan State University Press.

Winters v. the United States. 1912. 207 U.S. 564.

CONTRIBUTORS

LESLIE R. ALM is a professor of political science and chair of the Department of Public Policy and Administration at Boise State University. His undergraduate degree is from West Point (engineering), and his Ph.D. is from Colorado State University (political science with emphasis in environmental policy making). Professor Alm's research centers on environmental policy, especially as it applies to U.S.-Canadian cross-border issues and the implementation of North American acid rain policy. His most recent publications include *Crossing Borders, Crossing Boundaries: The Role of Scientists in the U.S. Acid Rain Debate* (Praeger, 2000) and journal articles in *The Journal of Environmental Systems, State and Local Government Review, The American Review of Canadian Studies*, and *The Social Science Journal*.

CAROLYN D. BABER is a librarian at San Diego State University. She is the author of numerous research guides and bibliographical reviews. She is working on an encyclopedic review of environmental policy in the fifty states.

WALTER F. BABER is an associate professor in the Graduate Center for Public Administration at California State University, Long Beach. He has published scholarly research articles and books on environmental politics, organization theory, and democratic theory, including *Deliberative Environmental Politics: Democracy and Environmental Politics* (MIT Press, 2005).

ROBERT V. BARTLETT is the Gund Professor of Liberal Arts in the Political Science Department at the University of Vermont. He is the author of many articles on environmental politics and policy and the author, coauthor, or editor of eight books, including *Deliberative Environmental Politics: Democracy and Environmental Politics* (MIT Press, 2005). He has twice been a Senior Fulbright Scholar (to New Zealand and Ireland). In 2003–2004 he was the Frank Church Distinguished Professor of Public Policy at Boise State University.

HUGH BARTLING is an assistant professor in the Public Policy Studies Program at DePaul University, Chicago Illinois. He is the co-editor, with Matthew J. Lindstrom, of *Suburban Sprawl: Culture, Ecology, and Politics* (Rowman and Littlefield, 2003). He has done extensive research on the politics of planned communities in the United States and has published in such journals as *Contemporary Justice Review* and *Mississippi Quarterly*.

MATTHEW A. CAHN is a professor of public policy and chair of the Department of Political Science at California State University, Northridge. His research interests include environmental policy, rule making, and the intersection of science and policy. His most recent book is *Strategic Planning in Environmental Regulation* (with Sheldon Kamieniencki and Steve Cohen, MIT Press, 2005). He is working on a book that examines the tension between science and democracy, using marine protected areas in coastal zones as a case study.

R. McGREGGOR (GREGG) CAWLEY is a professor of political science at the University of Wyoming. His primary research and teaching areas are federal lands policy, environmental politics, and natural resource administration. He also works in the area of public administration theory. He is the author of *Federal Lands, Western Anger: The Sagebrush Rebellion and Environmental*

Politics (University Press of Kansas, 1993) and co-editor of *A Wolf in the Garden: The Land Rights Movement and the New Environmental Debate* (Rowman and Littlefield, 1996). He has also published numerous articles and book chapters.

CHARLES DAVIS is a professor of political science at Colorado State University. His teaching and research interests lie in the areas of environmental policy generally and public lands policy more specifically. Professor Davis is the editor of *Western Public Lands and Environmental Politics*, 2nd edition, as well as book chapters and articles dealing with environmental and public lands policy.

SANDRA DAVIS is an associate professor of political science at Colorado State University. Her teaching and research interests lie in the areas of environmental policy generally and water resource policy more specifically. She has authored articles and book chapters dealing with water policy, public lands politics, and political behavior.

JOHN FREEMUTH is the Senior Fellow, Cecil D. Andrus Center for Public Policy, and professor of political science and public administration at Boise State University. Dr. Freemuth's research and teaching emphasis is in natural resource and public land policy and administration. He is the author of an award-winning book, *Islands under Siege: National Parks and the Politics of External Threats* (University Press of Kansas, 1991), as well numerous articles on aspects of natural resource policy. He is the author of six Andrus Center white papers on public land policy, based on center conferences in 1998, 1999, 2000, 2001, 2002, and 2004.

SHELDON KAMIENIECKI is dean of the Division of Social Sciences at the University of California, Santa Cruz. He was chair of the Department of Political Science at USC for six years and the founding director of the Environmental Studies Program for eight years. He has published several books and numerous journal articles and book chapters on local, state, federal, and international environmental policy issues. He is the recipient of the Lynton K. Caldwell Prize from the Section on Technology and Environmental Policy of the American Political Science Association for the best book published between 1995 and 1997 on environmental politics and policy. Professor Kamieniecki received the Raubenheimer Award for Outstanding Senior

Faculty in the College of Letters, Arts and Sciences at USC in 1999. He recently coauthored a book on strategic planning in environmental regulation for MIT Press and published a second book on the influence of business on environmental policy with Stanford University Press.

MATT LINDSTROM is an associate professor of political science at St. John's University in Collegeville, Minnesota. From 1997 to 2005 he was a member of the Political Science Department at Siena College in Loudonville, New York, and the founding director of the Siena College Sustainable Land Use Program. He is coauthor, with Zachary A. Smith, of *The National Environmental Policy Act: Judicial Misconstruction, Legislative Indifference, and Executive Neglect* (Texas A&M University Press, 2001) and co-edited *Suburban Sprawl: Culture, Ecology, and Politics* (Rowman and Littlefield, 2003) with Hugh Bartling. He is researching the politics of local food systems and co-editing a book about activism and sustainability.

WILLIAM R. MANGUN is professor of political science at East Carolina University. He is the author, coauthor, or editor of ten books and monographs on wildlife policy, natural resource management, and environmental administration. He has published numerous articles and book chapters on environmental policy. Previously, he served as the manager for policy analysis as well as national resource management coordinator of the U.S. Fish and Wildlife Service.

DENISE McCAIN-THARNSTROM received her undergraduate degree from Duke University and her law degree from the University of Florida. A former litigation attorney, she holds a master's degree in public policy and has taught Public Policy Formulation at the University of Southern California's School of Policy Planning and Development. She is a doctoral student at the University of Southern California in political science, concentrating on environmental policy. She is studying environmental policy impacts on children's health and development. She has served as a member of a local environmental review board and is the chair for a local children's foundation's grant screening committee.

DANIEL McCOOL received his Ph.D. from the University of Arizona. His research and teaching focus on environmental policy, water resources management, American Indian policy, and policy theory. He is the author of

Native Waters (University of Arizona Press, 2002) and *Command of the Waters* (University of California, 1987; reissued University of Arizona Press, 1994), coauthor of *Staking Out the Terrain*, 2nd edition (SUNY Press, 1995), author/editor of *Public Policy Theories, Models and Concepts* (Prentice-Hall, 1995), editor of *Waters of Zion* (University of Utah Press, 1995), and co-editor of *Contested Landscape: The Politics of Wilderness in Utah and the West* (University of Utah Press, 1999). His journal publications include articles in *Political Science Quarterly, Political Research Quarterly, Publius, Policy Studies Journal, Policy Studies Review,* and *Journal of the Southwest.* He has served as a consultant for the U.S. Justice Department, the National Oceanic and Atmospheric Administration, and the Southwest Center for Environmental Research and Policy. He is working on a book concerning dam removal and river restoration.

JAINA L. MOAN is a Ph.D. student in political science at Northern Arizona University. She received a B.S. in chemistry and biology from NAU and is employed as a research associate for the Colorado Plateau Stable Isotope Laboratory. She is interested in the link between science and policy in the area of environmental politics.

ZACHARY A. SMITH received his B.A. from California State University, Fullerton, and his M.A. and Ph.D. from the University of California, Santa Barbara. He has taught at Northern Arizona University, the Hilo branch of the University of Hawaii, Ohio University, and the University of California, Santa Barbara, and served as the Wayne Aspinall Visiting Professor of Political Science, Public Affairs, and History at Mesa State College. A national and international consultant on environmental matters, Smith is the author or editor of nineteen books and many articles on water and environmental topics. He currently teaches environmental and natural resources policy and administration in the public policy Ph.D. program of the Political Science Department at Northern Arizona University in Flagstaff.

INDEX